SUN

SEA &

SPIDER BITES:

Three More Years in Andalucía

SUN, SEA & SPIDER BITES:
Three More Years in Andalucía

Drew Johnson

To my four beautiful daughters, Stephanie, Andrea, Rachel and Corrinne. Thank you for the grey hairs and the empty bank balance … and your unwavering love, of course, without which I'd be a much poorer man

This book is based on actual events and actual people, although the names of all Spanish characters have been altered as a courtesy. All other characters are real-life family members or friends who are happy to be exposed for their association with the author – more fool them!

"The only thing you have to fear is fear itself
... and spiders!"
(Anonymous)

CONTENTS

1 – We're Still Here   1
2 – Enchanting Estepona   6
3 – Run Ragged Round Ronda   13
4 – Wildfire Watch   19
5 – When the Cat's Away   23
6 – Extra! Extra! Read All About It   28
7 – Letting Our Hair Down   33
8 – I've Had a Bellyful of This   40
9 – Watching Paint Dry   45
10 – These Boots Are Made For Walking   51
11 – Daylight Robbery   55
12 – Glorious Granada   59
13 – Fiesta Time in Fuengirola   64
14 – Making an Exhibition of Ourselves   68
15 – Magical Mijas 70
16 – A Taxing Time 73
17 – The End!   77
18 – Sizzling Sanlúcar   80
19 – Fire!   86
20 – Cooling Off at the Beach   88
21 – Livin' La Vida Loca   90
22 – Antique Antequera   93
23 – Eye of the Storm   96
24 – Having Doubts 99
25 – License to Kill 102
26 – Fabulous Frigiliana   106
27 – Captivating Córdoba   110
28 – Home Alone 2   114
29 – No More Interviews   120
30 – Spanish Kiss   122
31 – I Can See Clearly Now 125
32 – Two Weddings and a Burglary   130
33 – Family Fun   141
34 – San Juan   146
35 – Horses and Hounds   148
36 – Nuptials, Newborns and Nuts   151

37 – We Have a Leak 155
38 – House Hunting 159
39 – Another Fine Mess 166
40 – Moving House 170
41 – Getting My Lip In 177
42 – The Patter of Tiny Feet 179
43 – Mojácar Out of Season 182
44 – Peak Perfection 186
45 – Something Weird is Going On 188
46 – Spider Bites 192
47 – Countdown to Lockdown 199
48 – Lockdown! 202
49 – Medical Mysteries 212
50 – Going Stir Crazy 216
51 – A Novel Idea 223
52 – Going Out 228
53 – Going Out Out 231
54 – Back to Borisland 236
55 – I'm Having an Identity Crisis 240
56 – Double Trouble 251
57 – And Relax 254
About the Author 258
Other Books by the Author 259
Acknowledgements 260

1

We're Still Here

Here we go again, then … strap yourselves in for another headlong hurtle through Andalucía and the chaotic life of two of Spain's newest residents, me and my dear wife, Chris.

It's September 2017, the sun is shining, the pool is full, and my new *career* as a writer (and I use that term very loosely until someone pays me a living wage for doing it) has begun in earnest: I've begun to write my first novel – yes, I can be serious and all grown up when the mood takes me – and I'm sure that's going to take up much of my time over the next six months or more.

Mum says she always knew I'd be a writer after she was called into the Mother Superior's office at my preparatory school one afternoon to be told I'd been a very naughty little boy.

'What's he done?' she asked.

Mother Superior slid an open exercise book across the desk where someone had written inside it "YOU ARE A PIG".

'He wrote this in a girl's book.'

'What a clever boy,' Mum said, pride in her voice. 'Look at his spelling!'

As the journalist, Christopher Hitchens, famously said, 'Everyone has a book in them and that, in most cases, is where it should stay'. Let's just hope he wasn't thinking of me when he said that.

I'm sure he wasn't, because this will be book two in a series of, well, two travelogue books so far, and I wouldn't be writing this now if I hadn't been encouraged to do so by the marvellous response I received from all you lovely readers of book one ... so if you haven't read the first book in the series, *Tapas, Tears & Tribulations: A Year in Andalucía*, then STOP! ... come back here when you've discovered how we fared in our first year under an unrelenting Spanish sun.

I also decided to write this second chapter in our Spanish lives thanks to what you might call a moderately successful extended run in the Amazon charts, with book one reaching #1 in the Travel Writing chart, and even making it to #2 in the chart for Adventurer and Explorer Biographies (behind Ross Kemp, no less), when all I'd done was bugger off to Spain to live the life of Riley! ... although after a hard summer session on the garden strimmer I do feel a bit like Sherpa Tenzing must do every time he conquers Everest.

Now I've brought him up, what I want to know is this: who the hell is this Riley fellow, anyway, and what's he been doing that must be so rewarding that everyone wants to emulate him?

I'd also like to give a quick mention to the lovely members of the Facebook group We Love Memoirs. As a reader of memoirs – yes, that's YOU, you're reading one now – you should check them out. They're a lovely group of people and very supportive of up-and-coming writers like me. It's a great place to discover new talent and get some free books on your Kindle. Thank you Victoria Twead and your faithful team of administrators.

So, yes, I've decided to document years two to four of our foreign adventure for your delight and delectation. And who knows how much future drama is going to be heaped upon us in the ensuing years, such that, dare I say it, there is a third book in this series.

Anyway, let's crack on.

First, a quick recap: my gorgeous wife, Chris, and I are living in the *campo* (Spanish countryside) about half an hour inland from Málaga, and an uphill walk into the thriving working town of Alhaurín El Grande, population circa 24,000, about 20% of which are non-native Spaniards ... or as the older Brit generation might call them, "immigrants", or "bloody foreigners". We of course count ourselves in that cohort and are delighted to be here.

We live in a rented, three-bedroom, white, chocolate box finca with an acre of land to manage, a big south-facing terrace, and a lovely refreshing swimming pool. We have an olive grove that we haven't figured out what to do with yet, all manner of fruit trees, and a lawn I laid which now seems rather foolish after the hottest summer on record. We're both in our mid- to late-fifties and have retired early from our jobs in the UK, and whilst I'm hoping to find gainful employment here at some point, I think Chris has quickly become accustomed to not being at anyone's beck and call.

We have lovely Spanish neighbours on either side. Our landlady Olivia's sister, Rosa, lives on one side with her husband Luis. We often receive gifts of vegetables from Luis's garden. On the other side live José and Alicia, a sweet, older couple with a gorgeous black cat that follows José round his garden. José likes nothing more than to complain about his workload in the garden, how poor he is (despite owning two homes), the Spanish government and the flies. He grows mostly fruit, and his pomegranates are amazing.

We are as content as we could be right now. As my birthday approached, I was being harassed by our four adult daughters back in the UK, asking me to make my mind up about what I wanted for my birthday. I'm a nightmare to buy for, apparently; I'm one of those men that when they see something they want or need, they just go and buy it (funds permitting), even if it's the week before Christmas. I'm trying to get better at waiting for shiny things as a birthday or Christmas approaches and put those baubles on a wish list for the family, usually for said wish list to be completely ignored, of course.

On this occasion, there was nothing I was desperate for, so I opted for trying to improve my golf handicap … if you can call playing golf off the maximum permitted additional shots of 28 a handicap rather than a perk – I think the handicap to my game was in fact *me*. Anyway, I asked some of the girls to club together (excuse the pun) so I could try out the local golf course at Alhaurín El Grande. It's not cheap to play golf in Spain, especially when there's nobody to share the cost of a golf buggy with you.

We had no golf-playing visitors staying with us and I had no golf-playing friends locally, so it was a round of golf for one – what a great birthday this was turning out to be!

There are reportedly just shy of 500 golf courses in Spain, and this will only be the second one I've played. The United States has the greatest number of golf courses, with over 16,000 and Spain doesn't even make the top 10. Despite the rotten weather we've left behind in the northwest of England, the UK are in third place (surprisingly behind Japan), but at least in Spain the weather is good enough that you can get out and play on them almost all year round, something my UK mate, Tony, is always complaining about.

Alhaurín Golf turned out to be a bugger of a course to play – it was designed by the renowned Spanish golfer, Severiano 'Seve' Ballesteros (although I'm not sure he ever played it himself), and mentioning Seve's name immediately makes me think of the fantastically funny film from 2021, *Phantom of the Open* (and no, I can't see into the future, but am writing this book retrospectively). It stars Mark Rylance as the hapless amateur golfer, Maurice Flitcroft, who after being made redundant from his job as a crane operator at the shipyard in Barrow-in-Furness, famously bought a set of golf clubs from the catalogue and conned his way into The Open golf championship in 1976, going round it in a record high of 49 over par, or 121 shots, leading to him being dubbed the 'world's worst golfer'. The film – a true story – is hilarious. What's not hilarious is I went round Alhaurín Golf on my 54th birthday in more shots than that and would consider a score of less than 120 a very good day indeed!

The Alhaurín course is built on the side of a mountain with breathtaking views of the Sierra de Mijas and the Mediterranean Sea in the distance. I can therefore attribute my poor performance to being distracted by the scenery – that's my excuse and I'm sticking to it.

I was accompanied on the round by three Swedish blokes I'd never met before, and my final tally included a loss of eight balls, and a whole lot more in terms of the respect of my fellow golfers. Over a beer in the clubhouse afterwards, I half expected them to ask me if I knew Maurice bloody Flitcroft! They didn't. But they did enquire if I'd be playing again next week, which I thought was nice of them … or were they perhaps hoping they'd be able to go home to their wives next week and tell them they hadn't lost the match again?

'How did you get on?' Chris asked when I returned home.

'Not so great,' I said. 'I've never played golf down a mountain before, and I lost eight balls.'

'Never mind, I'm taking you into town for a birthday dinner tonight.'

'Erm. Change of plan … we're going to the golf club instead.'

'Why? Will they let you go back on the course to look for your balls?'

'Now, now. No need to be sarcastic. Especially on my birthday. No, there's a dinner dance there tonight with live Soul and Motown music, so get your dancing shoes on, I've booked us a table for two.'

'How did you find out about that?'

'I was hoping you'd ask me that … I heard it through the grapevine!'

We had a lovely evening, sitting out on the clubhouse lawn as the sun went down, enjoying a delicious three-course dinner with wine. The entertainment was quite good too, and we had a boogie to a few classic soul numbers. I went to bed full of fine food and wonderful wine, my golfing nightmare already a distant memory.

2

Enchanting Estepona

The following day we had a trip planned down the coast to Estepona. Our friends, Tony and Sandra, were coming over for a long weekend on the first of many future trips to do a little house hunting in that area. Having seen how much we were enjoying the Spanish lifestyle, they wanted a piece of the action for themselves and were looking to buy a holiday villa. We were meeting up with them for a night out in Estepona. However, the trip planning hadn't gotten off to the most auspicious of starts a couple of weeks earlier.

'We're coming over to Spain for some sun and wine,' Tony had announced. 'Will you be around the weekend of the eighth to meet up with us?'

'Yeah. We can come down to Estepona on the Saturday and stay at your hotel.'

'Great. I'll let you know when we've booked something.'

Now, Tony is a man who has been quite successful in business and has begun to appreciate the finer things in life. So, a little while later, it was no surprise to learn he'd booked a room in a place on the outskirts of Estepona called the Healthouse Hotel, a five-star luxury spa hotel. After looking at the prices, we soon came to the conclusion that our budget didn't quite stretch that far. However, rather fortuitously, the property had a sister hotel across the road called the Healthouse Apartments that was about a third of the price, and after applying a discount I had with

Hotels.com, I bagged us a room for less than €50 – I *am* currently unemployed, don't forget!

Afterwards, we had a nosy at Tony's hotel to see what he was getting for his money and were surprised to learn that it was actually one of those 'adults only' hotels where they espoused healthy eating and spa treatments (although the name should have given us a clue!).

Now, I don't know if there's a link or not, but The Priory in Bristol, where the rich and (in)famous go for rehab, is located on "Health House Lane". So we dug a little deeper, only to discover that it's not only a "dry" hotel – no booze on offer – but according to the information we found online, they actively discouraged you from leaving the premises for a crafty glass of red. One Tripadvisor reviewer gave it top marks but ended their review with a warning to future guests that said: NO pool bar, NO buffet, NO sugar, NO salt, NO alcohol, NO flour, NO fast food or dishes high in fat.

What kind of bloody holiday is that?! I couldn't think of anything worse!

So I fired off a message to Tony sharpish …

'You do realise your hotel is alcohol free don't you, and it's a healthy eating hotel?'

'You're kidding me?' came the reply.

'No, but if you like, we can try and pass you a bottle of Rioja through the fence on our way out to dinner?'

'We're changing it!' he said.

The following day a message pinged in …

'Drew. We've changed to Hotel Elba. Apparently, the health spa even discouraged you from leaving the hotel.'

'I KNOW!'

I then had to go back online to cancel our hotel, as Tony was now staying in another five-star hotel nine miles away on the other side of Estepona. I wasn't complaining as our new hotel only cost us €10 with the same discount voucher – as I just said, I *am* currently unemployed you know!

Estepona is just under an hour away from Alhaurín El Grande, and the A7 coast road that takes you there is a busy affair at most times of the day, skirting as it does some of the

Costa del Sol's more upmarket locations, like Marbella and Puerto Banús. Having said that, if you go out and buy a Spanish Monopoly game these days, the highest value property square on the board is in fact Estepona, making it the equivalent of Mayfair on the UK board, whilst Marbs and Puerto Banús don't even get a look in.

We went straight to the hotel to check in and drop the bags. We were in an aparthotel that overlooked one of Estepona's many golf courses. The accommodation was relatively basic, and as with most hotels in Spain, breakfast isn't included, and you don't even get tea and coffee making facilities, something we can't do without when we travel, so we'd planned ahead and brought our own kettle and supplies. As Chris unpacked, I got a brew on the go. It was a pretty gusty afternoon, and you could hear the wind whistling through gaps around the patio doors.

'I hope that's not going to keep me awake tonight,' I said.

'Don't worry, *nothing* keeps you awake at night,' came the reply. 'I, however, have to listen to you gnashing your teeth and snoring most nights, so the wind will be a welcome distraction for me.'

Charming, I thought.

A short while later, suitably refreshed, we headed off to meet our friends in their five-star luxury accommodation. We got out of the taxi with the imposing Sierra Bermeja mountain range making an impressive backdrop behind us to the north and walked into a luxurious lobby that was lavishly furnished with ornamental Buddhas and mood lighting throughout – a bit like I imagine a top-end hotel in Bangkok to look.

'I bet these two have got bloody tea and coffee making facilities,' I opined, casting my eyes around the spacious interior.

'Well, you get what you pay for,' Chris said, a little too pointedly.

We sauntered through to the bar area and found our friends drinking wine in the hotel bar. *Quelle surprise*, as the French would say!

'*Hola chicos*,' I greeted them, showing off my outstanding command of the Spanish language.

'*¡Holaaa!*' came the rather enthusiastic reply.

It was hugs and kisses all round, and then Tony ordered four more glasses of whatever they were drinking.

'How's the house hunting going?' I enquired.

'Erm, not so good. We haven't done any yet,' Tony said. 'But we have found some good restaurants.'

'And a nudist beach!' Sandra added.

'Tony won't even get in a hot tub with me with his trunks on, so I can't see him getting his meat and two veg out for every Tom, Dick and Harry to gawp at on the beach,' I said.

'We were quite shocked,' said Sandra. 'We only went for a short stroll along the beach and it's right next door!'

Sandra was apparently referring to the aptly titled Costa Natura Family Naturist Resort – although I find the inclusion of the word "Family" a little disturbing – situated just a few hundred metres up the beach from Hotel Elba. Nudist beaches are very popular along the Costa del Sol, and you won't need to travel far to find one if that's what you're into. Clearly, Tony and Sandra weren't.

We had a quick catchup while we sipped our wine. It seemed this house-hunting trip was destined to be the first of many unsuccessful such trips, due in large part to their reluctance to get out of the bar and go and poke around in an estate agent's office. We supped up and headed off into Estepona to see what delights it had to offer, this being our first trip to the town.

Like most of Europe, there is a rich and diverse history to Estepona, which can trace human activity as far back as 5,000 years ago; a few miles out of town, on the way up the Sierra Bermeja, you'll find *Los Dólmenes de Corominas*, (the dolmens of Corominas). A dolmen is a cave-like structure that's usually regarded as a tomb, and you'll find good examples of these in many parts of Spain, perhaps the most famous of which are the ones found in Antequera that are on our 'To Do List'.

Originally called Astapa by its Phoenician founders, Estepona was taken over by the Arabs after the Muslim conquest of the 8th century. One of their most celebrated rulers was an ambitious man called Abd al-Raḥman II, who oversaw a massive public works programme in Andalucía, works that included a new fortress in the area they called Estebuna, and while the town at that time was known as Astabbuna, you can now see the origin of its current name after the Spanish had conquered it in 1456.

Today, Estepona continues to cover a much larger area than just the town itself; you drive past the proverbial "Welcome to Estepona" sign on the A7 a long way before you reach any sign of the town. With many beaches to choose from, and a population that trebles during the summer months, Estepona boasts a beachfront covering some 13 miles of coastline.

As we drove into town past the marina, one famous landmark we failed to spot was the *Plaza de Toros*, the bullring. We didn't spot it as it's so well hidden from whichever direction you approach it. With over 1,500 bullfights a year in Spain, the sport is still clearly loved and revered by many Spaniards – and to some extent other parts of the Spanish-speaking world – and regardless of your views on bullfighting, you can't fail to still be impressed by the architectural beauty of Estepona's bullring. You'd need to either get up close or see it from the air to appreciate it fully. It's actually unique in its construction, being the only asymmetrical bullring in the world – i.e. the opposite ends of the structure are different in size and shape, with one side (the western end) built with an increasingly steeper rake and higher wall. Designed as it was by Juan Mora Urbano and opened in 1972, despite having no roof, this 8,000-capacity venue offers more seating in the shade than it does exposed to the searing heat of a late-afternoon summer sun.

In the centre of the town you'll also find Europe's biggest orchidarium housing a vast array of different species of exotic orchids – not something that floats *my* boat, especially.

We disgorged ourselves from the taxi on the edge of the old town and meandered its quaint streets, bustling with early evening drinkers and people just out for a stroll. The whitewashed, lime-rendered houses of the old town are synonymous with those you'll find throughout Andalucía, and this architectural style is one of the key attractions to visitors from around the world, us included.

It also serves a practical purpose, as the white walls reflect the light and heat of the day and keep the interior considerably cooler – which of course has the opposite effect in the winter and makes the inside feel like you're sat in a bloody fridge!

We eventually found ourselves in the *Plaza de las Flores* (Flower Square), a part of the town completed in the 19th century and, historically, the location for some of the most important houses of the time. There's a central fountain surrounded by colourful flower beds, and it made a perfect spot for us to stop for dinner in one of the pavement restaurants. If we were doing this back in Manchester, we'd have been huddled under a patio heater with our "big coats" on!

We finished the evening off with a stroll along the promenade with one last pit stop before taking a taxi back to our respective hotels, with plans to meet up for lunch the following day.

Returning to our budget accommodation, we found the wind still whistling through the patio doors, now stronger and colder than when we'd left.

'Bloody hell,' I said, shivering in my birthday suit, 'I feel like a character from a Bronte novel on top of a bleak, windswept Haworth moor.'

'Shut up, Heathcliff, and get in bed,' Chris replied.

So with a full belly and a hazy head, I hunkered down and was soon fast asleep (and I made a special effort not to gnash my teeth all night).

After making a morning cuppa and reading the newspaper online in bed, we headed down to try and order some breakfast, only to discover that we'd missed the breakfast serving times and were also late checking out. Throwing everything into our overnight cases and hustling out of the place, we drove back into town and found a nice little café for a decent cup of coffee and some *tostada con tomate y aceite* (a traditional Spanish breakfast of a lightly toasted bun smothered in olive oil, freshly grated tomato and a generous helping of salt) – an instant pick-me-up.

Later, we walked up and down the prom again a couple of times, stopping for another coffee while we waited to meet up with Tony and Sandra. I'd done my usual thorough research on local eateries along the beach and found the ideal spot for lunch, a *chiringuito* called Palm Beach, run by some Dutch lads with a good reputation for offering something a little different.

My research also threw up a little nugget of pop history as the beach bar was used as the venue for the video shoot of the hit single *The Ketchup Song (Aserejé)*, recorded by Spanish girl trio Las Ketchup in 2002, which went on to reach the number one spot in 20 European countries. Like the *Macarena* song of the early nineties, it had its own popular dance routine.

The food was excellent, a real mix of Asian and European cuisine. Definitely a place we'd be returning to on another visit. We left our friends and Estepona behind and headed back up the coast to our inland retreat, happy that my birthday weekend had turned out so well in the end (if we discount my round of golf, of course!).

3

Run Ragged Round Ronda

'Around the rugged rock the ragged rascal ran', or so the tongue-twister goes. Well, we created our own Spanish version according to Chris when we took my parents on a daytrip and I had them 'run ragged round Ronda' ... in search of the perfect lunch, I might add.

Dad had just celebrated his 80th birthday a month earlier, and Mum wasn't far behind him, and we'd all four of us just flown in from the UK where we'd been celebrating the 60th birthday of my brother's girlfriend, Ann, on the Isle of Wight. That lavish bash (as Ann certainly knows how to throw a party) had been a test of staying power for the hardiest of us, never mind these two octogenarians.

It had all started with brunch at the White Horse Inn at Whitwell, then 'The Old Girl' – not Ann herself, but the name affectionately given to the open top bus – took us on a ride through the island's quaint countryside en route to Cowes, before finally depositing us all quayside to embark on a dinner cruise aboard a splendid party boat named The Princess Caroline ... although given the amount of booze we got through, it might have been more appropriately named The Princess Margaret!

As an aside, one of the most off-the-wall birthday gifts I've ever seen was presented to Ann by Mike's two grown up prankster children: a portrait of Ann, painted by Pricasso – no, not the renowned Spanish artist who'd been dead for more than 40 years (so that would have been impressive in itself), but by an

Aussie artist called Tim Patch, aka Pricasso, who paints portraits with his penis (which in my view is even more impressive), and for the doubters amongst you, he throws in a video of the entire process for good measure.

If you're now thinking this would be an ideal gift for someone *you* know, then I can attest to the fact it was very impressive and life-like, regardless of how he'd got the paint on the canvas!

Anyway, back to Ronda ... What? You want a break while you go and google Pricasso at work? You saucy lot – go on then! ... right, happy now? Let's continue ...

It was a beautiful sunny day, and we'd decided to visit this historic mountaintop town, one of Spain's oldest and most visited places, lying not much more than an hour's drive away. It sits atop sheer cliffs that straddle an enormous gorge, rather fittingly named *El Tajo* (the pit). Photos taken looking back up at the town from the gorge are instantly recognisable as Ronda.

The original settlers, the Celts, named the town Arunda in the 6th century B.C., and today, we'd come to explore its pretty streets and marvel at the impressive views down into the gorge. The *Puente Viejo* (old bridge) was built in the early 17th century and is the smallest and oldest of the three bridges that cross Ronda's Guadalevin river; which rather begs the question, was it originally just called <u>El</u> *Puente* (<u>the</u> bridge) when it was built, and had its name changed to the <u>old</u> bridge when they built a new one?

Indeed, it's the rather unimaginatively named *Puente Nuevo* (new bridge) that is the iconic one you see on the tourist photos. Built in the 19th century, this one rises 98 metres from the foot of the gorge and is a popular stopping off point for a photo opportunity.

After parking up in the centre of town, we began our visit by wandering through Ronda's characteristically narrow streets until they eventually spewed us out alongside the *Plaza de Toros*. A little further on and we arrived at our destination, the *Mirador de Ronda*, the main viewing point from which there are terrific vistas down into the gorge and out across the verdant valley floor below.

Chris was hanging well back from the edge as she has a deep fear of heights – she imagines she's a lemming and would happily throw herself off for no apparent reason ... I hope she doesn't as I don't think our insurance covers that ... and can you imagine all the paperwork involved?

The rest of us lingered a while, wandering around the mirador, taking in differing views from each vantage point. I'd done a bit of research on Ronda's history before leaving home and now was the ideal time to drop it into conversation I felt.

'What do you reckon, Dad? Great views, aren't they?'

'Yes, it's pretty stunning,' he said. 'And a long way down, too.'

'I know. Have you seen the movie *For Whom The Bell Tolls*?'

'With Gary Cooper? Yes, a long time ago, though. Why?'

'Apparently, the scene where Franco's fascist sympathisers are tossed over the cliffs by the Republicans was inspired by true events in Ronda, although Hemmingway never admitted it.'

'Was it really?'

'He's probably just read that this morning, David,' Chris chipped in from behind us.

'Busted!' I admitted.

The Spanish Civil War (1936-39) is a blemish on Spanish history that is rarely talked about in Spanish society today. It pitted General Franco's Nationalists against the incumbent Republicans of the time. Franco was supported by Hitler's Nazi Germany, Mussolini's fascist Italy and Portugal's dictator António de Oliveira Salazar. The Republicans received aid and support from Stalin's Soviet Union, along with International Brigades composed of European and US sympathisers.

It was a very brutal war (if you'll excuse the tautology), that divided families up and down the country, and I'm told it's not uncommon when turning over the soil in Andalucía to come across bones of questionable origin, as thousands were killed and buried in shallow graves throughout the region.

The sun was beating down on us, and my stomach was beginning to rumble.

'Right,' I said. 'Is anyone hungry?'

'I thought you'd never ask,' said Dad. 'Where are we going?'

'Well, I've checked TripAdvisor…'

'Oh, here we go,' said Chris.

'What?'

'Why can't we just stop somewhere that looks nice?' she said.

'Because it might be rubbish.'

'Where are you taking us, then?'

'There's a lovely tapas bar in the centre of town called Bodega San Francisco. The locals eat there, so it must be good.'

'And how far is it?'

'About five minutes away,' I lied.

'Well it had better be worth the walk.'

Off we trotted, back up past the bullring. Chris stopped almost immediately, however, to read the menu outside a place called Restaurante Jerez.

'This place looks nice,' she said.

'Looks can be deceiving. It's not very busy.'

'It's only half past one.'

'No wonder I'm starving,' said Dad, who has his lunch at noon on the dot back home.

'Keep moving, folks. You won't be disappointed.'

I strode onward leaving stragglers in my wake. There was a slight incline on the street, so I slowed a little to let them catch up. Five minutes in, I took a left turn.

'It's just up here,' I said.

'We've been walking five minutes already,' Chris said.

'Nearly there now. Trust me.' I'm starting to sound like a politician now, I thought.

Five minutes further up another slight incline and I spotted our destination just up ahead.

'Here it is,' I shouted triumphantly over my shoulder at anyone willing to listen, ignoring the sweat dripping off me.

As we approached the bar, it was clear the place was popular as all the tables on the long pavement terrace were already occupied. I let the others catch me up. It looked nothing special from the outside.

'Is this it?' Chris said, with more than a hint of disdain.

'Yes. It's your quintessential Spanish tapas bar. The food's good, and the beer's only a euro.'

'And you found this on TripAdvisor?'

'Yes, although it looks like we might have to wait for a table,' I said, sheepishly.

'What? You've dragged us all the way across town in the heat of the day to a no-frills bar in the middle of nowhere that's full?'

'It could be a long wait,' said Dad, helpfully.

Whose side is he on, I thought.

'Right,' said Chris. 'We'll let Mum catch her breath and then we'll go back to that nice restaurant we passed … 10 minutes ago!'

I don't know – you can't win! You try and give someone an authentic Ronda experience, and you're vilified when the place you chose just happens to be very popular.

Ten minutes and 500 metres later, we were back outside Restaurante Jerez, where Chris was already in conversation with a waiter, securing us a table in the shade of their covered terrace.

We had a long, leisurely lunch, finishing off with coffees, and to be fair, the food was good and went down well with the old folks.

'Did you enjoy your lunch?' Chris asked me.

'Well it wasn't tapas, but yes, the food was good.'

'Well done, Chris,' Mum said. 'Good choice. We'll put you in charge of choosing the restaurant in future.'

Bloody traitor!

After lunch we went to find the car, but I had one more pit stop in mind on the outskirts of Ronda. As we pulled out of the car park it was time to test the water.

'Anyone fancy a spot of wine tasting?' I asked, before the older members of our party had a chance to fall asleep.

'I never say no to a wine tasting,' Chris said.

'Whatever you want to do,' Mum said, ever the diplomat.

The Phoenicians were the first settlers to exploit the rich soil in this area for wine production, and it remained famous for its quality wines until production was wiped out at the end of the 19th century by the phylloxera blight, a North American insect pest that laid waste to much of Europe's winemaking industry – since Chris and I arrived on these shores, we've been doing our level best to lay waste to it ourselves, but they must be making it faster than we can drink it!

Wine production has bounced back with spectacular results in recent years thanks to what's known as the Ronda Wine Revival, after French grapes were introduced to Andalucía 30 years ago.

Five minutes outside town, I turned off the main road and up the driveway for Bodegas Lunares. It looked very quiet as we rounded a corner into a small car park, ours being the only car there.

'Are you sure it's open?' Dad asked.

'There's only one way to find out for sure,' I said. 'Me and Chris will just nip in and see if they're open for a wine tasting. You two stay here a minute.'

I opened all the car windows to let some air in for Mum and Dad while the two of us went to find someone. We had a quick scout round and found a doorway, and after a few loud inquisitive shouts of *hola*, a woman appeared.

We were out of luck. Wine tastings were by appointment only. But she was happy to sell us a few bottles. A few minutes later we returned to the car carrying two bottles of red and two bottles of rose.

'Advance bookings only, I'm afraid. But we can do our own private tasting with these when we get home,' I said, holding the wine aloft.

'Not having a very successful day, are you?' Chris said.

'What do you mean?'

'Well, the restaurant you chose was full, and the vineyard was shut.'

'Well if that's your measure of success, then I can't argue with you.'

I didn't say that. In fact, I didn't say anything. I bit my lip, because what I wanted to say would have just got me in trouble, and we had a long drive ahead of us. And sure enough, all three of them nodded off as the car journey – or more accurately, the long boozy lunch – put them in a dreamlike state and left me pondering how best to dispose of a dead body!

4

Wildfire Watch

'I've got a job!' Chris announced as she walked through the door.

'Congratulations! How much does it pay?' was my first reaction.

'Nothing. It's voluntary.'

'Well that won't pay the bar bills!'

'Neither will what you're doing,' she countered.

'Erm. I'm a writer now, thank you very much.'

'And how many words have you written this week?'

'I'm still thrashing out the plot at the moment.'

'Exactly!'

'What's the job, Chris?' Mum asked, more reasonably.

'Reporting on wildfires and adverse weather events.'

'On the telly?' Dad asked, rather more naively.

'No, on Facebook.'

Dad looked a bit puzzled as he didn't use Facebook and had only just got used to using his tablet.

'That thing we do video calls with on my tablet?'

'No, Dad. That's Facetime.'

'Oh. I get my weather forecasts off the telly and the internet, anyway,' he said.

'It's not for you, David.' Chris explained. 'It's for people living up and down the Spanish Costas who are at risk from wildfires or severe flooding. I have to monitor some Spanish Twitter accounts…'

Oh no, she's going to confuse him even more now.

'...and when they post an alert, I have to translate it into English for people on a Facebook group.'

He was still none the wiser.

'It will alert people if there's a wildfire just started up in their area and let them know if they need to get ready to evacuate.'

'Ah, I see.'

The penny had dropped. Either that or he was just out of questions!

'Do you get a lot of fires?' Mum asked.

'Yes, they're a serious problem in Spain, especially in the summer months when the ground is so dry.'

Spain suffers an average of 13,000 wildfires every year, and readers of book one may recall that you need a licence from the town hall to do most things in Spain, like retile your bathroom or burn your garden waste. And the restrictions on fires are more severe in what's known as 'wildfire season', when you can't even light a barbecue if your house is within a given distance of an area with a particular tree density, and especially near forested areas. In fact, forest roads are often completely closed to all vehicles during the summer months as the heat of the exhaust can easily ignite the forest floor.

Between 1961 and 2016, forest fires in Spain have devastated as much as eight million hectares – and if you're struggling to comprehend how big an area that is, in true British journalistic fashion, you could say that's four times the size of Wales! That represents about 16% of Spain's total land mass, over half of which is forested.

This year seems to have been particularly bad, as so far, the country has lost more than five times as much woodland in the first half of the year compared to the same period last year. You can therefore understand the urgent need for people to be fully aware of any wildfires developing in their area. Hence, Chris applying for this volunteer role.

Our local mountains are mostly covered in ancient pines, and pinecones make for perfect kindling, so a pine forest is particularly prone to conflagrate rapidly – or in layman's terms, go up in bloody smoke.

Adding to Spain's problem was Franco's erroneous post-war forestry policy which oversaw the planting of far too many pines and eucalyptus (another remarkably combustible species). He reportedly chose those two species in order to quickly obtain a large mass of wood suitable for construction after the civil war had decimated much of the country – a civil war he started, I might add.

Another issue was the change of use of much of the forested areas. Where earlier, sheep and goat herders were free to graze their herds in the woods, thus helping to clear scrub from the forest floor (which is usually the source of any fire), the forests have been given protection over time, and access to the land for grazing has been severely limited, or become cost prohibitive for the shepherds.

'So, what hours are you expected to work?' I asked.

'Well, there are four other people plus me, and we have to monitor 13 regions. Basically, the whole Mediterranean coastline, plus the Canary Islands and Balearics. We work in two-hour shifts and have to make sure that there is someone monitoring the fire service information channels from 10am to 10pm.'

'And what's Spanish for wildfire?'

'*Incendio.*'

'How did you find out about the job?' Mum asked.

'When I was on my own here last year during the floods, and there were cars floating down the roads of Alhaurín, I was hearing rumours about people being evacuated off roofs, and I was worried I didn't know what to do or who to contact if I got into trouble. Then I found this Fire and Weather Watch Facebook group that was giving out advice and sticking to the facts so as not to perpetuate rumours, and the moderators were doing a great job. Then in the summer, they were asking for more volunteers, so I thought I'd give it a go.'

It turned out to be quite a demanding job at times, especially when a wildfire kicked off. After some initial training, Chris was expected to keep refreshing the emergency Twitter accounts for every province, as they each had their own, and Andalucía also had a dedicated forest fire response body called Infoca, who were the specialist wildfire firefighting service – you'll have seen newsreels showing skilled pilots flying helicopters and planes, dropping water onto fires. In Andalucía, they're allowed to hover over your pool and fill their enormous bucket with your pool water if there is sufficient clearance around it to do so safely.

Once some information appeared (in Spanish, naturally, but also in Catalán, where every second letter seems to be an 'x'!), Chris and her colleagues had to quickly translate it, establish if it related to an existing or new wildfire, or a severe weather warning, and then post accordingly in English in the correct regional Facebook group where they could share that information and allow people to ask questions. You got the usual idiots asking dumb questions or posting unhelpful comments which then had to be deleted.

And if a member of the public spotted a new fire themselves, they could create a new post, and the moderators would try and establish if it was a wildfire affecting a forested area, or just a car fire or house fire (which weren't reported on), in which case it would be deleted.

They say you're never more than six feet from a rat in Britain but having lived in Spain for a year now and read some of the crap posted on Facebook, I think stupid expats outnumber the rats over here!

There are even occasions in the autumn when the part-time firefighters (as they get laid off at the end of the season) start a fire themselves so they can get called out again and be paid to fight the fire, but they are all too often found out and prosecuted.

'Who runs all this, then?' Mum asked.

'A local woman named Jill who set it up years ago after a severe wildfire in this area.'

Apparently, a huge fire in 2011 that started on the coastal side of the mountain was fanned by high winds and came racing over the top of the mountain range and threatened the local area. Jill was herself struggling to find accurate information about the spread and direction of the fire, and so later decided to set up this volunteer service.

'Can we call you Fireman Chris from now on?' Dad teased.

'Only if you want a slap!' Chris replied.

5

When the Cat's Away

'Will you miss me?' Chris asked.

'Of course, I will.' I just hoped I had enough clean underwear to last the week as I didn't know how to use the washing machine – not just this washing machine, any washing machine!

Chris was leaving me to my own devices in Spain while she went back to the UK to help with the childminding while our second eldest daughter, Andrea, had a small operation. As it happened, just after arriving there, the op got cancelled, but she was more than happy to stay anyway and see all our four girls and the grandkids, which at this point numbered five, four more girls and one solitary boy.

And I felt like a solitary boy myself without Chris by my side. This was my first solo stint in Spain, and it felt weird. No matter that my prior work commitments on our arrival in Spain a year ago had forced Chris to spend the best part of six months on her own during the working week. At least when I was working away, I had hotel staff feeding me, but now I had to plan my own meals and dress myself every morning – what a responsibility!

It was a strange week all round, really, as Catalonia held an unlawful independence referendum that turned violent and Monarch Airlines went belly up, although the latter incident couldn't be blamed on me for not flying backwards and forwards to the UK every week as I used to be an EasyJet flyer.

The Catalonia thing had been brewing for a while now. When General Franco's three-year coup rewarded him with power in

1939, Catalonia lost any autonomy it had at the time, and the Catalan language was dropped from the education curriculum. After Franco died in 1975 and Spain became a parliamentary democracy and a constitutional monarchy, Catalonia never recovered its autonomy. It has a GDP almost as high as Madrid's and feels that it would be better off keeping its own tax revenues, rather than send them to Madrid to be distributed to some other poorer autonomous regions (even though that's how democratic western nations are supposed to work).

It's the opposite to the UK really, as in Spain money flows down to the poorer areas, whereas big capital projects in the UK always seem to happen in London, and certainly not the northwest or northeast regions of the UK. I don't know about "levelling up" ... someone should level London - although the Germans tried that in 1940, and it didn't work!

The Scottish Nationalist Party were taking a keen interest in the Catalan referendum as they too sought independence from the rest of the UK. However, whereas Catalonia has the tax revenues and industry necessary to thrive as an independent state, I'm not convinced Scotland does. In fact, trying to explain the offside rule in football is easier than getting your head round the UK government's Barnett formula for funding public spending in Scotland!

In contrast, Andalucía's GDP is around two-thirds the size of Madrid's, but Andalucía ranks way down the table for average earnings, probably because the main industries are olive oil production and tourism.

So with the best part of a week to entertain myself, I booked some much-needed golf lessons for later in the week – just in case I ever had to play with those three Swedes again. And then I jumped in the pool to relax after a hard day's meal planning.

'What have you been up to today?' Chris asked when she called that evening.

'Busy day, really. I don't where the time's gone.'

'Have you been writing?'

'Still thrashing out the plot. It's a complex thriller I'm writing. You can't hurry perfection.'

I knew I wasn't convincing her.

'OK, now tell me what you've really been doing?'

'Had a swim and booked some golf lessons,' I said sheepishly – she knows I'm a rubbish liar.

'Very productive.'

A couple of days later, I had a wonderful golf pro show me where I was going wrong with my shots off the fairway and my approach play to the greens, and armed with my newfound iron skills, I booked a round of golf with the Andalucian Nomads Golf Society, a friendly group of international expats who get together twice a week for a round of golf.

I turned up at Mijas Golf for my Nomads debut and was partnered up with three other blokes with too much time on their hands who probably didn't know how to work a washing machine. I was sharing a buggy with a smashing down-to-earth fella called Brian, a businessman from up north – in fact, he hailed from Bolton, just down the road from us back home.

I finished my round with 20 points using Stableford rules, which is almost as complex to explain as the offside rule, but in essence, if you shot a par on every hole then you'd finish with 36 points, so I was quite chuffed with my haul of 20 points … although don't forget, for being such a crap golfer, my handicap affords me an extra 28 shots across the course, and without that handicap I'd have scored about three points instead!

However, the most important thing was I made a new friend in Brian. He had a holiday home on Mijas Costa and was here with his family. He had some other golfing friends arriving the following week. I was cordially invited to play a round with them and have dinner afterwards with the wives. Something to look forward to when Chris returned then.

'So, when the cat's away, the mice play golf do they?' Chris teased when I collected her from the airport.

'Actually, I don't know where the cat's been, but you've got three new kittens to gush over when you get home.'

'Aw, how cute. Who's the mum?'

'No idea, but she must be a bit of a tart as the kittens look like they've come from three different dads!'

We had several feral cats that we fed on a daily basis, none of which we'd given names, except for next door's tame black cat that we called … wait for it … black cat! So I nicknamed our three new little furry friends Spit, Spat and Spot. One of the kittens had a mix of white and tortoise shell fur and was one of those cats that liked to hiss at you, so "it" (I hadn't sexed them yet!) was christened Spit. There was a dark grey one that picked fights with the other two, so was christened Spat. And finally, Spot was so named because it was all white with a single black spot on top of its head.

'And what else have you being doing this week?'

'Well, there's always a bit of gardening to be done. Erm, I played my trumpet really loudly every day … and I bought a goat and a hen,' I teased.

'What?!' she protested loudly. 'What the hell are we supposed to do with a goat and a hen?'

'Nothing. They're for Arcadius's family in Uganda.'

I should explain … I sponsor a child's education in a remote Ugandan village called Nkuringo. I'd previously visited the area on a charity hike with my brother and nephew and went to sit with the mountain gorillas in the Bwindi Impenetrable Forest for an hour or so, which was the most amazing experience.

The village kids there had to walk for miles every day to collect dirty drinking water, and most of them didn't get any proper schooling as their subsistence-farmer parents couldn't afford the fees. Thereafter, a charity was set up to help support the village, build water tanks, extend the school and dormitories, and provide funding for more kids to get an education.

My little boy is called Arcadius, and he's been attending primary school thanks to my funding for the past few years. And I'd just bought his family a goat and a hen to provide them with milk and eggs. A short while later, I received a photo of Arcadius and his mum taking delivery of the animals, and they looked so thrilled. Eee! It warms the cockles of my heart!

Go and check out the charity's great work at "necs.org.uk" and get involved if you're so inclined.

'I see the washing basket's full,' Chris commented a while later when she was separating the dirty laundry into lights and darks.

'Yes. I'm a clean boy – I change my underwear every day.'

'I see you've not changed the tea towel in over a week – there's not a single one in the washing basket.'

'I hardly used it – the dishes come out of the dishwasher already dry.'

'Then why does it look like you've been doing car maintenance with it?!'

I had no answer to that, of course. All in all, I'd had a fun week on my own, and I did actually get some writing done on my novel, so it wasn't all golf, swimming and sunbathing (and buying livestock). The following day I nominated Chris as my principal proofreader, a role she was happy to take on ... when she wasn't fighting fires or washing my underwear, of course!

6

Extra! Extra! Read All About It

'What're you doing today?' I asked Chris.

'Working.'

'Any fires?'

'Not yet. What're you doing today?'

'Writing. Although we may get a visit from the *Guardia Civil* later.'

'What?! What've you done?'

'I downloaded the manual for operating a Glock 9mm pistol without switching on my VPN.'

'Why do you need to know how to operate a pistol? Is there something you're not telling me?'

'No. Just research for my novel.'

'Wouldn't you be better off getting a proper job?'

'This is a proper job. Just you wait until I'm doing book signings and making millions.'

Despite first impressions, I wasn't averse to getting a "proper job" in Spain. In fact. I'd been actively looking for something that was Monday to Friday with sociable daytime hours. What I didn't want to be doing was jumping on a plane every week for a living – I felt those days were behind me now.

Nor did I want a job in hospitality due to the unsociable hours. I didn't want to be serving food to punters in the evening when I could be sat in a restaurant myself shouting *Oiga* at the waiting staff.

So my eye was drawn to an ad in one of the local, free, expat newspapers – they wanted a proofreader/writer for their paper … well, of course, I was infinitely qualified for the job as I could both read *and* write! *And* I was writing a novel, so surely that would weigh in my favour.

I knocked up a covering letter and sent it off without delay and felt quietly confident I'd be given an interview. A couple of days later I got the email I'd been waiting for: an invitation to attend an interview at their offices.

I won't deny it, I was nervous. After all, I hadn't had a formal interview for 16 years; the few job changes I'd had in that time didn't need formal interviews as the hirers already knew me. I also reckoned they probably used Apple Macs in publishing, and I was a Windows man through and through.

One of the prerequisites for the job was to have a social security certificate so off I went to get one, armed with the usual photocopies of everything they might want a copy of. Readers of book one will be all too familiar with the ridiculous bureaucracy in Spain, and the fact that when I first got registered with the equivalent of a National Insurance number last year they put my name and surname the wrong way round and everything I've had done officially since then has also had to be issued the wrong way round, as that's how I'm registered in the system … although as I was (un)reliably informed at the time, I shouldn't worry as it happens all the time.

And sure enough, they refused to give me a social security certificate that was contrary to how I was recorded in the central government system. Hence, to add to my existing NIE certificate (Foreigner's ID Number), *Padrón* certificate (recognition from the town hall that I lived in this town) and Residency certificate, all with the names the wrong way round, I could add to that collection of misinformation my new Social Security certificate. I'm sure all this is going to come back to haunt me some day and I'll be strip-searched and extradited, never to darken these shores again!

The job interview was relatively informal with the office manager, and I was invited back at the end of the week for a trial day in the office.

'I reckon I've got that job in the bag,' I said to my Spanish teacher the following day as we sat drinking beer during our weekly lesson in the bar at the end of our lane.

'Are you sure you want it? I know a few people who have worked there briefly before leaving. They're a bit of nightmare to work for,' she replied.

'It'll be fine. I'm not averse to a bit of hard work.'

Trial day came and off I went to meet my new work colleagues and show them what a great proofreader and writer I was. The people I was seated next to were Spaniards with a good level of English, and as I suspected, they were all working on Apple Macs.

The supervisor I was assigned to was a bit of a humourless character … think Mona Lisa, without the smile (what, you don't think the Mona Lisa is smiling? Have another look). She offered no pleasantries on introduction and went straight into telling me what she expected me to do. I confessed to not knowing how to use a Mac, so there was a brief introduction given on how to navigate my way around. Then I got the briefest of instruction on what to do with the pages I was given to work on and left to it. As a former trainer myself, it was the worst piece of training I'd ever come across, but hey ho, I wasn't an idiot, so I just got on with it.

My tasks were to check articles the others had written and edit them where they bled into the next article on the page layout, correct spelling and punctuation etc. and then submit the finished article to the supervisor to check. We weren't permitted to use accented letters – so none of the usual Spanish characters á, é, í, ó, ü or ñ should be allowed through – with the only exception being someone's name. Money for old rope, I thought.

Due largely to the crap knowledge transfer at the start of the morning session, she and I had a few "misunderstandings" during the course of the day. In one article, I'd left a cedilla (ç) in as it was in someone's name.

'You can't use the cedilla,' I was admonished.

'You said special characters were permitted in names.'

'Not cedillas though.'

It would have been nice to have been informed of that during the "training" I pondered.

On another occasion I was pulled up for correcting "health-care" to "healthcare".

'Health-care is hyphenated,' she informed me.

'I've checked that with the online Collins English Dictionary,' I countered, 'and it's not hyphenated.'

'We don't use Collins, we use the Oxford English Dictionary,' she replied rather too curtly for my liking.

Something else she hadn't told me in the "training" session then. And it was a bit pointless telling me that as, at that time, the Oxford English Dictionary wasn't available online, nor had she supplied me with a printed copy, which she should have done if it was supposedly the newspaper's oracle for English spelling.

I could see if I was to take this job, I wouldn't be going for a beer after work with this sourpuss!

I soldiered on for the rest of the day and was then appraised briefly at the end of the day by the office manager I'd met earlier in the week.

'How did you find it?' she asked.

'Not too bad. There was nothing about the job I couldn't do. How did *you* think I did?'

'Well, I'm told you can be a bit pedantic.'

'What? Surely that's a bloody key requirement for the job as a proofreader,' I almost said, but didn't. You've got to follow language rules and a style guide in publishing – it's not subjective!

I should also have said 'and proofreader doesn't have a bloody hyphen in British English, but your job advert used the American English spelling. Pedant? You ain't seen nothing yet!'

The hours were 9:30 to 19:00, Monday to Friday, with two short breaks and a lunch hour … apart from publication days, when it wasn't unusual to work until midnight, I was informed … WITHOUT EXTRA PAY! I had my Spanish teacher's words of warning ringing in my ears.

So for a 40-hour week (or more likely a 50-hour week), the hourly rate worked out at around €7 per hour. Jeepers! I thought they'd abolished slavery in the EU. No wonder they were mostly Spaniards working in the office.

In the words of Touker Suleyman off Dragon's Den, 'I won't get out of bed for one percent', or in this case, €7 per hour.

In fact, there's a fable that goes something like this ... Pablo Picasso was in a restaurant when a man approached him, handed him a napkin, and asked: "Could you sketch something for me? I'll pay. Name your price." Picasso took the napkin, pulled a charcoal pencil from his pocket and started sketching. Using only a few strokes, he drew a goat that was unmistakably a Picasso. He held it up for the man to see. The man was delighted and reached out for it, but Picasso withheld it. "That will be $100,000," Picasso said. The man was astonished. "$100,000?! You drew that in 30 seconds!" Picasso crumpled up the napkin and stuffed it in his pocket. "You're wrong," he said. "It's taken me 40 years to do that." And the moral of the tale is: don't undersell yourself – and I wasn't about to.

As my appraisal came to a close, I was informed they were trying out two more people the following week and I'd be advised in due course. Which I interpreted as ... every week we get a couple of mugs just like you to come in and do a full day's work for us free of charge.

'How'd you get on?' Chris asked when I got home.

'They pay peanuts, employ monkeys and don't deserve a man of my considerable talent.'

'Well, you were warned.'

7

Letting Our Hair Down

'All work and no play makes Jack a dull boy', or so the old proverb goes. And if you've seen Stanley Kubrick's eerie 1980 adaptation of Stephen King's horror novel, *The Shining*, that phrase will send a chill down your spine ... Jack Nicholson's character hits writer's block while looking after an empty, spooky hotel over the winter, and after he starts acting weird, his wife discovers he's been typing that phrase over and over again in a variety of grammatical styles on reams and reams of paper.

Chris was about to start one of her Fire Watch shifts, and I was busy working on my novel in the spare room.

'How's the writing coming on?' Chris asked, poking her head round the door.

'Not so well today,' I said. 'Let's book a night away in Málaga before I start knocking the bathroom door down and saying *Heeeere's Johnny!*'

'You what?'

'Never mind. Give Kim a call and see if they're free next weekend.'

Kim and Martin were friends we'd met since moving here that lived on the other side of Málaga, high up in the mountains. They were usually up for a good night out. We booked a couple of rooms at the Ibis in the centre of Málaga (another budget accommodation until the royalty checks come rolling in), and I went back to my writing.

The weekend would soon come round, but more importantly, my novel was beginning to take shape at last. After the *Guardia Civil* never kicked our door down to ask why I was downloading operating instructions for a Glock pistol, I rather foolishly tempted fate by downloading technical data sheets relating to bomb disposal equipment – surely, we'd be surrounded by helicopters before the sun set! I thought it best not to tell Chris this time and leave it as a surprise if we did get raided.

After such a stressful job in international IT projects, burning the candle at both ends and flying here there and everywhere, I was finding the writing process somewhat cathartic. Only time would tell if I could turn this into a career or just a hobby, however.

Málaga is such a fantastic city and is fast becoming my favourite European city. It has a thriving old town full of independent bars and restaurants, a main shopping street with the leading designer brand names, a beautiful marina playing host to superyachts and a long beachfront. And boasting 22 museums, it's second only to Madrid in that regard.

For lunch we'd tried to book into a popular tapas restaurant in the heart of the old town called Casa Lola, but it wasn't possible to reserve a table, so when we arrived, we had a short wait to be seated. The restaurant specialised in serving a vast range of quality tapas, all made to order at a reasonable price, with an extensive range of wines that could be ordered by the glass.

The first thing I ordered to eat was a plate of tomatoes, drizzled in olive oil and salt – the tomatoes in Spain are on a different level and have always been a favourite of mine since moving here. These were washed down with a glass of Ribera del Duero. To accompany that we chose a varied selection of small, lovingly created tapas plates, from fish to seafood to meat and vegetables, some decorated with tasty salsas or a fried quail's egg.

So successful were the owners with this venture that you'll now find half a dozen of these eateries dotted around the old town, and since visiting the first one in the autumn of 2017, it's been our preferred destination for a tapas lunch. And with all of them, expect to have to wait for a table if you turn up at the peak hour of 2pm.

Afterwards, we had a gentle stroll through the city, admiring the Roman amphitheatre adjacent to the walls of the Alcazaba. An Alcazaba is a fortified palace, and the one in Málaga is considered to be one of the most beautiful in Spain. Constructed in the Middle Ages by the Muslims, the name comes from the Arabic and simply refers to a fortification within a walled town, from within which the city could be defended.

Built on the slopes of the Gibalfaro mountain, it's overlooked by another 14th century fortification called the *Castillo de Gibalfaro* (Gibalfaro Castle). The upper castle is connected to the Alcazaba by a series of walled corridors, protecting the soldiers as they moved between the two. When the Spanish Catholic monarchs, King Ferdinand and Queen Isabella, sent 70,000 troops to lay siege to the resident Arab population in 1487, the fortifications withstood the onslaught for three months, and they were only defeated when they ran out of food and were forced to surrender.

We decided to leave a more formal visit inside the Alcazaba and Gibalfaro Castle for another day, and instead we wandered over for refreshments at one of Málaga's most iconic bars, El Pimpi, so named after the young boys who helped sailors arriving in the port to find taverns and female company. Two hundred years earlier, it was the site of the stables for the Count of Málaga's palace, but these days, it's more renowned for the patronage of one of Málaga's most famous sons, Antonio Banderas.

Inside the rather quaint bar, lined with barrels of Málaga sweet wines, you'll find old photographs of Spanish celebrities visiting the bar. Since opening in 1971, the bar has extended to include a fine dining restaurant and is a popular stopping off point for a glass of Málaga wine or the city's much-loved Victoria beer.

After returning to the hotel to freshen up for dinner, we headed to the rooftop cocktail bar of the four-star AC Hotel Málaga Palacio and enjoyed the views over the marina and across the city. And after imbibing since lunchtime, I don't have much recollection of where we ended up for dinner, but suffice to say, we won't have been disappointed.

A couple of weeks later, Chris and I were back in Málaga to visit the rather beautiful *Teatro de Cervantes* (Cervantes Theatre). It was Málaga jazz week, and Chris rather indulged me as I wanted to go and watch the American double bass player, Ron Carter. His trio were on tour, and I was a fan of some of his earlier stuff when he played with Miles Davis and Herbie Hancock. For the bass players amongst you, Carter is the most recorded bassist in history with over 2,200 recordings to his name, which works out at a staggering 34 recordings per year. He must be minted from the royalties alone on that little lot!

It wasn't Chris's cup of tea, sadly – she calls jazz that music where everyone is playing a different tune at the same time. I pity her, really, for not being able to appreciate the finer points of jazz music, as it's certainly not easy to play well. Oddly, she likes traditional jazz … where everyone *IS* playing a different tune at the same time! Maybe it's the foot-tapping boozy ambiance of a trad jazz band playing in a poky, smoky (pre-smoking ban in 2007) room at the back of a real ale pub that is the attraction for her. Who knows, but our brains are clearly wired differently.

A few weeks later still, we found ourselves in Málaga with Kim and Martin for one last time that year to enjoy the Christmas lights. This time we pushed the boat out as Chris convinced us to book into the Parador de Málaga Gibalfaro hotel at €140 per night. Having stayed in a couple of these government-owned hotels earlier in the year on our drive south from the UK, we knew it would be a cut above the standard hotels, and it certainly was. I still maintain I'd have a very different view if the UK government started running hotels as they couldn't organise a piss-up in a brewery, but the Spanish seem to have got it just about right.

Perched high on the mountain alongside the Gibalfaro Castle, it has commanding views over the marina, port and city. It took us about 25 minutes to walk down the scenic paved path into the heart of the town as we headed for Calle Marqués de Larios, the main shopping street, which is decked out the full length in

Christmas lights that dance along to a music track, which this year concluded with the ever popular Spanish Christmas song, *Feliz Navidad*.

It's a very popular attraction as you might imagine, and people are packed in tightly together like sardines along the full 350-metre length of the street. We chose a less cramped position at the end of the street where it meets the main road and thoroughly enjoyed it. All that was missing was a glass of *glühwein* and a *bratwurst*, something we would have normally enjoyed at the Manchester Christmas Markets.

After an evening of Christmas drinking and frivolity, I was pleased to get a restful night's sleep in the Parador, with its generous bed and – being as it's on top of a mountain – tranquil location, away from the late-night revelry of the city. One of the best things about the Paradors is the plentiful and varied breakfast buffet, and although I didn't quite 'fill my boots', I didn't need any lunch later.

Christmas was memorable this year for all the wrong reasons. We did what would become the norm with us now living in Spain, which was to head back to the UK for a week or two to visit all the family. Last year, we had Christmas dinner with our youngest daughter, Corrinne, who not being the most accomplished of cooks, left it all to Chris and me to prepare and cook. This year we'd been invited to have Christmas dinner with our eldest daughter, Steph, who is a very good cook, so I was looking forward to not having to peel mountains of sprouts on Christmas Eve – in fact, to ensure I didn't have to, we arranged to spend Christmas Eve with one of our other daughters.

Arriving at Steph's late Christmas morning, she seemed to have most things in hand, even if she was looking a bit flustered. However, halfway through the cooking of the huge turkey, the oven decided today would be a good day to stop working. Blind panic ensued while we tried to establish what had happened and how to resolve it. After a while scratching heads and the odd expletive thrown in, we resigned ourselves to not being able to use the oven at all until an electrician could come out after Christmas.

With Steph upset about her carefully planned Christmas dinner being ruined by the oven malfunctioning at the most critical point, it was time for a level head to calm things down. The business analyst in me quickly assessed the situation and drew up a mental project plan. Then after considering any other alternatives (like ringing out for a takeaway curry) I was ready to deliver my verdict.

'Don't panic!' I said. I pointed to the large gas barbecue currently under six inches of snow in the back garden. 'Have you got gas in that bottle?'

'You can't barbecue a whole turkey!' Chris protested.

'No, but I can chop it into pieces and barbecue them.'

I dismembered the turkey, taking off the wings and legs, then the breasts, cutting those in half again as they were so large – Jeffrey Dahmer couldn't have done a better job! Then I carefully barbecued our Christmas dinner.

Thankfully, the stuffing and roast potatoes had already been cooked as there wasn't room in the oven for them with the turkey, so those were heated up in the microwave just before plating up, and we all enjoyed our BBQ turkey dinner with all the trimmings. I don't know if it was the disappointment and upset caused by the oven failure or if it was on the cards anyway, but by the following Christmas, Steph had a whole new kitchen extension and a new oven!

This was also the one year where all the items on my Christmas wish list were dropped down the chimney by Santa, so I knew I'd been a good boy, even it was just a pile of books I'd requested to help turn me into the next Michael Connolly. Amongst my new reading material were books with titles like *Self-Editing for Fiction Writers*, *Write To Be Published*, *How To Write A Novel* – although I found the very helpfully titled *How NOT to Write a Novel* much more useful – and the almanac for such distinguished 'authors' such as myself *The Writers' And Artists' Yearbook*. How could I possibly fail armed with such tomes of unsurpassed writing excellence?

But just in case I did, I sent my second Spanish job application off to do IT Support for a fashion company. I'm an

IT professional with 20 years in the fashion industry – it's in the bag, surely!

No sooner had we returned to Spain than we found ourselves driving up the mountain road to hell on our way to celebrate New Year's Eve with Kim and Martin in Árchez. When we arrived, we were welcomed vociferously by not one, but two podencos, a Spanish warren hound breed used for hunting in these parts. Sadly, Toby the grand old labrador had passed away, but Pod podenco had a new friend in Peter podenco, another rescue, but unlike Pod who was brown, Peter was a white podenco cross, where the cross was perhaps something akin to a bull terrier – he was all muscle, but quite friendly once he'd met you, especially if you had food in your hand.

We'd been invited to join them at one of their favourite restaurants in Cómpeta, El Pilón, who were having a special all-inclusive New Year's Eve dinner party. It got a bit raucous as you might imagine, and by the end of the night people were up singing and dancing on the tables. Thankfully, the local taxi driver was sober and doing a roaring trade and safely dropped us back at their finca in the early hours.

So then, that was 2017, was it? Theresa May had pulled the trigger on Brexit, a deranged gunman killed 58 people and wounded 500 more in America's deadliest mass shooting in Las Vegas, Spain recorded its hottest day on record not far from here, and the world had witnessed the first total solar eclipse since 1918 – I don't know about you, but I can't help feeling the world is ending. If it does end though, I want to at least go out with an empty wine rack … anything less would be a crying shame.

HAPPY NEW YEAR EVERYONE!

8

I've Had a Bellyful of This

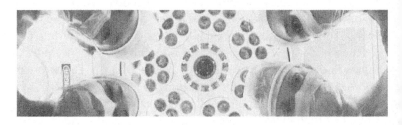

2018 started with me not making the shortlist for the IT Fashion job, but two more new kittens arrived on the terrace. They were so adorable and looked like a couple of raccoons; they had white faces and a dark Zorro mask across their eyes, just like their mum, whom we hadn't seen before either. It was like we were running a bloody mother and baby clinic for cats on our terrace.

Then again, we could have been running an old people's home too, as Mum and Dad arrived soon afterwards for another week of sun, sea and sangria. I think this was their fifth trip out to stay with us now, and we'd only been here 16 months. If this carries on, I might even elevate myself to #1 son in their will, although Dad is having a good go at spending it all while he still can – a man after my own heart, so more power to his elbow.

What was uppermost in my mind at the current time, however, was the need to book a gastroscopy appointment. After doing a passable impression of Linda Blair projectile vomiting in *The Exorcist* in a Scottish B&B 20-odd years ago – by the way, that was me in the Scottish B&B and not Linda Blair – I'd had a less than successful repeat operation to repair my hiatus hernia in 2015, and now I was expected to have a gastroscopy every two years to check that my pre-cancerous Barrett's Oesophagus was no worse. If it was, my life plan of having at least 10 glorious years of living it up in Spain before I pop my clogs might be curtailed somewhat (although Chris would be quids in as I was well insured!).

Hence, it was now time to see if my Spanish private health insurance would cough up for it, or if I'd have to raid my piggy bank. It would have been covered if we'd still been in the UK, but since moving to Spain, of course, everything you've already got is considered a preexisting condition. Regardless, you don't get anything in this world if you don't ask for it, so I thought I'd chance my arm and put in a cheeky claim. I was completely open and honest with them and sent them all the reports from my UK surgeon, and by some miracle – or administrative error – the procedure was approved.

Within the week, I was off down to the private clinic in Marbella. I must admit, I wasn't feeling the best as I had a bit of a head cold and a tickly cough after mixing with the great unwashed in the UK over Christmas. I was given a sedative injection – which felt more like a general anaesthetic because I didn't remember a thing after counting from one to about six – and when I came round, the news wasn't what I expected to hear.

'We had to halt the procedure,' my surgeon said.

'Eh, uuum, bah wooor foor?' I asked, still a bit dopy.

'He wants to know why,' Chris helpfully translated into my native English.

'You were coughing and choking on the camera. We'll have to repeat the procedure when your cough has gone.'

'Awwwkaay.'

'But we did find something concerning while we were in there.'

Oh shit, I thought. That's me a goner inside six weeks.

'What did you find?' Chris asked.

'We found a bezoar in your stomach.'

What in the name of all things holy is that, I wondered. I'd never heard of a bezoar, let alone knew how to spell it. Was it some kind of parasite, like a tapeworm? Was my stomach about to explode like that bloke in *Alien*?

I was still too spaced out to string a proper sentence together, so Chris asked him what it was.

'You've a mass of undigested vegetable matter that has collected together in a ball, and you need to get rid of that as soon as possible before it causes you a bigger digestive problem.'

If you google a bezoar, it says it's caused by eating hair, fuzzy materials or plastic bags, and is more commonly found in teenage girls. Well, I'm neither a pubescent female, a cat or a bloody turtle, so how have I ended up with one.

'Here's a photo of your bezoar,' the surgeon continued.

Then it all became clear to me. I was looking at a mostly orange ball of vegetable matter. It was thinly sliced carrots from that bloody big stir fry I had for my tea last night. Chris wasn't too hungry, so I had extra helpings as I don't like to see food thrown away. I also eat faster than is normal (or healthy), thanks to my early school years in a boys' grammar school where your lunchtime food intake was directly proportionate to how fast you could eat on a table of eight boys who were expected to share equally a big tray of whatever constituted lunch for that day. Hence, I often didn't chew my food enough, and Chris was always on at me about it.

'How does he get rid of that then?' Chris asked.

'I'll need to see him in hospital rather than the clinic where we have fully staffed recovery teams.'

Recovery teams? I might not even have six weeks left!

'We need to repeat the gastroscopy, and if the bezoar is still present, I'll need to remove it.'

'And can we do anything in the meantime to alleviate it?'

'Yes. You could try coke.'

What? I'm not turning into a crackhead just to get rid of a ball of carrots.

'Normal or diet?' Chris asked.

In my still hazy state that had me puzzled even more as I didn't know Weightwatchers promoted a healthier version of cocaine.

'It doesn't really matter,' the surgeon said. 'Coca-Cola has been proven to help agitate and break down vegetable matter so it can be digested properly. I recommend he drinks a can of Coke every day as a preventative measure from now on.'

We wandered out onto the promenade and found a café to digest the news (excuse the pun), and a waiter sauntered over to take our order.

'*Café con leche*,' Chris said.

'*Coke para mi*,' I replied, still not fully compos mentis.

I sat quietly for a while pondering my fate.

'What are you thinking?' Chris asked.

'That I'd better write all my passwords down for you and show you where my life insurance is. You'll be fine. I'm worth quarter of a million dead!'

'Don't be silly. You're worth much more to me alive. And you're going to be fine, anyway.'

A few weeks passed with me arguing the toss with the insurance company who had finally realised they probably shouldn't have approved the first gastroscopy, never mind a second one, complete with a crash team! I countered that, in principle, they'd paid for the first one so had set a precedent and should pay for this one, as it was a repeat of the procedure they'd already approved. And for another thing, the bezoar wasn't preexisting, and those carrots were Spanish carrots fresh off a Spanish supermarket shelf last week. But it was no good, I was met with a wall of intransigence and the computer had said NO.

They claimed the bezoar was related to my preexisting condition. I thought it was more likely to be related to the dining practices of a Catholic grammar school than anything else.

I'd previously won compensation from a Welsh council for pothole damage and successfully fought off a speeding conviction, but in the words of Desiderius Erasmus, 'in the land of the blind, the one-eyed man is king' … or rather, when you're in Spain with neither a perfect grasp of the language, Spanish contract law or an in-depth medical knowledge, it's almost impossible to take on a Spanish private health insurance company and come out the victor. I therefore had to accept defeat and cough up (literally) for the second gastroscopy.

And the cost of the follow-up procedure, presumably with a crash team on hand? A mere €750 – pocket change for a Marbella drugs kingpin, but not for me … I could have had a fortnight at the Ibis in Málaga for that!

My hospital visit proved largely uneventful – the crash team weren't needed, and the bezoar had gone thanks to my new coke habit. The only worrying moment was when the nurse told me she was going to put a *catéter* in, and I panicked – was she expecting me to pee myself in theatre? I thought I was only having a gastroscopy, not a triple heart bypass! I pointed to my groin and tried to clarify.

'A catheter? Are you sure?'

The nurse laughed and pointed to my arm.

'*No, un catéter en su brazo.*'

Ah! They must call a canula a *catéter* in Spain. She wanted to put a canula in my arm so the anaesthetist could inject his happy potion into me. Phew – that was a close one.

We popped along to visit the doctor a week or so later for the results of the oesophageal biopsy and the news improved further – there were no traces of cancerous cells. I breathed a sigh of relief and made a mental note to tell Chris to throw away that sheet with all my passwords on.

And one final piece of good news was that I'd only have to cough up the thick end of €800 for a gastroscopy every three years instead of two. I was so blessed, I felt like I'd lost a tenner and found a fiver.

9

Watching Paint Dry

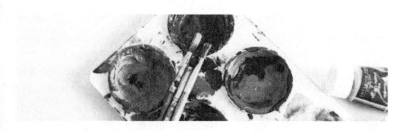

Not long after my "near-death" experience in a Marbella clinic, I was headhunted for a three-month IT contract in Wales. It would mean jumping on a bloody plane again though every week for three months.

Having only just survived a brush with death [*Chris: you're overreacting now*], seeing my life expectancy plummet in front of my eyes [*Chris: rein it in – I'm not telling you again!*], having a few restless nights mulling it over [*Chris: that's more like it*], and regardless of however lucrative it might have been [*Chris: more than €7 per hour and worth getting out of bed for was it?*], I decided to turn the job down [*Chris: at last!*].

In all honesty, having woken after another broken night's sleep with all the advance warning signs of a stress reaction coming on, I thought it was best for my health if I didn't return to a transient life in the IT world, even if it was only for three months. Plus, the journey from Alhaurín El Grande to the client's site in South Wales would have been like the plot of *Trains, Planes and Automobiles* twice a week. I was starting to enjoy my new life in Spain, or what little I might have left of it [*Chris: you've been warned once already*], and I wanted to continue with my foray into the world of creative arts.

'Do you fancy coming to art class with me?' I asked Chris.

'What? Where did that come from?'

'I've always fancied painting. And I heard there's an art class at El Bichito.'

El Bichito was the name of the bar at the end of our lane where we went for Spanish lessons.

'But you're writing a novel. And I've never even seen you draw anything.'

'I know, but I can do a bit of painting as well, can't I? And who knows, I might be the next Picasso.'

'Aren't you setting the bar a bit high? Why don't you aim for Pricasso instead?'

I was undeterred. The old girl that seemed to come primarily to disrupt our Spanish lessons every week had said she did a bit of painting. I'd even seen a couple of photos of her work, and what she lacked in linguistic dexterity she made up for (in part) with a paint brush in her hand. So I got the contact details and messaged the art tutor. Sadly, there was a waiting list to get in, so I had to wait for one of the old girls to either peg it or get banged up when the next illegal bingo session was raided by the *Guardia Civil*.

As it happened, Chris's new boss/friend, Jill, that ran the Fire Watch group used to do a bit of painting with another tutor, and there was no waiting list for her group.

'Right, I'm off to the shop to buy a canvas and some acrylic paints. Do you want some?'

'No. You paint, I'll just watch you.'

We arrived at the venue, a bar in the next town, just before 10am for my first three-hour art class. The art teacher, Julia, was a very talented, bohemian-looking artist who ran a relaxed, unstructured art session. Basically, she didn't stand at the front of class and make everyone paint the same thing; you could choose your own subject material and paint in your own medium.

Julia was just there to advise you in all things arty, from working with different mediums to which brush to use to achieve a particular artistic effect, generally offering support and guidance. I'd been told acrylics were easier for beginners as the paint dries quickly so you can paint over your mistakes.

'Right, Drew. What are you going to paint for your first painting?'

'Well, I thought I'd start simple with just a few colours. I've got a photo out of the paper of a full moon rising over

Glastonbury Tor, with a few silhouetted characters out for a moonlit walk.'

'Excellent,' she said, encouragingly, then looked at my meagre 12-inch canvas. 'Didn't you fancy a bigger canvas?'

'No. Let's start small. I may be useless.'

'Ok. And do you have an easel? If not, I can lend you one.'

'I'll be fine just painting on the tabletop.'

'And Chris, what will you be doing?'

'I'm just watching. I'm here for moral support.'

'Well, find a table and sit yourselves down. I'll be over in a minute to help you get started.'

We shuffled a few chairs around and plonked ourselves down on the end table, next to Jill, who had come along to do a spot of painting too. She must have been a pro, as she was using oils and had a much bigger canvas. I unpacked my plastic tablecloth and laid everything out ready for Julia to advise.

'Right, Drew. Where are you going to start?'

'Erm. With the sky?'

'Well, yes, but you'll need to mix your black and white paints to get the grey and then start by painting the whole canvas in that one colour.'

Julia showed me what to do. I had a plastic plate ready to squeeze my paint onto, but she advised me to cover that with a sheet of kitchen towel and give it a quick spray of water to moisten it – that would stop the acrylic paint from drying out so quickly on the plate.

'I'll come back when you've got your base layer down. You'll need a couple of coats as the canvas will suck up the first coat. You can use a hairdryer to speed dry acrylics, but I haven't brought mine this week, and everyone else is using oils.' Julia wandered off to go and help someone else.

'See,' I whispered to Chris, conspiratorially. 'Priceless advice already, and I've not even got the top off my paint.'

Chris rolled her eyes and carried on chatting with Jill.

And I didn't need much paint either – it seemed to go a long way on the canvas. I had my first two coats on in no time (having used the hand dryer in the gents to speed things up), and my little brush was soaking in a jam jar of grey water. I had a sip of coffee while I waited for Julia to share her next pearl of wisdom with me.

'Right, what do you need to do next, Drew?'

'Erm. Paint the hill in?'

'Well the hill's the same black as the tower, so you can paint the hill *and* the tower in next if you like. Just make sure your brush is clean, so you don't get any of the grey in the black.'

This bit proved harder than filling in the grey background. I'm a perfectionist and my own worst enemy at times. The lefthand side of the tower was easy – it was a straight line – but the righthand side was stepped in layers where the wall must have become wider – it was hard to tell as it was nighttime in my photo, and I'd never been to Glastonbury. Every time I painted the righthand side, I wasn't happy with it and had to make it a little wider all the way down to cover up my mistakes, till it started to look more like Windsor Castle.

'What're you doing?' Chris said, looking over the top of her coffee cup.

'I've had to make the tor wider because I messed it up.'

'You do know what a tor is, don't you?'

'Yeah,' I said bullishly. 'It's old English for a tower.'

'No. A tor is a hill. Glastonbury Tor is the hill. The tower is called St. Michael's Tower.'

'Oh. I didn't know that. Well, they might want to rename it St. Michael's Castle now.'

Julia was soon along to advise again.

'That's looking good so far,' she said, without the merest hint of a patronising tone, which I found comforting. 'You can put the moon in now if you like. Start with the yellow paint and we can mix up some orange highlights later. And as it's a full moon, you can probably draw the outline using the lid of your jam jar.'

To be fair, I'd already thought of that – I wasn't about to start freehand drawing a circle on day one … after all, I wasn't a complete idiot. I soon had the moon in, and even mixed my own orange without further advice … it's just yellow and red in case you were wondering.

'That's looking great, Drew. Just the silhouettes to do now.'

'Yeah, just the hard bits left,' I said.

'Well, just take your time. Use your smallest brush.'

I had two people walking dogs, a couple sat down facing each other, some bloke gawping up at the tower, and a little tree on the far side.

'I might need another week to finish this masterpiece,' I said to Chris.

'Really? You've got an hour and a half left yet.'

'Don't rush me. It might be hanging in the Louvre one day.'

'You're not even hanging that in the loo.'

Undeterred, I soldiered on. In fact, when I'd finished, I thought my little silhouette characters were the best part of the painting. I ordered a beer to celebrate while it dried naturally.

'Are you happy with that, then?' Chris asked.

'Yeah. Not bad for a first attempt.'

'I might have a go myself next week, then, if you're coming again.'

'Yeah. Fill your boots.'

I was pleased I'd shown her how easy this painting lark was, although having seen my effort, she probably thought she could do a much better job.

In fact, before I packed up, I had a wander round to see what everyone else was painting. One woman had been painting a huge Highland cow with its tongue sticking out on a four-foot canvas for weeks and it looked amazing. I thought I'd done well finishing my first painting in one session, but even Jill had knocked out a Bob Ross in oils in the same amount of time.

Ah well, there was always next week. I just had to find a subject matter and settle on a painting style. I know this isn't as easy as it looks, and I'm no Rolf Harris – although that's surely not a bad thing – but there were times this morning when I felt like asking Chris, 'can you tell what it is yet?'

The following week I knocked out my next masterpiece – three cartoon birds on a telephone wire looking bemused at their mate who was dangling upside down next to them with the caption 'There's always one' – unfortunately, it's usually me!

Meanwhile, Chris was enjoying herself painting a cartoon owl in acrylics. She was a much slower artist than me as it took her three weeks – I couldn't work out if she just wasn't as good as me, she was more careful, or if she was doing far too much chatting with Jill while I just got my head down and cracked on.

I must admit, when she'd finished it, it was difficult to tell the difference between her effort and the original. We might have a master forger on our hands.

'How much do you reckon you could sell that for?' I asked her.

'I wasn't planning on selling it. But I don't know. Ten euros, perhaps.'

'We're not going to make a killing in the art world, then, are we? It's cost you fifteen euros in art lessons, ten euros in drinks and at least a fiver on materials.'

'Well, I'll just have to keep it for myself, then.'

After a few weeks of knocking out stuff and nonsense on little canvases, I felt it was time I upped my own game now – I'd come across a colourful oil painting of the famous trumpeter, Chet Baker, so I thought I'd swap Chet for me, and paint a self-portrait of me blowing my trumpet.

'Are you going to be using oils this week, then, Drew?' Julia asked.

'No, I'm going to stick with acrylics, thanks. Let's not get too giddy!'

'You could make it mixed media. That would look good.'

'What's that?'

'Well, you can paint it in acrylics and then add some oils over the top of the acrylic background to bring it to life more.'

That sounded like a good idea, actually.

'And I see you've gone for a larger canvas this time.'

'Yep. This one's going to be special, so it was worth the extra euro.'

Chris rolled her eyes at me again. Hey! You never know, my great-great-grandkids might be admiring this long after I'm gone.

10

These Boots Are Made For Walking

As if I didn't have enough on my plate, what with me trying to write a novel and find a painting style I was good at, Chris thought it would be a good idea to go hiking at the weekends, so we signed up to join a local rambling group.

I was also still busy trying to find gainful employment and had just sent off my third application, this time for a job as a Ground Operations Training Manager with Jet2 at Málaga airport – I'd written and delivered training courses, I was a seasoned flyer and former card-carrying member of the Speedy Boarding club [*Chris: wrong airline – I hope you didn't put that on your application!*], so it was another job I should have been a shoo-in for, really. I'd have probably got the job if they hadn't decided a month later that the position was being put on hold – I'm a glass half full kind of guy normally … unless I've got a hospital appointment, as you've seen!

Undeterred, I dug out the walking gear and gave it a shake, as it hadn't seen the light of day since leaving the UK.

'Who runs this walking group, then,' I enquired.

'Someone called Rambling Al,' Chris replied.

'Well I hope the nickname is due to his walking prowess and not his bedside manner.'

I was actually looking forward to seeing a bit more of the area in which we lived. We'd been on the hunt for maps or walking guides to the area, and there wasn't much to be had in the bookshops in Málaga. You could probably step out of your front door and go for a walk, or drive a few minutes away and then go off on foot, it's just that you never knew if after walking a mile up the road there was going to be a way of returning to the start point without necessarily coming back the same way.

I had an excellent Garmin handheld GPS hiking device with Ordnance Survey maps on it, but a detailed map of the Yorkshire Dales was of no use to me in Andalucía. As it happens, I've since discovered that there is a Spanish OS equivalent, but it wouldn't have worked with my Garmin anyway.

This wasn't our first hiking experience in Spain actually, as we'd been walking in Andalucía's Grazalema National Park in Cádiz Province over New Year in 2010. On that occasion we'd booked a trip with InnTravel who specialized in walking, cycling and touring holidays around the UK and Europe. We booked our own flights, while InnTravel arranged our accommodation and supplied us with a range of recommended walks and local maps.

We had lovely sunny weather for our Grazalema trip, which in hindsight was rather fortunate as it's the wettest place in Andalucía, and one of the wettest places in Spain, with over two metres of rain a year, most of it falling in the winter months – I think we dodged a bullet on that trip, then.

Thankfully, today's walk was on the outskirts of our neighbouring town, Coín, where the annual rainfall is less than a quarter that of Grazalema, and this morning there was a bright clear sky and the customary nip in the air first thing. When we arrived at the meeting point it was evident this was a popular group – when we set off at 10am there were no less than 33 like-minded souls strung out along the track in small groups, deep in conversation.

Although the vast majority were expat Brits, we did have a few other nationalities there, including Dutch (who are born travellers) and a couple of Spaniards. Al was a friendly chap who had trodden these paths many times before. If we'd have attempted this on our own, there were a few occasions where I wouldn't have been sure it wasn't a dead end, so it was a good idea doing this kind of thing with a local leader in Al with expert knowledge.

We started and ended the walk in the area known as Los Llanos Woods, which was the location for a rather naff British soap opera on BBC1 called Eldorado that only aired for one year in the early nineties. They built a filmset in the middle of the woods which has been operating as a paintballing site recently. Apart from a few seasoned actors, the rest of the cast were mostly unknown with little or no acting experience, and the show was a big flop for the Beeb.

The rest of the walk was mostly on tarmacked small roads down to the edge of the old town and back out a different way. Remains of a settlement in the area of Coín have been traced as far back as 1BC. Originally called Lacibis by the Romans, it was the Arabs who turned the town into the most important in the area and named it Cohinede, from whence the current name is derived. They built fortifications on the site of the old Roman town, and walking around Coín today, you'll spot tiles depicting a castle embedded into the pavements at intervals, and these mark the original placement of the town's defensive walls. The walls are no longer here, as what was then Cohinede was completely destroyed after being besieged by a Catholic army.

That walk down to the town had been an easy downhill stroll, although very steep in places, and sadly, what goes down must come back up again – that's if you want to get back to your car at some point – and the second leg of the walk was indeed very strenuous. Nobody was in a hurry, though, so we had time for a tea break and biscuit stop, and lots of little pauses to stop and "admire the views" (or catch your breath).

And there were indeed wonderful views to be had around Coín, with the Sierra de Mijas on one side and the Sierra de Las Nieves on the other. Staggeringly, there are no fewer than 1,098 named mountains in Málaga province, and 83,377 in the whole of Spain, making it the country with the most mountains in the whole of Europe.

After the success of week one for us, we decided to go with them the following week, this time out on a bit of a road journey first. A 45-minute ride away further inland, past what we call our local Lake District – a series of large reservoirs feeding the Guadalhorce valley – lies the small hillside town of Teba.

The group this week was a slightly different mix of people with some new faces (to us, of course, as ours will have been the newest). As we approached Teba, the town and its castle (the largest in Málaga) were clearly visible perched up high overlooking the surrounding plains.

From the outskirts of the town, we headed out through the olive groves to the mouth of Teba Gorge, a limestone canyon formed during the Jurassic period. Heading upstream, we passed the *Cueva de las Palomas* (Cave of the Doves) on the right, which dated back to the neolithic era, before crossing the slow-moving *Rio de la Venta* (River of the Wind) a couple of times to continue our climb. We paused by the remains of an old mill that use to produce anis, an aniseed-flavoured liqueur, and after completing the climb out of the gorge, we passed once more through farmland dotted with olives and almonds before arriving back at the town. After covering 10km with lots of up and down, it was time for us to find a local bar for a well-earned lunch.

The walking group seemed to be a good place to meet a variety of people, some who'd been here for 20 years or more, and other newer arrivals like us, so it was a more reliable source of local knowledge than any expat group you'd find on Facebook. They were a sociable bunch, and the walks were certainly interesting, and exactly the kind of thing we enjoyed doing back home, although usually in less clement weather. So it was a big thumbs up from the both of us, and we became regular participants every Saturday morning.

11

Daylight Robbery

Tax Accountant? Bloody thief, more like. In the words of that great political thinker (and bacon butty aficionado), Ed Miliband, 'even Dick Turpin had the decency to wear a mask when he robbed people'.

Now that we were Spanish residents, we had certain obligations to report on our financial situation. In addition to the usual tax returns that we'd need to file in a few months, a more pressing deadline was approaching for us to report our offshore (non-Spanish) assets, including properties, investments and bank accounts (which would fill nothing more than the back of a fag packet, I assure you!). Hence, we needed to find ourselves a reputable accountant (assuming that's not an oxymoron) to handle all of our tax affairs going forward.

We'd in fact started that process a year earlier, although I was less than satisfied with how it all went at the time. I presumed we'd be better advised by an accountant on the coast where more UK expats lived, and that they might better understand the crossover between UK and Spanish fiscal requirements.

We'd arranged an initial, free, face-to-face consultation with a firm in Marbella. The first thing that went wrong is she gave me the wrong day for the appointment, but thankfully I checked with her the day beforehand and discovered she'd actually booked us in a day later.

'I don't like her,' I said to Chris after we'd left that first free meeting.

'Why not?'

'Every time I spoke to her and asked her a question, she didn't look at me when answering but looked at you instead. I found that very strange. In fact, I think she was quite rude and off-hand with me.'

'I'm sure it'll be fine. She seemed to know what she was talking about.'

'She may know very well what she's talking about, but I didn't like her at all. She was also very evasive when I asked her about the cost of her services.'

In many relationships, there's someone that handles all the nitty gritty of tax returns and financial planning. In our relationship, that was me, perhaps because I'm a Virgo and quite particular. Oh, really? … like one-twelfth of the world's population that were all born around the same time of year … how convenient is that?! Or maybe it's because I've always loved working with numbers and spent a career analysing and organising stuff. Or maybe it's because Chris is just happy to let me get on with it.

Anyway, after some pressing – bearing in mind this accountant now knew everything about our financial situation and how relatively uncomplicated it was – she told me it would cost around €200 each to submit our annual tax returns and our first offshore asset declaration, both of which weren't required until after the end of that current financial year.

So here we were, one year on, and we now needed to submit our offshore asset declaration first, otherwise known as a Modelo 720. This requirement has developed a certain notoriety, not least for the ridiculously high punitive fines for late or incomplete submissions. For instance, the fine for missing off or inaccurately reporting a piece of information is €5,000 for every piece of information concerned, and that's if you're upfront and admit it before they find out – if they find out before you tell them, the fine doubles to €10,000!

To add insult to injury, any forgotten or misrepresented asset is then considered a full capital gain and taxed accordingly, along with a fine of 150% of the unpaid tax. Unsurprisingly, this malpractice by the Spanish tax authorities became the subject of a protracted legal challenge in the European Courts soon after coming into force in 2012, thanks in large part to the ludicrous fines. The tax and fine regime of the Modelo 720 was finally ruled unlawful in 2022. You're still obliged to declare your offshore assets, but if you miss something off or declare it inaccurately, these days they can only fine you €20 instead of €5,000.

I dropped the accountant an email asking if an appointment was needed or if she wanted me to submit the required information by email. I also pointed out we'd be in the UK over a given week in February and therefore unavailable. She replied saying a meeting was needed and could we come in on a date that was in the middle of our UK trip – well done for not reading my email … we were already getting off on the wrong foot again. I pointed this out, and she acknowledged that my email did note the dates of our trip, and then proceeded to offer me another appointment the day after the first one, while we were obviously still in the UK.

And I'm still supposed to put my trust in this person who can't read or just can't be bothered, am I? Finally, we agreed upon a meeting the day before our trip.

When we arrived, we'd clearly been fobbed off and demoted to dealing with the trainee accountant – maybe he'll be more pleasant and thorough though, I thought. In my usual fashion, I'd itemised everything in each asset category in the required level of detail and presented it to him as a *fait accompli*, so he had bugger all to do really, other than convert the figures into euros and tap them into the online system. Oh, and they couldn't find my correspondence from last year with copies of our passports etc. so I had to send that through again.

I won't state the name of the company, as they'll probably sue me (although I noticed another unsatisfied client was brave enough to leave a scathing review), but they might have been better calling themselves 'Ooh Betty Tax Accountants'. Our trainee accountant later did a 'whoopsie in my beret' when he said he was going to charge us €500 each plus 21% VAT for the privilege of converting my figures to euros. 'Mmmm – nice!'

I went all Alf Garnett on him and called him a 'silly moo' and that we'd been quoted €200 each and that was to include our forthcoming tax returns too. I asked for a full written quote for the provision of both services and told him to go and speak with his boss.

He duly spoke to her and came back to me without a written quotation for all the required services we were expecting, instead saying his boss had agreed to drop the fee for the Modelo 720 to just €200 each plus VAT – that was kind of her. They wouldn't submit or share the final Modelo 720 with us until we'd paid their fees, and it was too late to try and find another accountant, so I paid them just to get rid of them as quickly as possible.

When I finally received a copy of what they'd filed with the authorities I found a glaring error where he'd undervalued my pension by over €5,000 by mistyping the result of the exchange rate conversion with two of the digits the wrong way round. After correcting him and having to request he make an urgent resubmission I felt like sending him an invoice for my own time – about €400 plus VAT should cover it.

I thought he'd have read between the lines and left us alone after that, but a month later he was after another pound of flesh – I received an email reminding me it was time to do our tax return now. I told him to 'eff off in the nicest possible way as I'd found a local firm to do our tax returns for €30 each, and that he should try touting for business by standing on the side of the marina at Puerto Banús and singing Adam Ant's "Stand And Deliver" instead!

Accountants, eh? Can't live with 'em, can't live without 'em.

12

Glorious Granada

We arrived back on Spanish soil to find the stray cats we'd been feeding had told all their mates we were a soft touch – maybe word had got out about us being fleeced by the accountant. Either way, there were now 12 feral feline furballs waiting to be fed. I don't think they appreciated I was unemployed and currently living off my savings.

Seeing as Alhaurín El Grande's cat population were now eating better than we were, I applied for another job. It was a dead-end admin job, but I felt I was at least being active in the job market. Suffice to say I was clearly overqualified and didn't hear back from them.

Whilst I got back to writing my novel, we continued our art classes. I finished my self-portrait, knocked out some African art, and then decided I still hadn't found my style. I did a bit of research and discovered I quite liked pop art, and especially paintings of famous singers.

I found a great painting of Bob Marley using just black paint for his silhouetted image painted over a background in the colours of the Jamaican flag, and after knocking that out the following week to great acclaim from my fellow artists, I decided that was going to be my thing. Chris, meanwhile, had spent weeks painting a rather splendid picture of nine bee catchers huddled up together on the branch of a tree. But even she loved my Bob Marley – now proudly on display in the living room of Chris's sister, Dee – and she said I should stick to that style now.

A few weeks later we flew back to the UK to celebrate Mum's 80th birthday with our immediate family – thankfully, there were no surprise Pricasso paintings this time around (and I was even more grateful Dad hadn't tried to knock one out for her, complete with video evidence!). When the festivities were over, we flew them back to Spain with us for their sixth visit (but who's counting?!).

Andalucía was experiencing some fine spring weather, and we had another cultural day trip that had been planned well in advance: we were taking them to Granada to visit the Alhambra Palace. To avoid disappointment, as it's difficult to get tickets on the day, we'd booked ours three months earlier. Tickets were about €15 and €10 for concessions.

Granada is a two-hour drive and 100 miles away from Alhaurín El Grande. Because of the topography around Málaga, you first have to head towards the city and then turn inland towards Antequera for a long uphill drive through the *Montes de Málaga* national park, but it's all motorway driving, and the traffic is light. Just shy of Antequera, you're directed eastwards onto a huge plateau behind the mountains. It's a nice scenic run that way, as opposed to taking the coast road to Motril and then up a long, winding road through the mountains.

We'd had an early start to the day and headed straight for the car park at the palace in order to complete our visit before lunchtime and the hottest part of the day. The Alhambra – or Red Castle as the Arabic translates – was so called due its reddish walls. Set high up in the city, about 800 metres above sea level on the Sabika hill, an outcrop from the imposing Sierra Nevada, the palace has commanding views over the surrounding area.

The Alhambra Palace is one of the most important and best-preserved examples of Islamic architecture you'll find anywhere. There's so much to see and admire of the palace and adjacent Generalife gardens that we decided it was worth getting the audio guides which gave you a commentary when you arrived at each point of interest.

Although there were certainly settlements here beforehand, given its prime location, works on the site as we know it today were begun in 1238 by Muhammad I Ibn al-Ahmar, the first emir of the Nasrid dynasty that ruled the Emirate of Granada for 260 years, up until all land was ultimately surrendered to the Catholic queen, Isabella I of Castile, at the conclusion of the Christian Reconquista.

In book one, you may recall we stayed at a rather gorgeous hotel in Salamanca that played host to Christopher Columbus and the Catholic Kings of the time as he tried to obtain their financial backing for his explorations of the New World. Well, we were now visiting another significant meeting point between Columbus and Isabella, as it was at the Alhambra Palace that he was finally given the royal endorsement for his trip that he'd been seeking some years earlier in Salamanca.

Although he expected to find a new western route to the Indies, he obviously discovered that the twin continents of North and South America stood in his path and rather fortuitously provided him and his Catholic backers with untold riches from the Americas.

The Alhambra Palace has undergone hundreds of years of development and remodelling, making it difficult to determine the exact chronology. Suffice to say, there are glorious examples of Arabic architecture throughout, from the mullioned windows of the Hall of the Two Sisters to the intricately sculpted stucco and tile decoration synonymous with the Nasrid rule.

If you've ever visited the Mayan city of Chichén Itzá on Mexico's Yucatan peninsula, you'll know that the shape, size and orientation of the main Temple of Kukulcán is a marvel of engineering and architecture, given that at the times of the spring and autumn equinoxes the shadows cast by the northwest corner evoke the appearance of a serpent wriggling down the staircase. Equally mesmeric is the fact that clapping at the base of the steps to the structure initiates an echo that sounds like a birdcall some say resembles that of the native Quetzal bird.

Similarly, the design of the Alhambra Palace and its courtyard gardens also incorporate architectural features and mathematical calculations that not only give the buildings a harmonious visual quality but also had the comfort of the occupants in mind. For instance, the orientation and layout of the courtyards, the positions of their windows and the inclusion of water features were all designed to provide cool relief from the heat of a Spanish summer, whilst maximising the internal light during the winter months.

A highlight of any visit to the Alhambra is the Palace of the Lions, which exemplifies the Nasrid architecture. Bookended by beautifully ornate pavilions at the eastern and western ends is the instantly recognisable Fountain of the Lions, a marble basin and fountain standing on the backs of 12 marble lions.

A later significant addition was the Renaissance-style palace of King Charles V. From the outside, the building looks square, but once inside, there is a unique circular patio. Sadly, the works were never fully completed.

Once you've visited the palaces and courtyards of the Alhambra, you'll need time to stroll around the extensive gardens of the Generalife, which occupy the slopes of the *Cerro del Sol* (Hill of the Sun). A much simpler and less ornate construction, the Generalife was a place of retreat for the kings of Granada. Originally, it would have been conceived by the Nasrid rulers as a country villa estate upon which to grow fruit and vegetables but has undergone extensive changes over the years.

The current condition of the Alhambra Palace owes little to Napolean's French army who, following their rout by the combined forces of Spain, Portugal and Britain during the Peninsular War at the start of the 19th century, tried to blow it all up with dynamite so it could no longer be used as a fortress. They succeeded in demolishing eight towers, but the remaining fuses were disabled by a brave Spaniard named José Garcia.

So with the sun beating down and our stomachs rumbling, we thought we'd go and drink a toast to José and find a bar to rest up and have lunch.

'Where are we going for lunch, then?' Mum asked.

'Don't look at me,' I said. 'I got told off last time, so it's Chris's decision.'

I was no mug; I'd learnt my lesson in Ronda.

'So you've not googled anywhere?' Chris asked.

'I haven't even TripAdvisored anywhere.'

'Well, we'll just have a walk down into town and stop at one that looks nice,' Chris decided.

Fawlty Towers looked nice from the outside, I thought, but you wouldn't want to stay there! I could feel the hairs standing up on the back of my neck – stopping at the first place that looked nice was (to me) like running a multimillion-pound project without a project plan. At least I was out of the crosshairs today. So we just meandered down the hill into town, past myriad souvenir shops until we stumbled across somewhere Chris liked the look of.

I can't remember the name it, but at the bar she chose we had a lovely tapas lunch, washed down with the local Alhambra Especial beer on tap, and as the self-appointed driver on such trips, my intake was limited to just the one small one, of course.

Granada is also famous for the flamenco shows that take place in the caves of the Sacromonto and Albaicín neighbourhoods. Flamenco has its roots in Moorish musical traditions but is strongly influenced by the Andalucian *Gitanos* (Gypsies). If we'd have been staying the night, we might have sought out one of the shows, as I would say it's the kind of thing best enjoyed at night with a large glass of red wine and some olives. But we had to head home, so passed up the opportunity on this occasion … and Chris wasn't fond of all the wailing and stomping anyway!

Back in Alhaurín, as it was Easter week, we took Mum and Dad to see the religious parades that they missed out on last year. People lined the route with their own plastic chairs, but we thought the council had put them out for general use. Dad sat down on one with a dodgy leg, and it collapsed, sending him crashing to the floor, much to the annoyance of the fella sat behind us who must have put them out for his own family to use. With it being Easter, it's a wonder Dad wasn't crucified.

A few days later, we had a brief daytrip down to Estepona with the old folks. Mum wanted to visit the orchidarium (whoopidoo!), and Tony and Sandra were back in town "villa hunting"! On our fleeting visit to the UK last week I'd stuffed some Spanish property brochures through his letterbox to gee him up a bit, but when we met them for lunch at Chiringuito Palm Beach, it was obvious there was no serious intent on show yet.

13

Fiesta Time in Fuengirola

As far as festivals go, as soon as you tell me that there's one that mixes the cuisine, drink, music and dance from some faraway exotic lands, then you can count me in. What could be more fun than sampling food from Argentina, drinking Guinness from Ireland, listening to rock music from the US, and then watching some Bhangra dancers from India? Exactly – not much!

So when I heard that Fuengirola was putting on its 24th such *Feria Internacional de Los Pueblos* (known as the International People's Fair) – later renamed *Feria Internacional de Los Paises* (International Fair of Countries) in 2022 – we just had to go and check it out. The festival is held in the spring each year and takes place across five days and nights. In addition to a fun fair at one end, the main attraction is the 30 or more *casetas* (small single-storey buildings) that line the main thoroughfare of the *feria* ground, each representing a different country, serving its regional food and drinks and offering entertainment into the early hours of the morning.

For our first experience of this particular *feria*, we went along on the first afternoon to see what it was all about. There'd been a procession through the town at midday to open the festival, but we'd missed that and got there mid afternoon when all the *casetas* were operational.

It was truly an assault on the senses, with huge barbecues roasting whole meat carcasses outside some of the South American *casetas*. There were bars inside and out, with food offerings from German bratwurst to Turkish kebabs, Australian kangaroo burgers to Belgian waffles. Not just a feast for the eyes and nose, but your ears were assaulted by a different style of music as you passed from the doorway of one *caseta* to the next.

We popped into the Aussie bar for a beer and a listen to some guy playing guitar and singing rock songs. They had a life-size crocodile at one end against a backdrop wallcovering of a billabong. Next, we popped into downtown Havana in the Cuban bar for a Cuba Libre, where a DJ was playing salsa music, and people were up on the dance floor. The Mexican bar had a Mariachi band playing, a Beatles tribute band were rocking the British bar, and doing nothing to eradicate stereotypes, Peru had some blokes in ponchos playing nose flutes!

We decided to grab something to eat. Chris naturally went for a bratwurst from Germany (because her mother was German), while I got a plate of grilled meats from Uruguay (because I'm a meat eater!). Afterwards we called in at the Dominican Republic, a country we'd visited twice before, although this time we didn't have to endure a nine-hour flight in economy first before we could swing our hips to some of their native bachata music.

And what does everyone do just when it's time to go home after a good night out? That's right, we nipped over to India for a bottle of Cobra and a "Ruby Murray", while a semi-naked temptress did a belly dance with a sword, and some dashing bearded chaps with curly toes showed us how to change a light bulb with one hand whilst petting the dog with the other ... or if you had no dog, they demonstrated how to change two light bulbs at once – just amazing!

We enjoyed it so much, we came away vowing to return again next year, along with the million or so other revellers that come to enjoy this fabulous festival.

The following day, I'm back on the job hunt, but there was nothing new that piqued my interest. Then I had a brainwave. Rather than apply for a crappy office job, why don't I get a job working outside? No, not sweeping roads or digging holes – it's far too hot to be working in direct sunlight during the summer months. No, what I could do is be a golf marshal ... that just involved driving a golf buggy all afternoon, making sure people are sticking to the paths and not slowing play up, etc.

And you don't even have to be any good at golf, which is just as well!

A new cv was required, as they don't want to know chapter and verse about my working life. They don't even need to know my golf handicap. They just need a brief one-page introduction with my contact details. I printed half a dozen off and spent the afternoon dropping them off at my nearest golf courses.

Oddly, one of the receptionists in the pro shop quoted data protection laws at me and said it wasn't possible to leave a physical piece of paper with my information on, it had to be emailed to the boss. Crikey! They park on roundabouts and zebra crossings over here without fear of reprisals, so why are they fussed about my name and phone number being written down? Bizarre!

While I waited for the job offers to flood in, I went back to writing, painting and hiking. My writing was starting to flow, and my proofreader was giving me lots of encouragement, even though my novel wasn't Chris's usual reading material.

I knocked out a few more pop art paintings in Marilyn Monroe (not a musician as such, although she did sing Happy Birthday to John F Kennedy), a rather splendid John Lennon and a colourful Jimi Hendrix. Lennon was whisked off to the UK to adorn our son-in-law Graham's bar in his back garden, and Marilyn eventually ended up in Sandra's living room, both as gifts. Hendrix is still lying undiscovered in a wardrobe somewhere – not that he's no good, just that nobody's claimed him yet. In fact, I liked the John Lennon one so much I did another one twice the size a while later that Sandra took a shine to.

Meanwhile, Chris presented her latest masterpiece to the art class, a close up of a black cat's face with piercing yellow eyes. It wasn't our next-door neighbour's lovely black cat, just some random image she'd found online that she wanted to try and recreate, but it was pretty mesmerising.

'Wow!' said a friend of ours when he saw a photo of it on her phone. 'That's the spitting image of my cat. How much do you want for it?'

'It's not an original, I'm afraid,' Chris confessed. 'I'm only just starting out. It's just copied from an image online.'

'That's alright. I love it. I'll give you fifty euros.'

Chris was gobsmacked and thrilled in equal measure, but more so that someone had appreciated her work.

'I'll bring it next time we're over in the UK,' she offered.

Our daughter, Corrinne, and her husband, Graham, nipped over for the weekend, and Corrinne loved the cat so much, she asked Chris to paint their black labrador, Max. Chris was delighted that she'd found her own style and vowed to paint people's pets from now on.

Meanwhile, Tony and Sandra announced their engagement – how wonderful, they're perfect for each other – still no sign of a holiday home, though! And to celebrate the occasion, they booked a stay in Málaga a couple of weeks later, this time staying at the recently renovated five-star Gran Hotel Miramar.

We went out for dinner with them, and Tony asked me if I'd do him the honour of being his best man. I was thrilled, of course, and accepted the invitation in a heartbeat. Tony had done me proud as my best man when Chris and I were married, and I now hoped to be able to do an equally fine job for him. We'd been best mates for knocking on 40 years, and I'd never seen him happier … and living in Spain, nor him me, probably.

14

Making an Exhibition of Ourselves

'How do you two fancy seeing your paintings exhibited?' our art tutor asked us.

Wow! Some people wait a lifetime to get their own art exhibition, and here we were, three months after picking up a brush. Perhaps we were better at this than we thought. The rest of the art class were going to be really jealous. I almost felt guilty.

'We're having our own art exhibition at the cultural centre next month,' Julia continued. 'Just choose your best two paintings and we'll display them for a week.'

'So the whole group are displaying paintings?' I clarified.

'That's right. We have an exhibition every year. It's just a bit of fun. We have a grand opening and lay out some buffet food for everyone.'

That popped my balloon! As if the good folk of Alhaurín El Grande were that bothered about seeing a couple of pop art paintings I'd copied off the internet. Get a grip, son.

All the same, I was looking forward to it. You never know, Alhaurín TV might be there wanting me to do a quick piece to camera, so I must remember to get my haircut. Buoyed by the news, I knocked out a silhouette of Prince on a purple background, then buggered it up by painting in some purple raindrops.

The following week, I tried my hand at landscapes, and painted a treelined Parisian avenue, but it turned out more Paul Gascoigne than Paul Gauguin.

The day of the exhibition arrived, and everyone was on buffet-making duties. Given the group was exclusively expat Brits, the buffet naturally included a range of triangular-shaped sarnies (including egg mayonnaise), chicken goujons, sausage rolls, mini pork pies (someone had been to Iceland!), that old favourite, quiche Lorraine, a bowl of ready salted crisps and a few vol-au-vents. Ah, the culinary splendour of a British buffet – we were just missing a Bird's trifle with hundreds and thousands on.

On the art front, there were some decent efforts on display, to be fair, and I don't think we'd disgraced ourselves with our own offerings. It was all very civilised, with lots of compliments being passed around, and when the buffet had all but gone, a few of us wandered up the street to a local bar to continue the celebrations.

The following week, undeterred by my previous landscape, I had another go, this time painting Mount Fuji with some cherry blossom trees in the foreground. I even got a palette knife out and did some 3D textured snow on top of the mountain. As I stood back to admire it, Chris leaned over.

'Your clouds could be better,' she said.

'Have you tried painting clouds? They're a right bugger to get right!'

'What're you going to do about it then?'

Was there a touch of menace in that question? Had I dishonoured the family name so much that because of a few crap clouds she now wanted me to commit hara-kiri? Or was she offering me another way out?

'I think I'll go back to painting pop art,' I conceded.

'Very wise,' she concurred.

And the following week, I did a really great Amy Winehouse. Stick to what you know, I told myself after that.

15

Magical Mijas

There's something about the whitewashed hillside town of Mijas, perched about 400 metres up the side of the Sierra de Mijas that keeps drawing you back. One of the more famous of Andalucía's *pueblos blancos*, it's only a 20-minute ride away for us, although the winding road that clings to the mountainside in places is not a journey Chris looks forward to, especially with so many blind corners and no weight restrictions for vehicles, meaning it's also a bus route.

We stayed in the town for two weeks when we came over on our first scouting mission, and despite it being the middle of winter and the apartment only warmed up when you opened the fridge door, Mijas Pueblo always has a special place in our hearts.

Since we stayed here on that particular visit, the town hall has completely remodelled the main square, the *Plaza Virgen de la Peña*. Now closed to vehicles, there is a bandstand where they have free flamenco shows every week at certain times of the year, a children's playground and some water jets to cool off the kids in the summer.

It's also where you'll find the horse and carriage drivers, with the horses having shade and a water supply. Mijas's famous *burro-taxis* (donkey carts) are also based here and pull small carriages of tourists around the narrow streets of the town.

As you'd expect, opinion is divided over the use of donkeys for tourist transport, but in recent years their facilities have also been upgraded significantly and their welfare has been a focal point for those that wish to see their use banned. If you want to be escorted round the town in something other than a carriage pulled by a four-legged beast, there are also a few licensed tuk-tuks.

There are regular buses to and from Fuengirola if you fancy getting away from the beach, and it's a very popular stopping off point for the many Asian tourists that are bussed in on coach tours. My main beef with those visitors is that you rarely see them spending money in the shops and café bars so bring precious little to the local economy, except perhaps for the horse and donkey taxis.

We always drive here, of course, and there is a large multi-storey car park opposite the main square. We often have a run over here for a wander round and a spot of lunch, especially when we have visitors in tow. A particular favourite for its location and inexpensive, simple fayre is Oscar's Tapas Bar.

Another favourite place to visit when we have the grandkids with us is the Mayan Monkey Chocolate Factory and Ice Cream Parlour, where the kids love making their own bars of chocolate.

There's a bullring in Mijas, although they don't use it much for bullfighting these days. It's unusual in that it's oval shaped rather than the traditional circle, and you're more likely to see a flamenco show there than a bullfight.

If you're one of those people that like visiting off-the-wall museums like the Kendal Pencil Museum in the Lake District (no explanation required), Cuckooland in the Peak District with its plethora of cuckoo clocks, or the world's largest collection of teapots at Teapot Island in Kent (over 8,400 at the last count), then Mijas has something for you too … it's the home of *El Carromato de Mijas* (the Mijas Caravan), a yellow hut housing over 360 curious miniatures curated from more than 50 countries. Otherwise known as the Museum of Miniatures – or simply Max's Caravan, thanks to a Spaniard called Max who collated his miniatures during his travels around Europe and Africa – it contains items like Leonardo da Vinci's Last Supper on a grain of rice, or the seven wonders of the world engraved on a toothpick.

It's only €3 to get in (kids half price), and all the money goes to an association for children with disabilities, so as well as a bit of a fun way to while away some time, you'll be contributing to a good cause.

And just down from there at the end of the viewing area down to the coast is a tiny hermitage carved into the rock by a Carmelite monk in the 17th century. Inside, as well as a small chapel with an ornately decorated altar, you'll find the *Virgen de la Peña* (Virgin of the Rock), the patron saint of Mijas, a figurine of the Virgin Mary reportedly discovered in 1586 by shepherd children who were guided to its discovery by a dove.

Today, I was here to meet up with one of my best friends, Gary, and his wife, Caroline. Although I was best man at Gary's wedding 18 months earlier, I don't think there was much I could reuse from my best man's speech at Tony's forthcoming wedding. Tony and Gary were different creatures from different spheres of my life ... Gary was a musician like me, and Tony claimed he once played the bagpipes, so no possible crossover there!

Gary and Caroline were currently on holiday down the road in Benalmádena, and we'd agreed to meet here so they could follow us back in their hire car to our little corner of paradise in Alhaurín for a spot of lunch. We had a stroll around the pretty cobbled streets, with their uniformly-painted blue flowerpots adding some colour, and after reaching the top end of the town, we ambled back through the paved gardens of *Parque La Muralla*, built in and around some of the old, fortified walls of a more ancient village time under Arab rule. Before we left the town, we stopped for a well-deserved beer at a shady pavement café.

Suitably refreshed, we headed back to Alhaurín for one of my homemade paellas, which are always well received by visitors. I hadn't seen the pair of them since the wedding, so it was nice to spend some time with them and show them why we loved living here so much.

16

A Taxing Time

It was time to file our tax returns in both the UK and Spain and hope that the authorities took pity on us, or at least didn't screw us over. The two countries operate very different tax regimes, and to add to the confusion, they operate different financial years too.

Just like we drive on the opposite side to most of the rest of the world in the UK, by some cruel twist of fate, the UK also operates under a different tax year too. Whereas most sensible nations like Spain base their tax year on the calendar year, the UK tax year starts on 6th April. It's as if someone had put every day of the year in a big cloth bag, given it a shake and asked some random passerby to "pick a date, any date"!

To be fair, the UK is not alone in having a fiscal year that is not aligned with the calendar year. Australia's starts on 1st July (at least it starts on the first of the month, though), as do many other countries. Some start on 1st April (e.g. Japan), but there are other UK-like fiscal basket cases like Nepal (16th July), Afghanistan (30th July) and Iran (21st or 22nd March – go figure).

Some smarty-pants always has an explanation though, and the UK's reasoning is something to do with changing from the Julian calendar to the Gregorian calendar in 1752 – and no, I don't know the difference and I'm not about to try and explain it to you, either. Suffice to say, it's a right royal pain in the bum when you have to do two tax returns against two different fiscal calendars, especially when you're trying to get your head round how a double-taxation agreement might work to your benefit.

We'd already had our fingers burned (and our pockets robbed) by that bunch of thieves in Marbella, so I wasn't looking forward to going through a similar process so soon afterwards. This time I had to be on the ball and make sure I wasn't being led a merry dance again.

I'd already done our UK tax returns, and wonder of wonders – and I still don't understand how the calculations worked in HMRC's big computer – but we didn't owe them anything this year. That was the first year since I'd got my National Insurance number at the age of 16 that I hadn't meaningfully contributed to the smooth running of the United Kingdom, although to be fair, we hadn't lived there for about 18 months so weren't even having the bins emptied.

Surely, Spain would want its pound of flesh, though? Chris had special dispensation because, as a former NHS nurse, the pension she received was classed as a crown pension and only taxable in the UK. When I told the accountant this, she said they might need evidence of that in the future, but for now, until someone higher up the food chain asked for it, we were good to go.

She was still benefitting from half the rental income on the UK property though, and with a miserly personal tax allowance of just €5,550, equivalent to £4,900 (that doesn't appear to increase from one year to the next), there would surely be something to pay.

My situation was a little more vulnerable to a tax raid as I'd been paying myself a small salary all year and getting some rental income. We were sitting in the accountant's office in Coín with our paperwork spread across the desk and she was entering all the information directly into the system of the *Agencia Tributaria* (Spanish HMRC).

'Is there any other income you've not mentioned?' the accountant asked as she reached the end of the form.

'Not for this year, no,' I said. 'But I'm writing a novel and hope to have it published, so would I just add any book royalties on to my annual tax return?'

'No, you'd need to register as *autónomo* for that.'

Oh, bugger! I'd heard bad things about being self-employed in Spain. The social security fees were astronomical for one (upwards of around €300 per month) and you were charged irrespective of your earnings, which explains why there is such a thriving black labour market in Spain.

That had come as a bit of a shock to me – surely, a new author can't possibly know if they're going to sell 10 books or 10,000 books. This was going to be a nightmare scenario for my new career as a writer in Spain – I didn't know how it was possible to make that work. And I wasn't far off finishing the book either.

I'd have to worry about that in the future. Right now, I needed to know how much the Spanish government were going to fleece me for.

'OK,' I said, beginning to gather up my papers. 'Let's leave that discussion for another time. Just tell me how much the computer says we owe it, please.'

'Well, when I press this button to submit the figures, the computer will work out if it's better for you to file a joint tax return together or individual tax returns.'

Go on then, I thought, let's roll the dice and see if we get to pass 'GO' and collect €200 or we land on 'Income Tax' and pay them €200 – which might only be marginally more preferable than having to 'Go To Jail, Go Directly To Jail'.

'OK,' she said. 'If you make a joint submission, you have to pay X.'

X didn't sound too bad to me – it could have been much worse, and I didn't come here this morning with any high expectations. X was doable … we had been using their bins, after all.

'And if we do two separate submissions?' I asked, expecting that to be an even higher figure. 'What does the computer say we have to pay?'

'Zero.'

'Nothing?! Are you sure?'

'Yes, zero.'

I thought she was going to add 'the computer doesn't lie' at the end, but she didn't.

'So, you are advised to make two separate submissions, and you won't have to pay any tax this year.'

I really couldn't believe what I was hearing. I had 300 days of sunshine a year, lovely beaches, fantastic food, I was paying less than €2 for a glass of wine in the bars, and now they didn't want any tax from me? I was as happy as a pig in … or a dog with two … I couldn't think of an expression right now that didn't have a naughty word in it, so I just smiled at the accountant, who must have thought I was a bit deranged.

'Right then, we won't waste any more of your time,' I said, turning my head to Chris and giving her the same deranged grin.

We paid the accountant's bill – the princely sum of €60 plus VAT – and we hightailed it out of there. After a brief supermarket pitstop to buy a bottle of cava (for less than €3), we arrived home, stripped off, jumped in the pool, and celebrated our good fortune by sipping cava from plastic glasses.

'Remind me again why we moved to Spain,' beamed Chris, trotting out her favourite expression.

17

The End!

DON'T PANIC! – if you're reading the paperback then you'll know you're not even halfway through this adventure yet, but it's not so obvious if you're reading the ebook. It's not the end of this book, but I have reached the end of my novel – I'm done writing it, and it's now ready for its first edit.

In the words of American life coach, Tony Robbins, 'The only impossible journey is the one you never begin', and when I started writing the thriller nine months ago, it did seem like an impossible journey, but started it I did, and finished it I have – crikey, I sound like Yoda now.

I wondered how long it would take me to complete, and for a first effort, I didn't think nine months was too bad, really, especially when I factor in almost three months in that period where we either had visitors in Spain or we were away visiting family.

The sense of achievement at typing 'THE END' on the last page was quite something. In fact, I went to the fridge and cracked open a beer to celebrate and reflect on completing my first book (as I completed my thriller before I wrote the first book in this travelogue series).

There will be writers reading this now who will recognise that feeling of completing a first draft of a new book, and especially their first book. The feeling doesn't last that long though as you realise you have more mountains to climb in editing it innumerable times, contacting agents or publishers, and no doubt getting rejection after rejection. There are no guarantees in this business.

As a matter of interest, I googled some stats on publishing … the results made me realise that if I thought it was going to be hard to get a job in Spain, it was going to be much harder to secure an agent and a publishing deal in the UK. There are apparently almost 160 million unique book titles in the world, with two million more new ones published each year. TWO MILLION!

The UK actually accounts for around 10% of those two million new books and publishes more books per inhabitant than any other country in the world. In fact, the UK publishes three times more books per inhabitant than the US (which quite surprised me), and over 50% more than the second and third placed nations … have a guess who they might be … you were almost certainly wrong, it's Taiwan and Slovenia.

From what I've read, the chance of getting a book published the traditional route via an agent and publishing house stands at around 1%, so not good odds … about as much chance as Foinavon had of winning the Grand National in 1967 … but win it did, so don't be disheartened.

For all you budding authors out there, the first milestone is to actually write the book. If it gets published and sells millions, or you self-publish and it sells less than 100 copies (which sadly is the more likely outcome), then to a large extent, that's out of your hands. Just enjoy yourself writing the book, and when it's finished, give yourself a huge pat on the back.

The following day I set to work doing the first edit, which was a case of reading each sentence through carefully and deciding if there was a better way of expressing myself. It took me a couple of days to do that and make the changes, and then I read the new draft through one more time.

My friend, Martin, up in Árchez asked me how the book was coming along, and when I told him the first edit was complete, he was keen to read it. He must have had some time on his hands, as after I'd sent him an electronic copy, he'd finished it and sent me his thoughts within the week.

I knew the genre wasn't Martin's usual thing, but he's very well-educated with an eye for detail, and his comments were a useful starting point for the second edit. Overall, he was thrilled by the work, as I guess when you're friends with someone and they say they've written a book, you're probably not expecting much. So I took his encouragement as it was intended and proceeded with the next edit.

At the time, of course, I knew I could write, but you're always anxious to know if your storyline and plot are engaging and with believable characters. Since publishing my first travelogue now and seeing it succeed as well as it has done, then I now know that I can indeed write and keep my readers entertained, which is any author's primary objective. Only time will tell if I'm as good at writing thrillers as I am at writing amusing travelogues.

18

Sizzling Sanlúcar

Speaking of guests and travel getting in the way of my writing, we'd just said goodbye to my brother and his fiancée, Mike and Ann, who'd visited for a week of excessive eating and drinking. They'd arrived the day after our niece and her husband had just spent a week with us (where the eating and drinking was a little less excessive!). We then had a week of downtime before we headed off ourselves again, only this time we were exploring another part of Andalucía.

Our friends, Karen and Rick, arrived in Málaga on the late flight, and after breakfast the following day, we headed off in my car to spend a week in Sanlúcar de Barrameda, a beachside town lying at the mouth of the Guadalquivir River in the neighbouring province of Cádiz. Karen and Rick's daughter had a spacious holiday apartment on a nice complex with its own pool.

The quickest route there for us was down the A7 coast road towards Algeciras, and then hanging a right just past Gibraltar to head inland past Cádiz, which would take around two and a half hours. However, we wanted to include a suitable stop for lunch, and as we'd never been to Tarifa – the closest point to Africa on mainland Spain, about nine miles away as the crow flies (which one assumes is in a straight line!) – we decided to head there first. It would add an hour to the journey time to Sanlúcar, but we were in no hurry, and fancied lunch on the beach.

It's quite a nice run down to Tarifa, apart from getting through Algeciras, which is very built up and not worthy of a stop unless you're planning to take the ferry across to Morocco. As we wanted a beachfront *chiringuito*, we bypassed the relatively small town of Tarifa and headed straight for the beaches of its Atlantic coastline.

Tarifa is where the Atlantic Ocean meets the Strait of Gibraltar at the mouth of the Mediterranean Sea, and it seems that wherever two large bodies of water meet, there is liable to be a very stiff breeze. The beaches of Tarifa are indeed whipped by strong winds, and it's therefore a very popular destination for people who like their wind sports. If you're so inclined, it's a great place to learn windsurfing or kitesurfing.

Our friends, Laura and Shell, once went on a three-day kitesurfing course on Tarifa beach and said they thoroughly enjoyed the experience, although they found it so difficult that they didn't get out onto the water until day three, and even then weren't successful – the first days are spent learning how to handle the kite on the sand.

I once tried windsurfing on a lake when I was in my late teens, and I just kept getting on the board and falling in until I found myself having been blown to the far end of the lake. It was then a real effort to swim and drag the board back up to where I'd started from. I've also never been any good on a pair of skates or a skateboard, so I think I'll pass on kitesurfing, thanks.

When we arrived at the beach, the weather was typically blowy as we wandered down to Chiringuito Waikiki. We found a table and watched with amusement as the bottles of spirits kept rolling off an armoire located on the edge of the sand thanks to the strong winds. We spotted some kitesurfers having fun further up the shoreline and raised a glass to their endeavours. It was a hot summer's day at the end of June, and temperatures were in the mid thirties. The winds on Tarifa beach were therefore most welcome to us while we ate lunch.

Getting back in the car, I thought I knew where I was going once we were a little closer to our destination as I'd studied the map, and Karen and Rick had been before so knew the area a little too, so I just lazily punched Cádiz into the satnav. My plan was to follow my nose up the N340 for an hour and then bypass Cádiz to reach Sanlúcar.

An hour in, Chris piped up from the back, 'Where are we going?'

'Eh? Why?' I replied.

'I don't think we should be heading into central Cádiz, should we?'

I'd been enjoying the trip so much and blindly following the satnav instructions, that we were about to drive across the spit of land that joins the city of Cádiz to the mainland. What we should have been doing was heading round the eastern edge of this enormous lagoon and not driving across it at the western edge.

'Bugger! I'll have to do a U-turn,' I said, which was easier said than done off this road.

'Too busy talking in the front, you two,' Karen said.

'Hey,' said Rick. 'If your novel doesn't take off you could start running mystery tours.'

I took the next *cambio de sentido* (change of direction) junction and came back in the other direction, adding another half an hour to the journey – oops! We made it to the apartment complex very late in the afternoon and the temperature gauge on the pharmacy we'd just passed was reading 35°.

While the girls began unpacking, Rick and I had a mooch to the local shop to buy essentials (beer) and some bread. On the way, we noted the bars were showing the football – the FIFA World Cup was in full swing in Russia, and England were due to play their second group game against Panama tomorrow lunchtime, having beaten Tunisia 2-1 in the opening game, so we had to factor that into our plans for the day.

Returning to the apartment, we headed onto the large terrace overlooking the pool and gardens and enjoyed a couple of beers after the (unnecessarily) long car journey. The apartment was lovely and only a short walk from the beach.

That evening, we had a leisurely stroll into the heart of the town, and I was quite surprised how large it was – it appeared to be much larger than Alhaurín El Grande and was really lively. We were spoilt for choice with restaurants and bars spilling out onto the pavements and plazas, as they so typically do in Spain. The food was great, and we tried one of the regional specialities, *tortillitas de camarones*, a crispy fritter made from chopped up prawns that are coated in a flour-and-onion batter and deep-fried – absolutely delicious.

The following day, we headed down to the beach with deckchairs and parasols from the apartment. As I've noted, Sanlúcar de Barrameda is at the mouth of the Guadalquivir River, the only navigable river in Spain – which is surprising for a country of this size – and is only navigable from Seville down to here. And when we arrived at the beach, the opposite bank of the river was easily visible as it was less than half a mile wide at this point.

On the other side of the river was the Doñana National Park, a renowned wetland area where the King of Spain reportedly spends part of his summer holidays. The park straddles the intersection of three of Spain's provinces, Cádiz, Seville and Huelva.

The beaches at Sanlúcar are famous for their horse races, two 3-day events that take place in August each year and have done since 1845.

We found a good spot on the beach and began setting out our pitch. There was a decent breeze blowing along the beach and I could see Rick thinking intently about the position of his chair and parasol. Apparently, he had a tried and tested way of securing his beach brolly so it couldn't be picked up by the wind, hurtle down the beach and impale a toddler.

After twisting the corkscrew end of his brolly attachment into the sand at a slight angle into the wind, the brolly was attached and opened out fully. He then pulled out a plastic bag and proceeded to load it with sand by hand. Once half full, he set that down a metre from his brolly and began securing some chord from the handles of his plastic bag up to the main arm of the brolly and back to the plastic bag, nudging the bag further away until the chord was taut.

And do you know what? It was as secure as a camel's jacksie in a sandstorm – that brolly was going nowhere!

'That's brilliant, Rick,' I said. 'If Dorothy had known how to do that with a few bags of sand, her house would probably still be in Kansas!'

'It's never failed me yet,' he said. 'And the best part is, you don't have to bring your own weights – the sand is already here.'

The man's a genius. I use that method every time we go to the beach now, and I'm still surprised when I don't see anyone else doing it around me.

After a morning sunning ourselves on the beach, we packed up in time for lunch and took the stuff back to the apartment before planting ourselves in the nearest tapas bar with a TV to watch England put six past Panama. The euphoria was short-lived, as Belgium beat us in our final group game, and we went out at the semi-final stage to Croatia 2-1 after extra time. It wasn't "coming home" just yet then!

We really were enjoying our stay in Sanlúcar de Barrameda. We went for a wine-tasting session at one of the *bodegas* located in the centre of the town. It was all conducted in Spanish, and at that point our vocabulary around viticulture was a bit lacking, so whilst we didn't understand what they were telling us, we did enjoy the wines. We also tried the local *manzanilla*, a local *fino* sherry. After all, Sanlúcar is one of Spain's three better known producers of sherry, and the foremost one, the city of Jerez de la Frontera (after which sherry is named), is only a half-hour drive away.

One afternoon, we decided to take a tour of the Doñana National Park. Before we booked, we were advised the tour was only conducted in Spanish. Feeling bullish, we thought we'd understand enough of it between Chris and me that we'd be able to translate for Karen and Rick, or at least the important bits. However, we may have been a little too ambitious in hindsight.

I've seen clips on TV sometimes of someone blathering on for ages in a foreign language in response to a question from an unseen presenter until finally the translator turns to camera and says about three words by way of translation. Well, it was a bit like that with the commentary on our tour. It would typically go something like this ... the tour guide gives a two-minute speech about the section of park we are currently in, then Rick looks over at me expectantly for the translation.

'She says we're in a Mediterranean forest.'

'Yes, I can see that, we're surrounded by bloody trees!'

The park is apparently famous for its wetlands, a large area of freshwater marshes, but as it was summer, they'd mostly dried up, so we didn't see much waterfowl. We did see the odd eagle soaring high in the skies, but they can be found throughout Andalucía and are a common sight from our own garden in Alhaurín. It's also the perfect habitat for Iberian Lynx, but we didn't spot any.

We did pass a large, gated estate that was the King's summer residence, but even he wasn't home. All in all, it wasn't the best tour I've been on, and we'd have been better lay on the beach with a cold beer and a good book, really.

So the following day, we made a picnic and had a run out a short drive south to the beach at Chipiona, which was a little quieter than the beaches of Sanlúcar. And in terms of a good book, Karen had finished her paperback, so I lent her my iPad so she could read my thriller, only the second person to do so if we discount my proofreader, Chris. It kept Karen quiet for most of the day as she only seemed to surface for beer and food.

Being on the western edge of the Iberian peninsular, you get some great sunsets in Sanlúcar, and one evening we found a lovely bar at the top of the Hotel Guadalquivir and watched the sun go down. Afterwards, we found a busy tapas bar in the centre where we tried one of their signature dishes, a chorizo sausage, flame grilled by your own fair hand at your table. Alcohol is poured into a small tapas dish and ignited while a skewered chorizo sausage lies across it. When the flames have died out, your chorizo is ready to eat – very tasty.

All too soon, our time in this beautiful corner of Spain came to a close. The apartment was perfect; we'd used the outdoor pool area on a couple of afternoons and found it a quiet place to relax. We look forward to returning to Sanlúcar one day, possibly even for the horse racing on the sands, although August is school holidays, and we're usually full up with the kids and grandkids visiting us.

For now, we left Karen and Rick there as they were going to head up to Madrid to visit their daughter, and we set off home, with no unplanned detours into Cádiz.

19

Fire!

Since returning to Alhaurín, the temperatures haven't abated, and it's been 38° this weekend (which in old money is 100°F).

Temperatures get so high in the summer that the walking group abandons its walks. Our last trek was in the middle of June. We'd ambled through Los Llanos woods in Coín to visit the fire lookout post above Barranco Blanco in the valley below, an area that has a reportedly shady link to the postwar Nazis.

The lookout posts are manned through the summer months, and someone sits up there with a pair of binoculars looking out for smoke and evidence of a wildfire developing. You get a good view all the way down to the coast, and most of the walk up to the peak is in the shade of the pine forest.

It was that hot this week that even the old girls at art class were melting like a Mister Whippy ice cream in August, and getting their oils to dry from one week to the next is becoming a challenge. I'm sticking to acrylics for now, and so is Chris, who finally finished her painting of Corrinne's dog, Max, and she's done a really fantastic job of it.

Everyone is drinking *café con hielo* at the moment, hot coffee poured over ice cubes, except for me … I've been maintaining my new diet regime of drinking coke to keep my furballs at bay!

Chris and I were relaxing on the terrace on the Sunday night, finishing off the bottle of wine we'd opened with dinner – 'and almost at the point of opening another one?', I hear you ask. The sun had gone half an hour earlier, and I heard a distant bang over to my left. Looking over the pool and beyond the end of our garden I could see flames dancing high in the garden opposite.

My first reaction was that some pillock had lit a bonfire at this time of night. My first reaction, however, was wrong.

'Shit!' I said. 'Is that next door's trees on fire?'

Chris jumped from her seat and turned around to take a look.

'It is, yes.'

At this point I half expected her to dash inside, grab her fireman's helmet and run down the garden with a hose pipe.

'What do we do?' I asked. 'Put it on the Fire Watch group?'

'No, you idiot! We ring the fire brigade.'

Chris rang the emergency number and reported the fire in Spanish – there's confidence for you! Only then did she report it on the Fire Watch group. A few minutes later we heard sirens.

At the bottom of our garden is a small tributary that feeds the *Río Fahala,* and the neighbouring garden is on the other side. But the tributary is only a few metres wide and overgrown, and our enormous Eucalyptus trees that grab whatever moisture they can from it (on the odd occasion there's any water in it) overlap with the neighbour's Eucalyptus trees. So if the fire I could now see travelled down his garden as far as his Eucalyptus trees, then it would certainly jump across to our garden.

We watched as the flames leapt higher in the sky for a while until the *bomberos* managed to get it under control. We didn't know the neighbours over on that side as there was no possibility of casually bumping into them – the only time I ventured right to the bottom of the garden was when I was strimming, and even then, your view is blocked by two dense lines of Eucalyptus.

We heard from Chris's boss, Jill, that the house belonged to an English electrician. His gas bottle had blown up. He'd called her and said she could take the fire warning down, and that he wouldn't have needed the fire brigade as he had it under control.

Well, it didn't look under control to us!

We breathed a sigh of relief it hadn't been worse, and that the fire station was only a short drive away.

'That was a close one,' Chris said.

'It was. More wine to settle your nerves?'

'Is the Pope a Catholic?'

20

Cooling Off at the Beach

The following day, we headed down the coast to a beach we hadn't visited before at *Playa Guadalmina*, about halfway from Marbella to Estepona.

An old Scottish mate and work colleague of mine, Richard, who lived in Dubai, was back in the UK with his wife, Becca, for a while. They had two teenage daughters, Islay 17 and Charlotte 15, whom my daughter, Rachel (then 25), and I had had the dubious pleasure of looking after five years earlier in Dubai while their parents buggered off to a rock festival for 10 days. Getting these two (then 12 and 10) out of bed each morning for the school run – or what I dubbed the Dubai Whacky Races down the Sheikh Zayed Road, where the only way to change direction is to do a U-turn from the fast lane going one way to the fast lane going the other way – was an absolute nightmare … no wonder their parents needed 10 days of headbanging music to recover from banging their heads against a wall every morning the rest of the year.

Anyway, Islay (now with the responsibility of getting herself out of bed) was interrailing it round Europe with a bunch of her mates, and they were currently on the Costa del Sol. Becca had secretly flown out with Charlotte yesterday to surprise them, and we'd agreed to meet up for lunch on the beach.

Chris and I plonked ourselves on the beach for the morning while we waited for them to join us. I'd already rung ahead and booked us a table for lunch at Chiringuito Sol Beach, a well-regarded beach restaurant with the usual fayre of grilled seafood, burgers and salads.

We weren't sure what time Becca and the five girls would descend on us. A couple of days earlier when asked, she said she'd round them all up after breakfast when it finished at 10:30, and then they'd walk down from their hotel about 40 minutes away, but by the time she factored in teenage moaning, it'd probably take them an hour.

On arrival, Islay and her friends dumped an assortment of hotel towels on the beach and got ready to sunbathe. Being teenage girls who probably spent their daytimes sleeping off the effects of too many good nights out – and coupled with their naturally alabaster-like Scottish complexions – they were in danger of underestimating the power of the summer sun in this part of the world (regardless of Islay's more recent upbringing in Dubai), and so nurse Chris was happily on hand to keep an eye on them and ensure they kept applying enough suncream.

After a decent lunch, the girls all piled into the sea to cool off for a bit. We had a good old catchup with Becca and learnt that their time in Dubai was coming to an end. Richard had been working in Saudi Arabia, flying in and out each week from their apartment on Dubai's Palm Island, but he was ready to return to the UK. Islay wanted to go to university in Glasgow, and two weeks later was given a place on her preferred marine biology course. So it was all change north of the border, and back to Alhaurín for an easy life for us.

Having said that, I did apply for two more jobs this week, but to no avail, so I've decided to knock the job hunting on the head for a few months and go back to editing my novel. There's a lot of work to be done before I'd be happy sending it out to literary agents. I'd read that most successful authors re-read and edit their book as many as 50 times before a final draft is considered worthy of publication. I'm only up to seven at the moment, so a long way to go yet!

21

Livin' La Vida Loca

Since breaking up with her boyfriend recently, our daughter, Rachel, is looking for love again, but there's all the love in the world for her here in Spain, and we're delighted she's flying in to spend a week with us.

August is a great time to visit Málaga because it's when the *Feria de Málaga* is held, a weeklong festival of free daytime concerts in the city's squares. And when the sun goes down, the party migrates to the outskirts of the city to the main fairground where they hold the *Feria de Noche* (night fair). It's like the Fuengirola food fair on steroids – one huge party that goes on way into the early hours of the morning with all the usual fairground rides and stalls, and not forgetting the 180 *casetas* with their own bars and music.

The day after she arrived, we drove down to Málaga city and parked over at Muelle Uno car park by the marina as there are always spaces available there. From there, it's a nice stroll through the gardens of the *Parque de Málaga* to Calle Larios district which is the main hub of activities.

The *Feria de Málaga* is a commemoration of the city becoming part of Castille in August 1487 after the Moors were expelled by Ferdinand and Isabella. You'll find revellers dressed in traditional Spanish costumes (especially the older generation), and they'll be found partying in the main squares where the concerts take place. We headed to *Plaza de la Constitución*

(Constitution Square) at the top of Calle Larios, and later into *Plaza de las Flores* (Flower Square).

It's a real party atmosphere with everyone having a good time and dancing along to the music provided by live bands. One of the key sponsors of the fiesta appears to be a sweet white wine brand from Málaga called *Cartojal*. You'll see their distinctive pink barrels located around the area and people drinking directly from their pink-labelled bottles.

It was fun watching everyone in a party mood, but I was driving so couldn't partake of a glass or two. I made a mental note to try and make it back here another year on public transport so I could get the full party experience.

We had a late lunch and then decided to check out the main fairground before it got fully underway later – we had alternate plans for the evening and so wouldn't be here after dark. Parking near the fairground is difficult, even late afternoon. If you're visiting at night, there's a 24-hour bus service that will shuttle you to the fairground and back from the city centre.

Some of the fairground rides were up and running when we arrived, and we just meandered through the huge site, imagining what it must be like after dark. The *caseta* bars were closed, but they'd be rammed from about 10pm until 6am, and I bet there are some bleary-eyed looking characters taking the bus back home afterwards.

Having seen enough and walked quite some distance, we made it back to the car and drove down the coast to Fuengirola – Ricky Martin was playing at the MareNostrum castle this evening, and although we didn't have tickets, many people just congregate outside on the beach and have their own little party.

It took us about an hour of driving round the streets and local car parks before we were able to find a free space. We had a cool bag with us and stopped at a minimart to pick up some cold drinks. We tried to get in a couple of beach restaurants for something to eat but they were all rammed in that part of town, so we went back to the shop and bought some bread and a packet of sliced cheese to make sandwiches.

There was an air of excitement in the crowds as we found a good position on the beach to spread out our beach blanket. We couldn't see the stage as it backed onto the beach, but we had a view of one of the big screens inside the stadium and were treated to a free evening of *Livin' La Vida Loca* and *She Bangs*!

I can safely say I don't own a Ricky Martin CD, so it's not something I'd stick on to listen to in the car usually, but sitting on a beach with family in the dark, with the tide lapping up, Latin-influenced music blaring out and people dancing on the sand made for a memorable evening.

My most recent pop art paintings had been of Michael Jackson, Debbie Harry and Bono, but maybe next week I should try one of Ricky Martin … then again!

22

Antique Antequera

With the summer heat not quite so oppressive in September, we allowed Mum and Dad to visit again on the proviso Dad didn't get heatstroke and drank plenty of water – Mum was much more sensible (unless she'd had a couple of glasses of cava in the middle of the day and forgot to drink water with it!).

I'd always fancied heading inland towards Antequera to climb El Torcal, a mountainous region famed for its amazing limestone rock formations. However, even I wasn't stupid enough to attempt that with two octogenarians in tow and with temperatures in the mid eighties. So I thought we'd go and cool off in a cave instead.

Apart from El Torcal, the other thing Antequera is famous for are its neolithic burial caves known as dolmens, similar to the one I previously referred to in the mountains behind Estepona. However, the ones in Antequera were reportedly the dog's doodahs of dolmens, so we were anticipating being impressed.

Antequera lies an hour's drive away up the same steep motorway pass we took when we went to Granada with the old folks earlier in the year. We headed straight for the site of the dolmens which lie just outside the town centre to the northeast. Parking was free, and so was entry to the dolmens – you'd have been charged at least a fiver for parking in England and the same (or more) to get in.

You walk through the grounds on a gentle incline as the dolmens are buried into the hillside (or rather the hillside will have been built on top of the dolmens as a covering) ... a bit like Tellytubby houses! The earthworks covering the dolmens are basically an artificial mound of earth (so not quite a hill) called a 'tumulus'.

There are three dolmens in Antequera, and the oldest dates back almost 6,000 years. The largest (and oldest) of them – and indeed the largest in Europe – is the *Dolmen de Menga*. Inside, this megalithic tomb measures almost 30 metres in length, with a ceiling height that rises to 3.5 metres at the rear. On entering, it has a very spacious and airy feel.

'Ooh, it's a lot cooler inside than out,' said Mum.

'Shall we put your name down for a place in here then when you're gone?' I asked.

'You cheeky monkey,' she replied.

When the tomb was opened in the 19th century, they found the skeletal remains of several hundred people, and I'm sure there's room for one more.

Dolmens are constructed by laying very large stones vertically to form the walls, and in this dolmen, there are three central columns that help support the larger and heavier ceiling stones. The heaviest ceiling stone in the *Dolmen de Menga* weighs almost 200 tonnes, which is about five times heavier than the largest stone at Stonehenge – where they charge you about 30 bloody quid to go in, I might add!

One of the unique features of the *Dolmen de Menga* is that the entrance points towards the *Peña de los Enamorades* (Lover's Rock), a distinctive rock formation over which one could watch the sun rise at the summer solstice from the door to the dolmen.

According to local legend, the rock is so named because it resembles the face of a prone woman. During a battle between Muslims and Christians, the commander of the Christian army was captured and put in a cell. Whilst incarcerated, the daughter of the Muslim king visited him, and they fell in love. They fled together and were chased by the king, but on becoming trapped at the edge of the rock, they leapt to their deaths in a final loving embrace.

The rock formation can be seen from the A-92 motorway and (to me) looks more like the face of a Red Indian. In fact, the other name for this feature is *El Indio* (the Indian), so I'm not the only one to think that.

On the same site is the *Dolmen de Viera*, which has a slightly smaller chamber. The third one, the *Dolmen El Romal* is a couple of miles further out of town, so we passed up on seeing that one – I suppose once you've seen one 6,000-year-old neolithic burial cave, you've seen them all, right?

The visitor centre has some further information about the dolmens, and they're well worth a visit, even if it'll only take you about half an hour to go round the site and nip in the visit centre.

Archeologically, dolmens are very important structures, and the site at Antequera was awarded UNESCO World Heritage status a couple of years earlier in 2016.

Returning to the car, we drove into town, parked up in a car park next to the bullring, then strolled around the narrow streets of this pretty town for a while, checking out the lunchtime options. Eventually we settled on Restaurante Leila (after passing by it once) … nothing to do with me this time, we were just browsing!

Set in *Plaza San Sebastian*, a short distance from the fortress of the Alcazaba and its entrance point, the *Arco de los Gigantes* (Arch of the Giants), we sat outside under the shade of a parasol and had a leisurely lunch.

Antequera isn't an especially big town (although much larger than Alhaurín El Grande), and it doesn't take you long to navigate its streets. So after lunch and another stroll back to the car park, it was time to return home.

At an hour away, it made the perfect day trip for us, and we didn't have to exert ourselves to see the dolmens or wander around the town.

23

Eye of the Storm

Well, I didn't see that coming ... the week had started well – I'd knocked out another painting at art class, this time of the great Aretha Franklin ... and on Friday morning, all the good omens were aligned for me when I cracked two eggs into a frying pan alongside two slices of potato cake and they both turned out to be double-yolkers! That means something good is going to happen to me, right?

Double-yolkers tend to come from young hens who haven't learnt how to lay properly yet, and the odds of getting one are about 1,000-1, so that means the chances of getting two in the same pan must be around one in a million. Chris sometimes says I'm one in million, but I don't think she means it in a good way.

You can sometimes get triple-yolkers, but I've never had one – incredibly, the record for an egg is nine yolks, and I'm not sure I could have managed nine yolks and two potato cakes.

Feeling luck was in the air, after breakfast I nipped into town and bought a ticket for the Euromillions. Someone won €17 million that night, and the fact I'm writing this book tells you it wasn't me! – it was some lucky beggar in Belgium, who probably went out and gorged himself on *moules frites* washed down with a glass of Leffe Blonde.

Our daughter, Corrinne, and her husband, Graham, arrived the next day for a long weekend, and if I had been lucky enough to win €17 million, I'd have been tempted to give them the ticket to claim in the UK where lottery winnings are tax free; over here the state taxes lottery winnings over €40k at 20%, so I'd have had to hand over about €3.4 million to the Spanish government.

Our visitors had left a cold and wet St Helens to grab some autumn sunshine, but their luck ran out by Monday. The sun had gone and was replaced by endless cloudy skies, humidity was around 90%, and the temperature started to plummet from a high of 33° to just 20° by Tuesday morning. By lunchtime, we could hear the ominous sound of thunder in the distance.

As the sun was just going down, the rain started, slowly at first, but within half an hour the thunderstorm was upon us for real. We watched the light show from the safety of the villa as it flashed all around us, illuminating different sections of the town in the distance with each new flash.

The rain was biblical, and we were keeping a keen eye on local twitter accounts. In Alhaurín El Grande, the rain pours down off the mountain and rushes down through the town's narrow streets. We watched in horror as someone in the centre of town had posted a video of cars and vans floating down the street and crashing into other parked cars.

We were safe enough in the villa as our land was relatively flat, and the villa's terrace was raised above ground level with a tiled walkway all around the perimeter. With the TV signal out of action thanks to its reliance on a pretty slow microwave internet signal from the mountain transmitters, we turned into bed early.

The thunderstorm raged all through the night and finally ended at about 9:30 the following morning, 12 hours after it had started. The pool was full to overflowing and full of leaf litter and other debris. We also knew the pool pump housing and the adjacent below-ground electrical cable box (that our landlady, Olivia, had oddly drilled holes in the bottom of) were both going to be full of water again. Wisely, we'd isolated the electricity supply to the pool pump before the storm started, but only thanks to prior experience of this level of flooding.

When the rain finally abated, I gingerly made my way round to the shed at the back of the house to find my wellies, before wading through the mud to the pool pump. Lifting the lid, the water had reached the bottom of the electrics, so there was about two or three feet of water to be baled out again.

I set to work rigging up a portable electric pump to do the majority of the initial baling out for me, but after that it was a question of poking a mop down to the bottom a few hundred times and wringing it out into a bucket. It was a pain in the neck and tiresome work, but at least our cars hadn't been washed away like some of the poor residents in town.

The road network in Málaga was on red alert all day, with the torrential rain causing havoc to travel plans. A landslide had hit the main A7 coast road causing a six-mile tailback, and the town of Ojen above Marbella had recorded 174 litres of water per square metre overnight. Looking in our pool pump housing I could well believe it.

While I was clearing out the pool pump, Chris and Corrinne decided to head out to the shops for supplies, but when they tried to get out of the property, the electric gate had stopped working, so they had to get out and push it open. On closer inspection, the motor had blown up and the video intercom inside the house was no longer working. It took a couple of visits from the mechanic to replace the motor and intercom for us, thankfully paid for by the landlady, Olivia, but the motor wasn't cheap, and she wasn't happy.

When they returned from the shops, they said the town was in a bit of a sorry state, and our local bar at the end of the lane had been flooded thanks to its position at the bottom of the mountain opposite a gully on the opposite side of the road.

We don't know if our gate motor had been hit by lightning or just shorted out with water getting into the electrics. Either way, we were given strict instructions to turn it off at the fuse box next time storms were anticipated, just as we had learnt to do with the pool pump. An insurance company would have called the damage caused by the flooding an act of God, but I've no idea what God was thinking last night.

24

Having Doubts

I used to think Twitter was just a series of echo chambers for people with similarly extreme opinions, so wasn't sure about getting on there myself. However, as well as starting a little blog earlier in the year (as recommended in some of my reading material), I was also encouraged to build up a writing social media profile.

Hence, since setting up an account to connect with authors and the writing community, I've been deliberately choosy about who to follow and what I post. And thankfully, I now read about topics that interest me and that may help me get my novel out there. I'm connected with many UK literary agents to see what their interests are currently, but I'm also connecting with other authors writing in my genre of military based fiction.

Essentially, my novel is about an ex-army bomb squad operative whose family are kidnapped from a Spanish beach by perpetrators unknown to him, and he finds himself in a race against time to find and rescue them with the help of an odd mix of characters.

And I could really do with a little bit of advice on military procedure. The reason it was so important to me was that the novel was just about ready for my first agent submissions, and I needed clarification on a few points. In fact, I already had the submission letters ready to go, and this was the final piece in the puzzle.

I'm well versed in the genre but have never served myself, and hence the value of an experienced eye over a few things. Having now read a mixture of true wartime accounts and fiction written by ex-servicemen, it would be great if I could start a dialogue with one of them.

Well, this morning, my luck was in … Major Michael Jenkins MBE, a veteran of the British Army's bomb disposal division and UK Counterintelligence (and a bloody great author of counterterrorism novels) agreed to help me out. I emailed him the text I wanted him to review along with some questions I had. He replied the same day with a detailed response and with a most encouraging view of my writing. I was absolutely thrilled!

The following day, without further delay, I pressed SEND on submissions to my three preferred agents, the industry experts who represented the writing interests of people like Andy McNab, Chris Ryan and James Deegan. My small library of publishing books had informed me not to scattergun but to be targeted in my approach, tailoring the covering letters specifically to the intended recipients and their literary interests – just as you would a covering letter for a job advertisement (which I was *too* well used to writing since moving to Spain!).

The next day I couldn't help but send out a fourth, but then I promised myself I was going to wait for responses (and hopefully requests for more information). It was a nervy wait, and I wasn't sure what to do with myself in the meantime. Should I start writing a follow-up book, keep editing the first book, prepare some more agent submissions for if and when the first ones are rejected? Or should I just take some time out from writing and relax?

As it happened, it took the mechanic longer to fix the gate and intercom than it did to receive that first letter of rejection. Six days for a gate repair and only four for an agent rejection. Literary agents should start doing foreigners fixing gates at that rate.

I wasn't sure whether to be encouraged or upset by the speed of that first rejection, but the tone of the response was thankfully very encouraging, and I was wholly appreciative of the fact. Nevertheless, you'd have to be thick-skinned for it not to knock your confidence a little and for doubts to start setting in about your writing ability.

And at least that agent took the trouble to write a reply – two of the other agents I first approached didn't even bother replying. I can understand they probably get a lot of submissions sent to them, but it doesn't take long to say 'thanks, but no thanks', even if it's in a standard, impersonalised rejection email. Plus, those agents probably don't even see your submission, as the bigger agencies will have minions acting as a pre-filter and doing the first read.

Time to put things in perspective, so I googled how many rejections some famous authors received before finding success … Stephen King had his first novel, the chiller *Carrie*, rejected by 30 publishers … and even J.K Rowling's first effort, *Harry Potter and the Philosopher's Stone*, failed to cast a spell on the first 10 publishing houses to receive it. And maybe that's the thing: approach publishing houses first, and if you get a tickle on the line and a further approach, then get an agent on board. For now, I'd follow what appears to be the standard route.

History is littered with success stories that faced rejection before finding success. The fella that designed the Trunki suitcase for kids went on the UK's Dragons' Den in 2006 and came away without an investment, but he ended up being 'wheely' successful and sold five million of them. Then there's the guy that designed a hairbrush called the Tangle Teezer. He was again laughed off Dragons' Den, but his website crashed due to public demand on the night the show was aired, and he sold over 50 million of them before selling his shares for £70 million.

And even The Beatles were turned down by the Decca record label before they were snapped up by George Martin at EMI!

So the motto surely is, 'if at first you don't succeed, try, try again'. Or in the words of the American writer, Suzy Kassem, 'doubt kills more dreams than failure ever will'.

So I guess I'll just crack on and keep believing in myself.

25

License to Kill

'We need to get Spanish driving licenses soon,' Chris said to me one morning.

'Why? What's up with our British ones?'

'They become invalid over here in a few months.'

'Great! More things to have with my names the wrong way round. What idiotic Spanish bureaucracy do we need to navigate this time, then?'

Chris was scrolling through her phone to find a list of documents we would need.

'You need your NIE document, your passport, UK driving license, passport-sized colour photo and a medical certificate.'

'A medical certificate? Where do we get one of those from, the private health clinic?'

'No, there's a place in the centre of Coín that does them, and they send off all the information to the DGT. Apparently, it's really easy.'

'Famous last words,' I grumbled.

The DGT (*Dirección General de Tráfico*) is Spain's national traffic authority, the equivalent of the UK's DVLA (Driver and Vehicle Licensing Agency). They're responsible for executing the Spanish government's road traffic policies. These guys issue driving licenses and speeding fines, in essence.

The fixed speed cameras in Spain are not very conspicuous and are often difficult to spot, but on the motorways, there are usually signs warning you about your speed before you reach the cameras. Those ones are directly linked to the DGT, but you've got to watch out for mobile speed traps too that are operated by the *Guardia Civil*. We're unfortunate to have a training centre for the *Guardia Civil* in our area, and they often set up roadblocks at our local roundabouts to pull over anyone that looks a bit suspicious (or pissed!).

In order to get our medical certificates, we had to pass a 'psycho-technical medical aptitude test', whatever that was, so Chris booked us in.

'Do I have to revise for this test?' I asked.

'No, they'll just check your eyesight and reactions, probably, to make sure you're fit to get behind the wheel of a car.'

'Shall I show them that video of you driving a Subaru round a racetrack?' I joked.

'Hey, it's not me that drove into the back of a wedding party!'

'Alright, no need to drag that up.'

'Or got done for driving without due care and attention in Blackpool one week after I'd passed my test.'

'It was wet, and that copper was a jobsworth.'

'Or drove into the back of a car in Barcelona.'

'I get your point, you're a more careful driver than I am.'

Arriving at the test centre, we handed over copies of all our paperwork, and for once, there was nothing untoward or missing. She didn't even ask why my names were the wrong way round!

The first part of the medical was a blood pressure test – no problem there … fit as a butcher's dog, as they say.

Medications? Just a daily PPI for acid reflux … maybe not as fit as a butcher's dog, then!

Then she handed me on to a chap in another room for the eye test, which was a bit like being at the optician's – I just had to read smaller and smaller letters on a card at distance.

Now it was time for the hearing test. After a lifetime of playing the trumpet (or at least a pre-Spanish lifetime as I don't seem to get it out of the case much anymore) and listening to music too loudly – plus Chris generally thinking I'm deaf when I'm just ignoring her – I wasn't so confident about this one … I should have had a bit of an ear poke with a tissue before I left the house, maybe.

Then again, I recalled my Great Uncle Bob who was as deaf as a post, and had been as long as anyone could remember. He was in his 90s at the time and was as fit as a fiddle apart from his hearing. He used to walk miles to the shopping precinct every day to do the day's shopping, while my Great Auntie Annie hardly set foot out of the door. When Mum took us to visit them you had to shout at him to be heard. Anyway, at one point he had to go to the Ear, Nose and Throat department where someone finally had a good look in his ears and pulled out a long length of cotton wool from each ear that must have been about a foot long. When asked how it came to be there, he said he used to shove cotton wool in his ears when the Luftwaffe were dropping doodlebugs on Manchester, and some of it must have got stuck in there each time he did it – afterwards, his ear canals had somehow knitted a rope out of bits of cotton wool!

I needn't have worried about the hearing test – although you'll not believe what I'm about to tell you. The chap led me to a small booth … I thought he was going to hear my confession at first, and seeing as I hadn't confided in a priest for about 40 years, it would have been a long confession! However, this booth had a clear glass window in the front. He instructed me to press a little button every time I heard something through the speakers in this booth. But the comical thing about the test was that the thing that initiated a noise in the booth was him pressing a button on the other side of the glass, so even though sometimes I wasn't entirely sure if I'd heard anything or not, as soon as I saw him press his button I pressed mine – simples!

He handed me back to the first lady who was now ready to test my reactions. She seated me in front of a black and white TV screen that had two roads on it, side by side – I say 'roads' but they were just a series of vertical dashes either side of a bigger vertical dash (representing a car presumably?). I think they'd built this simulator with a ZX Spectrum! I had a joystick in each hand that moved only left and right, and I had to keep both 'cars' on the 'road' without hitting the 'kerb' (the little dashes on either side). If you hit the kerb, the machine would beep.

Off we went down the road, and the lefthand road veered left a bit and the righthand road carried straight on. Then the righthand one veered right at the same time as the other one veered right. Then for the next few minutes (although it seemed like an eternity) I was going left-left, right-right, left-right, right-left, straight-straight, straight-left, left-straight, right-straight, straight-right … it was a real effort not to burst out laughing at the graphics and the concept of the test in general – it was great fun.

'How did I do?' I asked when the 'cars' finally came to a stop.

'Excellent,' she said. 'You only hit the kerb once. You scored 99%.'

Wait till I tell Chris that, I thought. Wedding party my arse!

'And what's the pass mark?'

'Fifty percent, although if you're over sixty-five the pass mark goes down the older you get.'

I couldn't believe what I was hearing – and we'd already just established there was nothing wrong with my hearing. So, let me get this right … you're considered fit to drive on a Spanish road as long as you only hit the kerb 50% of the time you're driving, and if you're a bit doddery, you can hit it a few more times? That answered all my questions about erratic Spanish driving right there. Jeepers! I've never seen the bar set to low for someone being in charge of a lethal weapon. No wonder every panel of every car on the road had a dent in it.

And that was it – medical done. They would send all the paperwork to the DGT, and we'd get our driving licenses through the post in about a month. I drove home and tried not to hit the kerb, but I kept a keen eye out for Spaniards, and old Spaniards in particular!

26

Fabulous Frigiliana

Frigiliana is one of those picture-perfect, whitewashed, Andalucian villages that is usually listed in any guide's "top 10 most beautiful villages in Spain" list, and we found ourselves visiting it for our third time when my parents were over again (for only their fourth visit of the year – they must really love me). However, we were hoping on this visit that we'd actually find the town centre!

That's not as crazy as it sounds, as the signposting and some roadworks the first two times we came led us off a roundabout to the top of the town that was neither beautiful nor picture-perfect. However, we'd seen the place many times on Channel 4's travel programmes, *A Place in the Sun*, and more latterly *A New Life in the Sun*, and we knew that if we tried hard enough, we'd find it this time.

You shouldn't be able to miss it really as there's only one road up from the coast that passes through the town and out the other side, but miss it we had – twice!

To make sure we were successful this time we actually booked a hotel there for the night, safe in the knowledge that our satnav would find the hotel, which was in the middle of the picture-perfect, whitewashed part of the town centre we'd been so keen to visit on those other occasions.

As they were avid watchers of Channel 4's *A New Life in the Sun*, we thought we'd treat Mum and Dad to an early Christmas present and stay at a boutique hotel called Miller's that had featured recently on the programme. The owner, Tanya, had done a splendid job of refurbishing the building into this cosy, bijou accommodation using antique furniture she'd brought over from the UK – her family's background was in antiques, and she'd used her knowledge expertly to marry the furniture with her design ideas.

The hotel is located on Calle Real, the main artery through the old village, a narrow one-way street which is only accessible by car between the hours of 2pm and 6pm. Outside of those hours there are traffic restrictions in place. So after finding somewhere to pull in briefly, decamp the folks and their luggage and check in to the hotel, I carefully navigated the narrow streets round a circuit of the old town and deposited the car in the public parking garage.

The rooms at Miller's were chic and comfortable, and after unpacking an overnight bag we went to explore the town. We found a restaurant for dinner later that evening just a stone's throw from the hotel and booked a table – again, not my decision and no googling involved … once bitten twice shy.

Frigiliana is indeed a most picturesque town (when you can find it). In 1982 it was awarded first prize in the search for the most beautiful village in Spain, and it has a distinctly Moorish feel to its narrow, cobbled streets. Situated in the Axarquía region and originally part of Granada province, it's a very short drive up the road from the much larger seaside town of Nerja (from which there is a frequent bus service). Like most of Andalucía, the town has at various times been under the control of people from different cultures and religions, and as with larger cities such as Córdoba, the Arabs, Jews and Christians have at times happily coexisted in Frigiliana.

There is even a fiesta in Frigiliana towards the end of August named *El Festival de las Tres Culturas* (the Festival of the Three Cultures) to celebrate that time of peaceful coexistence. It was only when the Christian rulers of the time began to clamp down oppressively on the Muslim culture, banning their language and traditional clothing, and trying to convert them to Christianity, that frictions emerged.

Eventually, in response to the oppression and crippling taxes, the Moors rebelled in 1568, an uprising that spread throughout the Muslim population of Granada, and the rebellion culminated in *La Batalla del Peñon de Frigiliana* (the Battle of the Rock of Frigiliana). After 20 days of fierce resistance, the Christian armies defeated the rebels with the loss of thousands of Arab lives, making it one of the bloodiest campaigns in Spanish history. The remaining Moorish population was enslaved or driven out of the kingdom.

We took our time strolling around the old town, partly because there is so much to stop and admire, partly because we had Mum and Dad with us, and partly because it's so darn steep in places. Spanish old folk are used to living in villages on the side of mountains though. We've been overtaken more than once by an old dear carrying her shopping up a steep hill in Alhaurín El Grande.

There is a bohemian feel to Frigiliana, and many artists have settled here over the years. After a while, we stopped for a drink at one of the many restaurants on our route that had panoramic views down the hillside. It may have been the beginning of November, but the temperatures were still in the mid-20s and there wasn't a cloud in the sky, so it was nice to sit for a moment with a cold beer.

Later, we took dinner at La Taberna del Sácristan in *Plaza de la Iglesia* (Church Square). The temperatures had now dropped, and a warmer outer layer was called upon as we dined outside the pretty St. Anthony's church.

The following morning, we headed down into Nerja and had a stroll to the *Balcón de Europa* (Balcony of Europe), a popular viewing point in the centre of town perched on a rocky outcrop that looks out over the Mediterranean and was given its name by King Alfonso XII, of whom there is a statue on the promenade.

It was another cloudless, sunny day on the coast, and we mooched around the shops for a while, stepping inside the Art Gallery on Calle Pintada (Graffiti Street – although there was none in evidence), a two-storey gallery of interesting artworks through which you're allowed to amble at your leisure. I noticed they didn't have any pop art on the walls, so I made a mental note to contact them later to see if they'd like some … after all, I had 10 to my name now and could offer them a full collection.

On our way home, we met up with our friends, Kim and Martin, on Algarrobo Costa, which is the nearest seaside resort to them at the bottom of the treacherous mountain road down from Árchez. Martin had googled somewhere suitable for Dad's discerning palate – i.e. 'no bloody garlic!' – called Pippo on the promenade.

He likes his fish and seafood, and we managed to find him something on the menu that wouldn't ruin his chances with Mum later in the afternoon.

All in all, the weekend was a resounding success … we'd managed to find Frigiliana at the third time of asking, Mum and Dad hadn't been hobbled by its cobbles, and we'd sated their curiosity for a TV personality's boutique hotel.

Happy Christmas to the old folks.

27

Captivating Córdoba

I've just received my second agent rejection in the space of three weeks – ah, well, at least someone's reading it, even if it is just the cleaners. Onwards and upwards … to Córdoba, in fact. The parents had returned to rainy Manchester, and so we decided to have a few days away doing touristy things on our own.

Córdoba had been on our radar for a while. People recommend going in May to visit the *Patios de Córdoba* (Courtyards of Córdoba), when people open up their private courtyard gardens to visitors who wish to see the colourful flower and plant displays. However, although visitors have been enjoying that spectacle since 1921 (give or take a period of civil war that undoubtedly threw a temporary spanner in the works), that's not what I personally call fun.

I'd also heard from friends that there are large queues for the more popular courtyards, and the temperature in Córdoba in May can be stifling, especially when you consider that Córdoba is the hottest place in Spain, with summer temperatures regularly over 40°. So November was a much better time for a relaxing visit to the city.

Being a lover of them since we arrived in Spain – and wanting to cross another one off the list – we stayed at the Parador de Córdoba for a couple of nights. It's about 120 miles away and took us two hours to get there. Situated on a hill a couple of miles north of the city centre, and much more modern than what was here before it, namely the palace of Córdoba's first Emir, Abd al-Rahman I, the Parador de Córdoba is famous for having Europe's oldest palm trees in its garden.

We'd arrived late in the afternoon and seemed to be almost the only guests there, although we did arrive on a Sunday, which any seasoned traveller will tell you is a hotel's quietest night. We relaxed on the expansive terrace for a while with a complementary glass of red wine and olives, all part of the service at the Parador chain. We dined in the hotel restaurant that evening and were more than happy with the quality of the food.

Córdoba is such a culturally rich city with an amazing history that we had a busy schedule of sightseeing lined up for our only full day there, and after breakfast we headed straight for the main attraction, the Moorish architecture of the *Mezquita-catedral de Córdoba*, otherwise known as the Great Mosque of Córdoba, awarded the status of UNESCO World Heritage site in 1984.

Although converted into a cathedral following the expulsion of the Moors, the Catholics at least had the presence of mind and empathy with the outstanding Moorish architectural interior that they retained it all and built the cathedral around it. Anyone even vaguely familiar with the beauty of Córdoba would recognise instantly an image of the beautiful labyrinthine columns that flow in every direction when you stand in the centre.

The cathedral is a must see when you visit Córdoba, and with a €10 entry fee, it could be considered expensive by normal Spanish tourist site prices. Perhaps it has something to do with the fact it's owned by the Catholic church – as a disgruntled ex altar-boy, I'm allowed to say that – but it was worth it.

We stepped outside for a coffee at a pavement café and watched the world go by for a while. Then we headed off to explore the rest of the city. Next on our chosen tourist trail was the crossing of the river Guadalquivir via the Roman bridge – or *old* bridge as it used to be known, given that it was the *only* bridge in the city for 2,000 years.

At the other side of the bridge is the Calahorra Tower, originally built under Islamic rule to guard the entrance to the city over the river. We paid a few euros to go inside and visit the Living Museum of al-Andalus and learn more about the history of the city during its Moorish period. There are several floors of exhibits, and at the top, you come out onto a roof terrace with panoramic views of the city and beyond.

After the death of the first Emir of Córdoba, Abd al-Rahman I, the baton of ruler was passed not to one of his sons but to a favoured grandson, Abd al Rahman III, who 10 years into his 32-year reign founded the Caliphate of Córdoba. The city prospered and became a centre of excellence for education and learning under the rule of the Umayyad dynasty, and in its heyday was one of the largest and most prosperous cities in Europe.

After assuaging our cultural curiosities, we then meandered through the narrow streets of the city's historic Jewish quarter, itself designated as a World Heritage Site in 1994. Originally, this part of the city will have been walled off to protect the Jews from the Christians, but there are no such walls present today.

With stomachs rumbling, we found a nice restaurant called Taberna Deanes down a back street at the end of a narrow alley, a short distance from the Mesquita. Their three-course *menú del día* board tempted us inside to a smart, bright, courtyard dining area. Lunch was only €12 each and was washed down by a couple of bottles of Ribera del Duero (what else?) – we'd come on the bus before you lecture me about drink driving!

We then went back to the hotel for a siesta before venturing back out in the evening. Dinner was pre-booked at Restaurante Al Grano in the eastern part of town – sorry guys, I caved in and googled a good one this time! The restaurant is located in a small square outside the *Basilica de San Pedro* and is known for its paella and black rice dishes … so I had fish, and Chris had a steak for a change, just to be awkward!

The following day, we checked out of the hotel, but our visit to Córdoba wasn't over yet as we'd booked a guided tour of the Medina Azahara, a separate city built by Abd al-Rahman III over 1,000 years ago. Sited just a few miles to the west of the city, it now stands in ruins after it was ransacked in the early part of the 11th century during a Muslim civil war.

We were picked up by bus from a location just outside the city and driven to the site. The tour guide was bilingual, and he did a good job of explaining everything to us, although his

Spanish explanations seemed to go on for twice as long as his English translation – so it's not just me then!

The Medina Azahara was designed to be the administrative centre of the Caliphate, and after taking around 40 years to build, it lasted less than a further 40 years before falling victim to the incoming Caliph's desire to move the administrative centre to his own city across the other side of the Guadalquivir River. Since then, it was picked apart for building materials.

It sounds a bit like Manchester then, but they're still building Manchester – although the town planners have ransacked Piccadilly Gardens, and it's now a concrete hellhole with no plants in sight! It's called "Piccadilly Gardens" – for God's sake, put the "gardens" back! (Rant over)

Excavation of the ruins of the Medina Azahara began over 100 years ago, and they've only completed about 10% of it so far, but there were some magnificent facades on show, the most impressive of which is the Prime Minister's Gate, an ornately decorated entrance to the site with three horseshoe arches, so typical of Muslim architecture.

We would definitely recommend a visit to Córdoba, and there is too much to see in one day, so two or three days are needed to see everything worth seeing.

28

Home Alone 2

They say it's aways difficult making a sequel, so when I was left home alone again – for 15 days rather than five this time – I was determined to succeed where Macauley Culkin had failed with *Home Alone 2*. I was going to be what *Terminator 2* was to *The Terminator* franchise – better than the original. I would try and turn this solo experience into a fortnight of fun.

I'd just come back from a party, so I was already in the party mood – Chris had been due to fly over to the UK to look after our eldest daughter Steph's three kids while she went to Sri Lanka with her boyfriend. However, Chris and I had flown over together a few days beforehand to surprise her at her birthday dinner – her face was a picture.

But after flying back and leaving Chris wrangling three grandkids, I was now footloose and fancy free to do what I liked, although before I could be trusted on my own for so long, I'd been given a crash course on how to use the washing machine, as I didn't think I had enough underwear to last me until Chris got back … and she expected the bedding to be clean when she returned too.

The washing could wait though … the first thing I did was buy some lamb chops and smoked mackerel, neither or which are allowed to be cooked in the house when Chris is home. So it was a plate of lamb chops for my dinner and smoked mackerel for breakfast – delicious!

It wasn't going to be all fun and games, though – there was still a literary agent to find for my novel.

I'd also recently celebrated my 55th birthday and was now drawing money from my private pension, and I had to regularise my tax situation. The UK were taxing my private pension, but the Spanish would also tax it, and then I'd have to claim it back from the UK. I didn't fancy doing all the paperwork for that and then waiting ages every year for a refund from HMRC, who were not the easiest people to get a positive response from at the best of times. No, much better to stop the UK taxing it in the first place.

I contacted our new, Asda-price, Spanish tax accountant for some advice. She told me we had to fill some forms in and get a certificate from Spain – whoopidoo, more Spanish admin!

The next morning I went to the town hall to get a *Padrón Histórico* that would confirm from what date I'd originally been registered as a resident of Alhaurín El Grande – or at least I could request one, as I knew I'd no doubt have to come back another day to collect it … and I wasn't wrong. Then I had to sign a letter the accountant was sending to the *Agencia Tributaria* along with copies of my Spanish residency certificate, my passport, my last Spanish tax return – where I hadn't actually owed any tax – and my last English tax return – where I hadn't owed any tax either … there was half a chance they might just deport me on that basis rather than give me the certificate I needed.

I thought I was supposed to be having fun – I don't remember Kevin from *Home Alone 2* having to fill a load of forms in … he just used his dad's credit card to con a room at the Plaza Hotel in New York.

To destress, I took myself off to art class and painted a crazy multi-coloured frog wearing huge spectacles – why? I was running out of pop stars I wanted to paint and wanted to stick with a pop art kind of theme. It looked pretty cool, actually.

For dinner, I thought I'd have a go at making my own pizza from scratch for the first time. On a previous visit to the UK I'd brought back a bag of OO flour in my hand luggage, and what a surprise, my wheelie case was pulled off the line for inspection.

'I know what you're looking for,' I said to the woman at security as she unzipped my wheelie case.

'Drugs?' she said.

'No, OO flour,' I said.

'OO flour? Why are you taking OO flour on holiday?'

'We're not. We live there and you just can't find it in Spain.'

She laughed and then swabbed the bag and put it through the scanner one more time. She didn't open it and snort a sample. I'm sure it still looked like cocaine on the scanner, so as long as you're really careful bagging it up, if you ever want to smuggle a kilo of coke through security, just put it in a bag of OO flour and be very careful with any residue!

I tried the spinning-my-dough-in-the-air trick, but it's a lot bloody harder than it looks, you know – hats off to all you pizza dough spinners out there. Much respect. So I reached for my rolling pin instead. Why is it that when you try and roll a circle out of dough, you end up with a hybrid oval-triangle shape instead?

Never mind, I put my toppings on – passata, mozzarella slices, chorizo, salty anchovies and fresh basil. I sent Chris a photo. She'll be proud of me, I thought. Not so.

'What the hell's that?' she replied.

'It's my first ever pizza.'

'Looks like a map of Italy.'

She wasn't far out with that description, but it tasted great, regardless of the shape. I celebrated by sending out two more agent submissions for the novel.

Come the middle of the week, I was hungry for some culture. I had a look online to see if there was anything interesting going on at the *Teatro Cervantes*, Málaga's main theatre. If it was high brow entertainment I sought, then I was in luck: the Málaga Philharmonic Orchestra were performing Mahler's 9th symphony … and in the words of Maureen Lipman's character in *Educating Rita*, 'wouldn't you just *die* without Mahler?'.

I used to play in a classical symphony orchestra when I was a teenager, but I used to get fed up counting 300 bars of nothing but bloody violins before having to blow three loud notes on my trumpet. At rehearsals, the brass lads were usually chatting away, and we always missed our entry the first time through, so everyone had to stop and go back 20 bars and play it again so we could come in properly. I eventually left and started a jazz band instead, which was much more fun.

It's not often you get to see a full orchestra at work, though, so I bought a ticket in the cheap seats at the back of the top tier for just €12 and had a night out in Málaga on my own. I'm quite happy with my own company, actually … perhaps more than Chris is happy with my company, but she's still with me, so I must be doing something right.

Mahler's 9th was very good, actually – he'd obviously worked hard at it. I couldn't tell you if it was any better than the first eight or not, as I can't say I've sat and listened to them, although I believe his 5th wasn't bad. According to the BBC's *Classical Music* magazine, his 9th was in fact his best work, which is probably why it was the one chosen by Málaga's Philharmonic Orchestra. Mahler went out on a high, then, as he didn't finish writing his 10th before his premature demise at the age of 50.

I finished off my cultural night in Málaga with some Turkish cuisine – a kebab … Mahler would have approved, I'm sure, but maybe not Maureen Lipman!

A couple of days later I was out with Rambling Al and his walking group again, this time a little farther afield to the countryside around Álora, one of the larger villages in the Guadalhorce valley. It was a great day for hiking, and we had some spectacular views of the large viaduct carrying the train from Málaga.

There's always a good turnout of 20-40 people for Al's walks and you get to chat to a wide variety of people, mostly older but a few in my age group. I was having a good chat to a Scot called Allan who had retired early and was loving his single life on the Costa. He mentioned he was off to watch Málaga CF play football that evening, so I jumped at the chance of tagging along with him.

I love my football, and I come from the red half of Manchester (or more accurately the red three quarters) – although, since a certain opportunistic American family had bought my club and compulsorily purchased the few shares I had in them, I'd been a season ticket holder at breakaway non-league club FC United of Manchester instead. So I'd been missing a bit of live football living in Spain, catching just the odd game or two at FC United whenever I was back in Manchester.

Málaga CF had been relegated to the Second Division of La Liga the previous season but had started the season very well, winning all of their first seven home games, so this 8th home game against Granada should make it played eight, won eight. This was my first live football experience in Spain – in fact, my first live football game outside of the UK – and the atmosphere was great. Málaga had a very vocal home support, who were being rabble-roused by a guy stood on the fencing at the front facing the crowd and shouting indecipherably down a loudhailer.

There's a large contingent of British expats that have regularly attended the games (home and away) for more than 20 years and call themselves the Guiri Army, embracing the derogatory Spanish word *guiri* that translates as 'uncouth foreign tourist'. They've adopted the name as a badge of honour, and they're loved by the Spanish Málaga fans for their undying support of the club.

I think I'm a bad omen, though, as Málaga sadly lost this game 1-0. There wasn't much sign of their earlier season dominance on display, but it was great to experience, nonetheless, and I'd surely be back in the future. Allan was good company, and he showed me a few watering holes I hadn't visited before, including Málaga's oldest wine bar, Antigua Casa de Guardia, where they have barrels of Málaga sweet wine – not my cup of tea (or wine) – and your bar bill is simply chalked up on the old wooden bar till you're ready to pay.

Before I knew it, my fortnight of fun was finished, and Chris returned home to a (relatively) clean house, clean sheets and one or two more cats to feed.

'Have you missed me?' she asked, when I got her home.

'Of course. I've been moping round the house on my own for two weeks.'

'It's a shame you weren't *mopping* round the house too!'

Ah, I've really missed that acerbic wit. Glad to have you back … I think!

Chris was desperate to get back to the sunshine after two weeks of typically cold, wet, miserable weather in Manchester, and after a day getting back to normal (and mopping the floor), she insisted we head down to the beach for the day at La Cala to soak up the sun's rays. And with that simple act, normal service was resumed.

29

No More Interviews

Christmas came and went, and I didn't have to barbecue the turkey this year, although we had a power cut in Spain and the temperamental induction hob stopping working again and had to be replaced.

The build-up was busy with social engagements in Spain. We had Christmas lunches with the art group and the walking group, and we had a night out in Málaga again with Kim and Martin watching the Christmas light show on Calle Larios, with the now obligatory overnight stay at the Parador de Gibalfaro.

I was approached about a job in Málaga on LinkedIn but felt I wasn't fully qualified so passed it on to Martin, who was also looking for work and had everything the recruiter was looking for. In the meantime, spurred on by that approach out of the blue, and the fact I just received my third agent rejection, I applied for three more jobs myself, including one as a Junior Content Producer, where I hoped by Junior, they meant in terms of experience rather than age!

Three weeks later, after returning to Spain post-Christmas, I found myself waiting to be interviewed at their offices in Marbella. The job involved creating marketing content and required someone with a passion for writing (ME!), producing engaging content (ME, ME!) and with good analytical and numerate skills (ME, ME, ME!).

I didn't get the job. I think I came across as a bit too eager (see above) – well, I'd been in Spain for two and a half years now and wanted a job to pay some of the bills, so you can't blame a guy for trying.

They did say that, with my background in CRM solutions, I might suit a role they thought their UK IT director was looking to fill, but nothing ever came of it. I guess I'll just have to double down on my writing career then and make a success of that instead. As Katharine Hepburn once said, 'death will be a great relief. No more interviews'.

On the positive front, Martin got the job I sent his way, and he's delighted – he's clearly a bit more poker-faced in interviews than I am.

And with that in mind, after receiving a fourth agent rejection notice a few days later, I sent out my seventh submission. I shall not be deterred in my mission to become a writer. I shall from now on adopt the motto Ted Lasso pinned up in the dressing room of AFC Richmond … "BELIEVE"!

30

Spanish Kiss

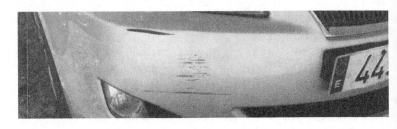

To take my mind off the rejections coming at me thick and fast from both sides, we welcomed our first visitors of the year in the shape of Chris's eldest sister, Dee, and her husband, Paul, who run a most excellent 'if Carlsberg did …' kennels and cattery in Yorkshire. This was only Paul's second visit (Dee having visited one time more with hers and Chris's other sister). Paul's a dyed-in-the-wool Yorkshireman with a good sense of humour, and he and I get on well, so I was looking forward to a few laughs with him.

One morning we decided to have a run out into town as they wanted to see how they could help raise some money for one of the dog charities, Animals In Distress (AID), that had a shop in Alhaurín El Grande. I was headed for where I thought the shop was when Chris said I'd taken a wrong turn, and the shop was somewhere else. I therefore had to turn around. There was a roundabout halfway down this road, so that would be the ideal place to do a U-turn.

I approached the small roundabout, which was built on a downhill slope with an adverse camber to it when you get round the other side, thanks to it joining another downhill slope to the fairground. I was pottering round the roundabout at a slow speed with my indicator flashing my intentions – which is usually enough to confuse the locals as they never indicate, especially on a roundabout. As I approached the halfway point of my move, the driver of a car coming up the hill from the opposite direction (at a not unreasonable speed, really) decided not to bother looking if there was anything already on the roundabout and instead just carried on at the same speed to join the roundabout.

I hit the brake pedal hard, and due to a combination of my forward motion, the front wheels being turned in and the adverse camber, my anti-lock brakes kicked in and the brake pedal juddered under my foot. At the same time, as well as yelps from my passengers, I'd pressed hard on the horn to alert the Spanish woman to my presence on the roundabout in the hope that she would take evasive action, as I had nowhere else to go.

I saw her startled face as she realised there was a car bearing down on her, then she veered over to the far edge of the roundabout and stopped, blocking the next entrance to the roundabout.

I couldn't believe we hadn't hit her, and as she came to a halt, I could see she must already have been a careless driver, as there was a big scrape down both doors.

'Jesus,' Paul said from the back. 'That was close.'

'I know. What a pillock – she never even looked. And judging by the state of her doors, it's not the first time she's done that.'

I set off again round the roundabout, wound my window down as I passed her, and I shouted angrily while pointing at my eyes, as if to say, "look where you're going". Then we left the roundabout and drove back up the hill.

A few minutes later, we pulled up opposite the charity shop. As I walked around the front of the car, I could see my number plate was out of shape a little, and worse, there were several scrape marks across one side of my bumper. That's when I realised, I must have hit her car, and the scrape marks on her car doors must have been created by our collision rather than an earlier accident she'd had.

'Did you hear us hit the other car?' I asked the others.

They hadn't. Thanks to the juddering of the anti-lock brakes, the radio being on, me pressing hard on my car horn as I tried to bring the car to a stop, and three passengers screaming, nobody had heard or felt the point of collision. I straightened out my number plate and took a photo of the scrape marks.

I don't know what I'd have done or said if I'd have stopped and remonstrated with her, actually, as my Spanish isn't good enough to be angry with anyone in anything other than my native English. We'd have both had to pull over somewhere out of the way of everyone to fill out the accident report we're supposed to carry around with us, which is easier said than done in the middle of town.

'Have you got any T-cut,' Paul asked.

'Why? Do you think that'll T-cut out?'

'Possibly.'

I had a tube of silver T-cut in the car, so when we got home, Paul and I tried to get the marks out. We did a reasonable job of hiding most of them, but you could still see some of the marks.

'Ah well,' I said to Paul. 'It had to happen sometime … my first proper Spanish kiss.'

I'd had people open car doors on me before, which is very common over here, but that was my first 'bump' on Spanish soil.

'What about Barcelona?' Chris chipped in.

Is she never going to let me forget that one? She's got the memory of an elephant!

When our visitors left after a week, I got back on the agent search and sent out four more submissions, a little over three months since I'd sent out the first ones. I suppose those that haven't replied yet won't be doing so now, which always winds me up, as it's just plain rude.

The following day, one of the agents with a conscience sent their rejection through, my fifth to date. And I guess that was a fitting end to a bad week.

31

I Can See Clearly Now

My brother got married this week – we didn't get an invite, though. Don't be too concerned for me. Mike and I get on great, but even Mum and Dad didn't get an invite.

They'd decided to get married in Sri Lanka with just a couple of friends as witnesses. It wasn't their first time, so they just wanted something quiet and private on a beach while they had the honeymoon before, during and after the wedding. There was an informal wedding reception planned at their house on the Isle of Wight when they got back, and we were looking forward to that. Ann is a great party planner, so we knew it would be a fun-filled family celebration.

In the meantime, Chris was due to have an operation on her left eye. She had cataracts in both eyes, and the left one was worse, so that was the one going under the scalpel first. I think that's one operation I would definitely not be looking forward to – although you do literally, don't you? … look forward, that is … you're bloody wide awake looking straight at the tip of a sharp knife coming for your eyeball.

Aaaarrggghhhh!! It sounds like a scene from the *Saw* movie franchise.

She should have had the op a couple of weeks earlier, but the surgeon's wife was being induced, so her need trumped ours, and the op got shoved back a fortnight. Probably for the best really. Imagine the knife going in and his phone goes off in his pocket because his wife has just gone into labour, and he was waiting for that call. I'm not sure anyone could keep a steady hand waiting anxiously for that kind of news.

Thankfully, the private health insurance was picking up the tab for the operation, although Chris chose a designer varifocal lens as an optional extra with a Gucci hallmark – only kidding, although for €1,200 for a bit of plastic, it should have been stamped with the Gucci mark.

She seemed quite calm on the morning of the op. I was more worried they'd probably do what they did with me two years ago when they got my names the wrong way round on my NIE certificate – or as the German car spares company had done when they sent us two lefthand headlamps to stick on Chris's mini before it had to pass its first ITV test ... I really thought she was going to end up with a right lens in the left eye and vice versa, or worse, two left lenses!

The surgeon had already measured the prescription for each eye ... in fact, when he wrote out the authorisation request slip for the health insurance company to approve, he specified the right eye and not the left. I only spotted it when I was scanning it to email across to them for approval. Chris contacted the surgeon, and he said it's alright, next time we'll specify the left eye when we're doing the right eye.

You couldn't make this shit up, could you?! Only in Spain! Fair enough, he's probably ordered the lens for the left eye, but what if he checks the authorisation from the health insurance company while he's gowning up and then thinks he's doing the right eye?! I mean, is it just me, or is this asking for bloody trouble? You read about enough people having the wrong organ taken out when they've got two of them, don't you?!

Chris got gowned up, removed her jewellery, said a few Hail Mary's, and then put herself at the mercy of the surgeon. As with anything that happens over here, and particularly in a hospital, you think you're going to be done and out again when they say you should be, but these things always take much longer than you're led to believe. Hence, I was quite anxious for her while I had to sit and wait in the café.

She had a mild sedation to numb her eye and dilate her pupil. but other than that, she said she was fully conscious throughout.

By the time I was allowed to go in and see her, I was a bag of nerves. After the surgery, they'd given her an intravenous painkiller and made us wait an hour before letting her go.

'How was it?' I asked when I went into the recovery room.

'A bit scary, but it all went fine,' she said. 'I didn't feel a thing, really – just a bit of pushing and pulling.'

She told me she'd been hooked up to a blood pressure monitor that was beeping throughout the operation, but the surgeon just put it down to her being anxious. Chris had told him she had white-coat syndrome, which although it's something about a quarter of the population suffer from, only 5% of them are proven to have high blood pressure.

She had to wear big, thick, black, Roy Orbison sunglasses for a couple of weeks and act like a vampire, staying out of the sun. He'd told her to stay off the beach and stay out of the *campo* to avoid getting dust in her eye, but we lived in the *campo*, so that was a bit awkward.

The following morning when I woke and found Chris's side of the bed empty, I wandered into the living room and found her staring at the rug, covering one eye with her hand and then the other.

'Are you alright?' I asked.

'Yes. Isn't this rug really purple?' she said.

'Well, yes. You bought it because purple is one of your favourite colours, remember?'

'I know. But I didn't know it was *this* purple.'

'If anything, it's probably faded a bit since we bought it.'

She carried on staring at the rug.

'You know what?' she mused. 'I think cataracts are Mother Nature's soft focus for when you get older.'

'What're you talking about?'

'Well, when I woke up this morning, the first thing I saw was you, and I thought, wow, I'm married to an old man!'

'Cheers. I'm only fifty-five!'

'And then I went in the bathroom to look in the mirror and thought, wow, I'm an old woman, too!'

'Well, you're not drawing a state pension yet, but you are three years older than me.'

'I am not, I'm only two years older. You were born in sixty-three and I was born in sixty-one.'

'Yes, but you were born in January, and I was born in September, so we're three school years apart and you're two years and eight months older than me.'

'Like I said, two years older.'

I wasn't going to win, so I went into the kitchen to make a brew while she carried on looking at objects weirdly with one eye covered up.

I took Roy Orbison to art class with me that week, but she refused to get up and give us a rendition of *Pretty Woman*.

I was finishing off a painting for Mum. She loves pictures of boats and has a few on the wall of their apartment in Manchester, so I was painting this as a surprise for her. It was a galleon battling a moonlit sea in a gale. It was the first time I'd tried painting waves, and they're not easy – they're almost as hard as clouds. I had four attempts till I thought they looked alright.

The surgeon was really happy with the result ... of the operation, not my painting! He booked us in for the second op a couple of months later, and that's when things started to go wrong.

This time, once she was gowned up, given she'd been hypertensive last time, the anaesthetist hooked her up to a blood pressure monitor straight away and gave her a sedative while I was still waiting with her. Before long, the machine started beeping and her blood pressure rose to 200/100. To put this into perspective for clueless twonks like me that know nothing about blood pressure, a reading of 130/80 is enough to suggest your blood pressure is high (classed as stage 1), and a higher reading of 140/90 is stage 2. When you're getting up to 200/100, you're in heart attack and stroke territory.

The nurses don't mince their words in Spain, and they're not known for their charming bedside manner, so when Chris asked if the operation would be going ahead, she got a very direct response.

'No, you can't have the operation. You will DIE!' she said bluntly.

They helped her into a wheelchair and carted her off to A&E for further tests and to put her on a drip with some magical elixir of life in to calm her down (probably grappa!). When they were happy to release her into the care of Nurse Drew, they gave us a diet sheet to follow. I read it out to her, as she still only had one good eye.

'No salt,' I said.

'Doable,' she replied.

'Walk for 30 minutes a day.'

'No problem.'

'Avoid alcohol.'

'Are they having a laugh?'

'No tobacco.'

'Does it mention vapes?'

'No.'

'Good.'

'And you need to cut out coffee.'

'Dream on. I might as well slit my wrists now!'

She was given Lorazepam and had to go and see her GP in 10 days. It was two years before they'd let her back in for the second operation (largely due to a certain global pandemic taking place), but I can happily report it was a huge success. So much so that now she won't drive at night because of the halos round car headlamps, and I'm the nominated teetotaller when we need to take the car for dinner.

Thanks!

32

Two Weddings and a Burglary

Mike and Ann's wedding reception was upon us, and I took my galleon painting over for Mum. She was thrilled when I presented it to her – she'd have still told me she was thrilled even if she wasn't … that's what great mum's do. But if I find it's hanging in the loo next time I visit her, I'll know she didn't mean it!

There are no trains involved in getting to the Isle of Wight from Spain – it's more Planes, *Boats* and Automobiles. You could probably get to America in the time it takes to get to the Isle of Wight from Málaga. After taking a flight to Gatwick, a hire car to Southampton, and the ferry across to the island, Chris drove onwards to the house while I had to meet up with the stag party on the other side of the River Medina. This involved running to catch another boat, this time the Cowes Floating Bridge, a little car ferry that is pulled across the 120-metre stretch of water by chains.

The wedding reception was fun, with all of Mike and Ann's family present. For something different, the catering was provided via a repurposed fire engine serving up great pizzas all night.

Apart from seeing my brother so happy, another unexpected highlight of the trip for me was meeting the Iranian comedienne, Shappi Khorsandi. She wasn't a wedding guest or booked to do a standup routine (more's the pity), she was just having a drink in the local village pub when the stag party arrived after a night out in Cowes. I'm a huge fan of her comedy and recognised her instantly. She was gracious enough to chat with us and let me have my photo taken with her. Apologies if we stunk of beer and were a bit lairy, Shappi!

Back in Spain, Chris could now see well enough to continue painting, and after having done such a great job of painting Corrinne's labrador, Max, she'd been implored to paint Steph's Weimaraner, Khali, named after the Game of Thrones character, Khaleesi. It was the usual labour of love that took a few weeks to complete, but once finished was the perfect likeness, and Steph was over the moon.

Meanwhile, I did a Banksy. To be clear, I didn't exactly sneak out in the dead of night and paint a million-pound mural on the side of someone's villa, but I did paint a Banksy in art class ... that one where a gorilla is wearing headphones. I'm sure I've not infringed copyright, because I'm not passing it off as a Banksy, and you can buy the same artwork from several sellers on Amazon.

Then we had to fly back to the UK for the second time this month – I had to go and try on wedding suits with Tony. We spent ages in Moss Bros trying on different morning suits and picking out a nice, pink-coloured cravat and pocket handkerchief to go with it, only for Sandra to ring the shop later and change the colour scheme after seeing a photo.

Brides, eh? Control freaks!

The wedding wasn't for another four months, but these things take time to plan, especially when the best man lives in Spain and the bride has to carefully vet the groom's sartorial selections.

We left them to sort it out and headed for Spain again. When we arrived home and drove up to the house, I could sense something wasn't quite right as the *rejas* (bars) from the living room onto the terrace were open.

Maybe Olivia had had reason to go in the house when she popped by to water the garden for us? Or perhaps we'd had a power cut, and she'd gone in to reset the fuse box so our freezer food wouldn't spoil? Although, she would probably have gone in the front door, not the patio doors on the terrace, and she certainly wouldn't have left them wide open.

The mystery was solved when we anxiously opened the front door – our belongings were spread across the floor of the living/dining room, and all the drawers and cupboard doors were open. It was a right mess.

'Oh my God! We've been burgled,' I cried, stating the bloody obvious.

We'd never been burgled before, so this was coming as quite a shock to us both.

I'd once had my Nissan Sunny Coupe broken into on my parents' driveway when I was a teenager … it wasn't quite broken into, it's just that I didn't remember locking the car that night. Some opportunist thief must have come up the drive to try the car doors and mine wasn't locked, so they had easy access and stole all my cassette tapes – kids, ask your parents what they are!

At that time, cars didn't have CD players, digital radios, Apple CarPlay or USB charging points, and most cars didn't yet have a cassette player, just a radio with about five preset station buttons. Hence, there was a fad for installing flashy aftermarket cassette players that were the must-have gadget, and this was the main reason your car got broken into in the early 80s.

The burglar must have been a bit thick, though, as the radio in the centre console was the factory-fitted one without a cassette player, and my new cassette player was tucked away beneath the dashboard on the driver's side with a piece of black fabric hanging over it so it couldn't be seen through the window. I don't know where he thought I was playing my cassettes.

This house burglary was on a different level, though. I hurriedly went through to the spare bedroom where I kept my trumpet and flugelhorn. They'd been removed from their cases but were otherwise intact. That was a relief, at least.

As we moved through the house, it was clear they hadn't missed anything. Every drawer had been turned out, the pillows had been taken out of their pillowcases, all the paintings had been removed from the walls, all the kitchen cupboards were open. The thieving buggers had even left the fridge and freezer doors open, spoiling the contents. I wandered round videoing the scene for the insurance claim, and then I went round again taking photos of all the rooms.

The burglars had forced open the bars over the doors to the patio, pulled up the shutter and then smashed through the patio doors, breaking the lock at the top.

'We need to ring the *Guardia*,' Chris said.

I was in a daze trying to process everything.

'Drew!' Chris said louder, trying to shake me out of it.

'Yes. I'll go and get Luis. He'll know what to do.'

Luis was Olivia's brother-in-law and one of our neighbours. I fired off a quick text to Olivia first to tell her we'd been burgled and then nipped next door. Thankfully, Luis was home. I explained to him we'd been burgled, and he followed me round to the house.

'*¡Madre Mía!*' he said when he saw the state of the place.

Madre Mía, indeed, I thought.

'*¿Puedes llamar a la Guardia, por favor?*' I asked him.

Luis proceeded to call the *Guardia Civil* for us.

'Any idea what's missing?' I asked Chris.

'They've taken some jewellery, like the ring my mum and dad bought for my sixteenth birthday, the diamond eternity ring you bought me, the earrings you bought me when we got married, and I think the watch I bought you for our wedding is missing too.'

Those were really special items to us both. I started to cry. I'd like to be able to tell you that that's not like me. However, it most certainly is – I'm a right emotional softie! I was supposed to be the strong one here, a shoulder to cry on for Chris, but it was me turning on the water works. I just felt so helpless. The fact some strangers had been in the house and through all our stuff.

We're not a rich couple; we don't have expensive tastes, lavish ornaments, priceless artwork (apart from my Banksy gorilla they hadn't spotted). But everything we have has a sentimental value to us. The watch wasn't a Rolex, it was a Citizen watch worth less than £300, but we'd chosen it together and it had a special place in my heart. It was quite distinctive, and I'd recognise it at a glance. The most expensive item missing was Chris's gold and diamond eternity ring, worth about £600.

'They've nicked the soundbar too,' I said, pointing towards the TV.

Poor Luis didn't know what to do with himself or where to look, especially with me having tears still running down my cheeks. Olivia messaged back and said she was in Tarifa with her boyfriend, so couldn't come round to help, but she told me not to worry as she had insurance to cover the damage to the doors.

'I'll call Jill and Ian,' I said. 'They'll know what to do.'

It was early evening, and there was still a bit of light in the sky. Jill, Chris's Fire Watch boss, had lived here over 20 years, and her Spanish was better than ours. She said they'd come over right away.

Thankfully, I'd calmed down a bit by the time they arrived, and then the *Guardia* turned up. They had a mooch round the house and looked at the point of break-in with me. We explained to them that the gates to the patio were locked and showed him how robust they were. There didn't appear to be any damage to the bars, and I started to doubt we'd locked them, but we were sure we had.

I told the *Guardia* that they shouldn't have been able to open them without a key. He laughed and asked me if I wanted him to show me how to get them open with a little force? There was already enough damage done so I didn't take him up on the offer. You'd be better getting a dog, he told me.

His mate was wandering round the garden and called us over to the fence. He'd found where they'd gained access to the garden as the chain link fence was bent out of shape here with footholds created. After making a final check over the place and telling us there had been a spate of similar burglaries in the area, they said we needed to go to the station when we had a list of everything that had been stolen so we could file a *denuncia* (police report), and then they left, along with Luis.

What happened to dusting for fingerprints and taking plaster moulds of the footprints in the ground? It didn't seem that the *Guardia* were as good as the squad of *CSI Miami*. I reckoned they just needed to send the boys round to the Gypsy quarter, and they'd find everything there, but that seemed more trouble than it was worth.

Jill continued offering words of comfort and advice while Ian was browsing my paperbacks.

'Have you finished reading this one?' he said.

'Yeah, take that one if you like.'

'What about this James Patterson one? I don't think I've read that one.'

'Yeah, I've read that. Take it.'

You've got to love Ian. He was an ex-copper who'd moved down from Glasgow to spend most of his career as a Detective Inspector in Manchester, back in the good old days when you could give the villains a bit of a seeing to in the back of the police van on the way to the nick. It seems he'd hung up his DI cap years ago and wasn't about to dust it off and go after the bad guys for me.

Ian's a bit of a character, as you can already tell. He once told me about the time there were roadworks near the entrance to their urbanisation. They were digging up one side of the main road and it was single file traffic for a long stretch. They had to wait for oncoming traffic to pass before a workman waved them through – this was before they had anything sophisticated like STOP/GO signs. Their car was the last in line, and when they drew level with the workman, he handed Ian a short wooden stick through the window, which he thought was a bit odd. Halfway along this section of road, Ian turned into their urbanisation. Later on, while chatting to the barman in their local bar, Ian told him about the stick.

'What did you do with it?' the barman asked Ian.

'I threw it out the car window. I had no idea what it was for.'

'You were supposed to hand it to the workman at the other end of the roadworks so he knows when to wave through the next line of traffic!' the barman laughed.

Simple is clearly not always best, especially when you throw a clueless expat in the mix!

After they'd left, Chris and I started to put the house back together again.

'Look,' said Chris. 'They've even been in my sock drawer and unrolled all my socks looking for cash. And they've nicked my new Touche Eclat concealer!'

I felt like ringing the *Guardia* again and telling them to be on the lookout for a couple of jewellery-clad Gypsies in heavy makeup!

'When do you think they broke in then?' I asked.

'Judging by the temperature of the food in the freezer, I'd say they broke in last night. We'll have to throw all the food out, but it's been no more than a day, I reckon.'

'Have you found your car keys?' Chris's Mini was still parked on the driveway.

'Yes, and I found the spare house and gate keys.'

'Jeepers. They could have loaded up the Mini, opened the gate and driven off with everything if they'd have wanted to.'

I started going through my own bedroom drawers, looking for more missing items.

'Most of my cufflinks have gone. What're they going to do with a load of cufflinks? Melt them down?'

'Are the silver trumpet-shaped ones still there that I bought you?'

'I carry those in my washbag, so those came to the UK with us. And I can't find my golf rangefinder watch.'

'What about your laptops?'

I had two laptops, an old work one and another one I bought two years ago that was worth a bit. In fact, apart from our house in the UK, the two old cars on the driveway, a few exotic holidays, the furniture and my trumpet, my laptop was the most expensive thing I'd ever bought.

'No, they're still here, but the laptop bag is missing.'

'Probably just used that to carry stuff away.'

And thankfully, they couldn't steal my novel, as that was in the digital cloud somewhere.

After tidying the bedrooms up, we moved onto the living room. There's a vase by the patio doors with fake flowers in, and I keep my spare car key in there. I fished out the fake flowers and put my hand in to check for the car key. It was there, but so too was something else.

'Some of my cufflinks are in this vase,' I said, puzzled.

'Perhaps they threw them in there as they were leaving as they weren't valuable. Maybe they were disturbed. Perhaps the lamp in the lounge came on with the timer and it spooked them?'

We used a timer plug on a lamp in the lounge for when we weren't home, and I think that's what maybe spooked them. In the end then, they'd made off with everything already mentioned, plus a Maglite torch, a mobile power bank, a Swarovski necklace I bought Chris in Milan, another inexpensive necklace, and a few pairs (or in some cases, singles) of cufflinks. We called the insurance hotline and reported the theft, and they said an assessor would be in touch to pay us a visit.

The day after the burglary, I went straight up to the *ferretería* (hardware shop) to buy some sturdy chains and locks for the bars over the patio doors. I proceeded to tell everyone in the store that there were burglars in the area. They seemed most concerned, and I wouldn't be surprised if they sold out of chains and locks after I'd left.

Back home, I started to make a full inventory of all the stolen items and the damaged food. I went looking for photos of us wearing the jewellery, etc. and trying to find receipts or get valuations online. It took me all day, and then I translated it into Spanish ready for visiting the *Guardi Civil* the following day. The total claim was about €2,500 with most of that being small items of jewellery. Like I said, we didn't own much of any value, but it was all precious to us in one way or another.

It was some time later that I discovered they'd also made away with my Barcelona football shirt with "Drew 50" written on the back that Tony had bought me (unsurprisingly for my 50th birthday). But by that time it was too late to add it my claim.

Our Spanish teacher, Michelle, agreed to come to make the *denuncia* with us as we thought we might struggle to be understood.

When the assessor came round the following day, he told us there shouldn't be a problem with the claim – other than our jewellery limit on the policy was €2,000 – and he said we should get paid out in about 10 days, which sounded too good to be true for an insurance claim. And it was.

Taking him at his word, however, I gave him 11 days before sending a reminder – too eager? … you have to push these guys if you want something! Then about three weeks later we had about a third of the claim amount paid into our bank account with no email or explanation as to what the amount equated to.

A week later after ringing the company to complain, they said they had some queries over the value of some of the jewellery and were waiting for a reply from the assessor. It took repeated complaints for about three months before we received the balance of the payout. Ten days my arse!

Four days after we'd arrived home to find the house burgled, we were watching television in the evening and heard a dog yapping repeatedly.

'Is that Lili barking next door?' Chris asked.

'Sounds like it. Maybe Olivia's there?'

'But she never barks like that.'

Olivia had a little pooch, Lili, and it was indeed unlike her to bark incessantly, and especially if Olivia was there visiting her sister.

'I'll go and check,' I said.

As I'd just had my Maglite nicked, I switched on the torch on my iPhone and crept out into the garden. I walked over to the fence and could see Lili in Luis's garden barking at the house. The house was in darkness, but I could see torchlight inside the house.

'Luis?' I shouted. Nothing. 'Luis?' a bit louder.

Two men came hurtling out of the house and ran down the garden.

'Oi!' I shouted, although I'm not sure what I expected them to do in response, other than shout 'eff off' in Spanish at me.

Chris was watching from the front door.

'Call Olivia,' I said. 'Tell her Rosa's house is being burgled. I'll go round there.'

We didn't have Rosa's or Luis's number, so I hoped Olivia picked up straight away. What was I going to do, though, if I came across two big blokes in the garden, probably with crowbars and hammers? I'll take the car instead!

I grabbed my car keys and drove round to Luis's. The gate was locked and there was no sign of anyone. From the direction the guys were heading, they could be garden hopping across to the industrial estate, I thought. I got back in the car and raced up the single track to the main road and round into the industrial estate, looking out for two big blokes on foot acting suspiciously, but there was nobody around, so I headed back to Luis's.

As I pulled up, Luis's son came haring down the lane in his car and screeched to a halt next to me. I told him what I'd seen, and we entered the property together. On the dining table was a watch and some items of jewellery, and there were a couple of bedside drawers open in the master bedroom. Other than that, the place looked normal, although I'd never been inside before to know what normal looked like. There were certainly no piles of stuff all over the floor like we'd come home to.

I reckon I must have disturbed them within a minute of them getting inside, and I assumed the watch and jewellery had been taken from the bedroom and placed on the table while they looked for other valuables, or more likely they purposefully dropped them on the way out in case they were nabbed by the police making a run for it – if they had no stolen gear on them, they couldn't be charged. Luis and Rosa arrived, entered the house and had a look round for anything missing. They'd all been eating in the bar at the end of the lane when Olivia had relayed our message to them.

The *Guardia* were called again, and the same two fellas came out. The two boozy coppers off *Early Doors* would probably have been more use, though. They asked what I'd seen and if I could describe them. I pointed out that I was using the torch on my iPhone because probably the same two blokes had nicked my Maglite earlier in the week, and they hadn't made a bust yet, so I didn't get a good look at them, other than one looked to be well over six feet tall.

We all had a wander down the garden and found the point of entry; Juan's fence was all pulled down in one section, and they'd probably made off up the back lane to the industrial estate. It's a shame I didn't spot them.

Rosa was in tears – she must be as soft as me! Her and Luis said it looked like nothing had been taken and they were ever so grateful for our vigilance. Perhaps we may not have been so vigilant if we'd not just been burgled ourselves, as although we lived down a quiet lane, a dog bark was not uncommon. It was good that we knew Lili wasn't normally a drama queen to make so much noise and we'd gone and investigated straight away.

I asked Luis if he'd ever been burgled before and he said no. I took comfort from that as I was thinking it was going to be something we'd need to guard against every year, but maybe it was just a rogue foreign gang operating in the area before moving on somewhere else.

In fact, there was a report in the local newspaper not long afterwards stating a warehouse in Málaga had been raided and found to contain lots of stolen gear. I wondered if it was worth ringing the *Guardia* and reminding them they hadn't found my stuff yet but thought it would be a waste of time. One of the useless coppers in *Early Doors*, the actor James Quinn, does the matchday radio commentary for my non-league team FC United … I'll have a word with him next time I'm at the match and see if he's heard anything!

Before I bade goodnight to Luis and Rosa, I created a WhatsApp group for the four of us so we could contact each other quicker and more directly if anything like this happened again. We vowed to post on the group if we planned to be away from home overnight, or just back late after a night out. We also used it any time we heard suspicious barking in the *campo*, and it allowed us to sleep a little easier at night knowing they would be extra vigilant if we weren't home.

I'll raise a glass to good neighbourly relations – *Salud*!

The next morning we had rain and there was a rainbow that looked like it finished in someone's garden about three houses down. I wondered if it was a sign … maybe that's where all our stolen gear was buried, but I didn't think it'd look good if I started furiously digging up some else's garden like a maniac.

33

Family Fun

The following week we had something to cheer us up – our daughter, Andrea, was arriving with her family, albeit just for a few days, but it gave us chance to have some fun with the grandkids. It was only the start of April, and the pool wasn't warm enough to get in yet, so we had to find other activities to entertain the kids.

For their first day with us, the weather forecast was for heavy rain in the morning, so we went down to Benalmádena. Someone had recommended the *Mariposario* (Butterfly Park). It was an indoor attraction – naturally, otherwise they'd all fly off! – so should be the perfect escape on a wet day.

We parked up next to the iconic Buddhist Temple, or Stupa of Enlightenment, which at 33 metres high is the tallest in Europe and looks out over the Mediterranean. It was lashing down, so it was a quick dash across the road to the Butterfly Park.

Inside, it had a tropical feel, with water features and exotic flowers. The temperature was much warmer than outside today, and the incessant rain was dribbling through cracks in the roof here and there, adding to the humidity. There were thousands of colourful butterflies flying freely and landing on you at will. The kids were amazed at the size and colour variations.

The lifespan of a butterfly is only two to three weeks, so they have a butterfly nursery to constantly replenish the stocks. Second only to beetles as the insect with the most species worldwide, Lepidoptera (made up of moths and butterflies) number 265,000 species, most of which are moths, but with 20,000 varieties of butterfly. The park has around 150 different butterfly species on show throughout the year, and it showcases some of the diverse plants needed to support them in the wild.

Each variety of butterfly has a specific host plant it has evolved to lay its eggs on and which the caterpillars can eat before they form a chrysalis and then become a butterfly. There are no caterpillars here though, as the insects are transported to the park in chrysalis form, as it's apparently the best time to transport them. This is the most exciting part, though, as you can actually see new butterflies emerging in the nursery. All the butterflies are then fed with artificial nectar, and there are little feeding stations dotted here and there.

It doesn't take long to see everything at the park, as it's all housed in one large building with pathways through the plants and water features, and an upper walkway to explore. We were all done after about an hour. The kids loved being up close with the butterflies, especially if one landed on them, and they were given a tick sheet with the butterflies on so they could mark them off as they went round and spotted them.

Then we drove up to Mijas Pueblo for lunch and more fun activities. When you've got young kids in tow, no visit to Mijas is complete without a visit to the Mayan Monkey Chocolate Factory where they can make their own chocolate bars. We'd been here before with Steph's kids, but this was the first time here with Andrea's little 'uns.

While the chocolate was setting in the fridge, we went off to grab some tapas for lunch. The weather had improved enough for us to sit outside on the terrace at Oscar's Tapas Bar at the mirador. The kids, Jessica and Caleb, were only five and three respectively, but they both have great appetites and weren't fussy eaters, usually trying anything, especially Mediterranean food.

We went back to collect the chocolate bars but couldn't resist an ice cream in their ice cream parlour first, where there are lots of delicious flavours to choose from. Ice cream parlours are an institution in Spain, and the one at Mayan Monkey is a great one.

The following day, we took the kids and Andrea into Málaga to visit the Museum of Imagination, an indoor attraction with lots of interesting, interactive, illusory exhibits. Things like a room where the décor and dimensions are designed to make a small person like Jessica in one corner appear much larger than her mum standing in the other corner.

There are lots of opportunities to get some bizarre, gravity-defying photographs of the family. It's a really great, fun, family activity, and the kids loved it. They change their exhibits from time to time, so we'll have to come back again in the future.

The weekend was over all too soon, and it was time to take them back to the airport. It's always a sad moment when the grandkids have to leave as they love coming over … although it's probably more to do with them being able to make their own chocolate and have butterflies land on them than it is to do with seeing their grandparents, and in the summer months, you can't get them out of the swimming pool.

We soon had more arrivals in the shape of our youngest, Corrinne, and her husband, Graham. No kids yet from these two, but Corrinne has a 'bun in the oven' as they say, which will be grandchild number six for us!

They arrived the day I got another agent rejection for my novel, so I needed cheering up. Having already put my John Lennon painting up in the bar in their back garden, the pair of them had a browse through my pop art and asked me to send over the Banksy and another one I'd done this week, a big dopy cow's face wearing glasses with a mosquito buzzing round its nose (although the mozzie was a late addition to the picture I was copying from as there was a blemish on my canvas, and I hadn't whitewashed the background first, so I covered it up rather artfully with the mozzie!).

They were only here for a few days, but wanted to go and see what Gibraltar was like. I told them it was a bit crap, and apart from the thieving apes on top of the rock (which I had no desire to traipse up to see … plus Corrinne was heavily pregnant), and a naff main square with fish and chip restaurants, there wasn't much they'd like in a throwback to 1970s Britain. We went anyway.

When you go to Gibraltar in the car, it's not worth queueing to drive over the border as (a) it takes ages, (b) it's not very big, and (c) you'd struggle to park – the only reason a lot of people from around here take their car over to Gibraltar is to go and do a 'big shop' at the Morrison's supermarket and stock up on home comforts like Yorkshire Tea, Vimto and Warburtons Crumpets, but you can get all that in Iceland in Fuengirola, so I don't see the point, even though it is a lot cheaper.

The alternative is to park on the Spanish side in La Línea de La Concepción, where there's a large car park adjacent to the border, and then you can just walk across, which is what we did.

Once you get through security, you walk past the airport, which only has about half a dozen departures a day, and the same number of arrivals, and then you have to traverse the single runway that cuts across Winston Churchill Avenue – they're big patriots the Gibraltarians. They close pedestrian access briefly if there's a plane about to land or take-off, but you can normally get across without a delay. Then you cross through Landport Tunnel, a pedestrian tunnel through the rock, and emerge into Grand Casemates Square, where you'll find the Lord Nelson pub (amongst other delights).

They wanted to see if we could get up to see the apes, but after walking through the main shopping street – where you can do some tax-free shopping for jewellery, sunglasses, beer and fags – and trying to get some more information, it all seemed too much of a hassle in the end and very expensive. Instead, we got on a bus and rode out to the far end, which doesn't take long, as Gib is only three miles in length. We got out at Europa Point to have a look across at Africa. We had a beer at the café, then took the next bus back to town and sampled the delights of Roy's Fish & Chips – and here's me thinking they'd just flown 1,200 miles from Manchester for a bit of Spanish culture, not fish and chips!

After leaving Gibraltar and heading home, the day had more drama in store for us. With just a couple of miles to go, and coming off the motorway, I approached the end of the slip road and came to a halt at the stop sign, waiting to turn right. Just before that, I'd peered to my left around the back of a transit van in the left lane as he came to a stop before attempting his left turn. I thought there was no oncoming traffic, but as I started to pull out and turn right, a car shot across in front of me and I couldn't stop in time – almost, but not quite.

I caught the rear wing slightly as the driver tried to take avoiding action. This one was completely my fault – I should have waited for the transit to get out of the way first. I thought it wasn't pulling out because of traffic coming from its right which didn't affect me, but apparently not. Oops! [*Chris: at least it wasn't a wedding party this time!*]

There were scrapes down the back wing of the other car, and I now had damage to both sides of my bumper. The funny thing is, after the roundabout incident (that wasn't my fault), I installed a dashcam which perfectly captured this second accident. At least it showed that I'd stopped at the stop sign and pulled out slowly, and I sent a copy of the video to the insurance company so they could see exactly what had happened, and that I wasn't driving recklessly or speeding.

I paid the excess on my insurance claim and had Lexus replace the bumper. Just as well I didn't bother repairing it after the roundabout bump, then, so all's well that ends well.

Although the month went from bad to worse when we received our Spanish tax bills. Sadly, last year's euphoria of having no tax to pay was a distant memory now. I'd started my pension drawdown from the UK, of course, so we were no longer living off our savings. Unfortunately, there's no concept in Spain of a 25% tax-free lump sum when you start dipping into your pension pot, and all of it is classed as income and taxed accordingly. I knew this before we moved, of course, but it still stung when the realisation dawned. The all-year sunshine, great food and cheap wine make up for it, though … you win some, you lose some.

34

San Juan

The summer solstice in the UK is a moving feast in that it falls somewhere between 20th and 22nd June each year and marks the beginning of summer, or the longest day of the year, when the sun is at its highest position in the sky in the northern hemisphere (or its lowest position in the sky in the southern hemisphere).

In Scandinavia, they call it *Midsommar*, but they can't agree when to celebrate it – while Denmark and Norway always celebrate it on the evening of 23rd June, as one of the year's biggest celebrations, the Swede's demand a public holiday and hold it on the closest Friday to that date. In Spain, they call it *San Juan* and celebrate it on 23rd June too, on the eve of the feast day of *San Juan* (Saint John), which always falls on 24th June. This year it fell on a Sunday night, and we decided to go and experience it for ourselves.

The summer solstice was of course a pagan festival originally, celebrated by druids, witches and wizards – although they stopped people of that persuasion using Stonehenge for their celebration years ago – until the Christians made the festival their own. Traditionally, bonfires were lit, and the flames were jumped through three times to purify the soul.

The celebration of *San Juan* takes place up and down Spain's coastline, and bonfires are lit on the beaches, with people partying all night until the sun comes up. We were going to head to Málaga's main beach, Malagueta, but we didn't think we had the stamina to stay up all night drinking, so I booked us in at the Novotel Suites hotel.

We arrived at the beach in the evening while there was still an hour or so of daylight. We found a good spot to lay out our beach blanket, and we cracked open a bottle of wine to go with the cheese and biscuits we'd brought to sustain us. All around us, people were doing likewise. The age range seemed to be mostly late teens to twenties and thirties.

Normally, there are beach bonfires up and down the coast of Andalucía, including here on Malagueta beach, but we'd read that this year they weren't allowing them in Málaga city, which is odd, as the Spanish don't care much for health and safety if that's what was behind the decision. Sure enough, there were none that we could see on this stretch of the beach.

As darkness fell and the volume of liquid being drunk showed no signs of abating, we discovered why seawater always tastes salty – all the young blokes were wandering down to the shoreline and openly peeing in the sea. According to legend, if you wash your face or bathe in the sea at midnight on the eve of *San Juan*, you will retain your beauty, but if you think I'm going to wash my face in everyone else's pee, then you can sod that for a game of soldiers – I'm no oil painting to begin with, and having never moisturised in my first 55 years, I think that boat has already sailed.

When we'd grown a little tired of the lewd behaviour (and the wine bottle was empty), we packed up and wandered over to a nice bar along the marina for a more civilised end to the evening. With there being no bonfires, the celebration seemed a bit of a damp squib this year, so we soon retired to bed, although we may have to come back and give it another try if they permit bonfires again, perhaps in a different resort along the coast next time.

35

Horses and Hounds

I've just got back from a flying visit for Tony's stag do in the UK. I'd arranged a trip to see the gee gees at Chester Racecourse. I had 15 hardy souls board the coach to Chester after a hearty breakfast, and all 15 were safely deposited back in Manchester afterwards for a traditional northern evening meal, a curry at Akbar's Indian restaurant – as the best man and organiser of said trip, that counts as a success in my book.

The stag do was unique in my experience in that Sandra decided to have her hen party there on the same day (different coach). She must have either loved my idea, or she didn't trust me to look after her beloved. I didn't come away a winner – I piled a load on the favourite, a horse called Puerto Banús in the first race (well, you would wouldn't you? ... the omens were all there for me), but it didn't come anywhere. And my luck didn't improve throughout the afternoon. It's always a nervy time organising a stag do, so I was glad when it was over, and I was back in Spain.

We got back the same day Steph arrived with her three girls, 16-year-old twins Grace and Lucy, and six-year-old Amelia. Amelia is like a fish, and the only time she's not in the pool is when she gets out to jump back in again. We had a contest to see who could jump in the pool and land on the lilo, and Amelia won that. The other two are growing up into fine young women (if still an untidy pair) – we're just lucky to have them with us after being born severely premature and weighing in at 2lb 11oz and

1lb 6oz. They're technically identical twins, but you wouldn't know it as they don't look identical, and they have different tastes in clothes and different personalities.

We took them all to a fundraising event in aid of a local galgo charity. Galgos are like Spanish greyhounds – they're hunting dogs used for catching hares. Just like podencos, they are badly treated by hunters and often left to die at the end of a season so the hunters don't have to bother feeding them. As a result, they're a prime candidate for a dog rescue centre, and this one dealt solely with galgos.

We knew some of the people that volunteered at the charity as they were fellow ramblers with our group. We had a tour of the kennels to meet all the lovely dogs, followed by a helping of freshly made paella, with all donations helping out the charity.

The girls are all big animal lovers, and the twins are incredibly talented artists. Grace, in particular, loves drawing animals, while Lucy prefers drawing Japanese anime and fashion.

When we got back to the villa afterwards, Grace found a good photo online of a galgo, and within an hour she had reproduced it perfectly in pencil. I loaded up her drawing to Facebook and tagged the galgo charity. Grace wanted them to have the drawing to sell. When I took her back the following day to hand over the drawing, an American benefactor of the charity had already contacted them and said the photo was of her own dog and could she buy the drawing. What a fantastic result, the drawing being shipped overseas to the owner of the dog in question. The power of social media.

A couple of days later, Grace sat there doing a commissioned colour drawing of someone's horse back in the UK, while Lucy busied herself drawing a female portrait. They really are exceptionally gifted artists.

As the girls were leaving, I received another agent 'thanks, but no thanks' reply, so sent out another four submissions. It seems it's as hard to secure a literary agent as everyone suggested.

Chris and I later attended another dinner dance evening at the local golf club, this time with friends, Jill and Ian. We were out on the lawn again for dinner, and after the plates were cleared away, we were entertained by a pretty good Freddie Mercury impersonator, complete with the moustache, buck teeth, balding pate and yellow jacket.

When the music started, I was up like a flash ... I wanted to break free with some fat-bottomed girls, but I just ended up in a bicycle race with a killer queen, and by 11 o'clock, it was clear I'd overdone the all-inclusive beverage package, and another one bit the dust!

36

Nuptials, Newborns and Nuts

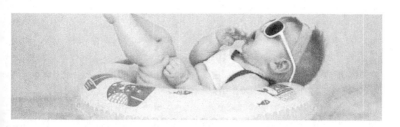

Tony and Sandra's wedding had come around quickly, and we had another trip back to the UK, our 6th this year, and it was only July. I was going to stay for the wedding (and hopefully the birth of my new grandson) and then get back to Spain, leaving Chris to help with the baby for a month.

I'd picked up my wedding suit from Tony's and took it round to Mum and Dad's down the road to try it on.

'Shirt's fine. Trousers a bit tight.' I messaged Tony.

'Fatty!' came the reply.

'Hey! That bloke in Moss Bros didn't know one end of this tape measure from the other – I didn't even get to try on any trousers, and we were there for 2 hours! And I've lost a few pounds since then ... although I have just been out for a big, two-course lunch with Mum and Dad.'

The wedding was a posh affair in The Cotswolds. Mum and Dad had bagged an invite – they get everywhere those two! To add some peril into the mix, Chris was Corrinne's nominated birthing partner, and her baby was due anytime now. On the eve of the wedding, things started to develop in St Helens, and Corrinne thought she might go into labour imminently, just as we were driving south to a hotel 160 miles away.

The following morning, Corrinne went into hospital and started with slow labour pains, so we were in a bit of flap wondering how Chris was going to get from the wedding venue back up to Corrinne in a hurry if needed. I couldn't take her – I was best man, and Chris had already missed my last best man's speech at Gary's wedding after taking ill during the wedding breakfast, so I dearly hoped she wasn't going to miss this one!

We agreed that she would have to hang on until after the wedding breakfast and the speeches – Chris that is, not my poor little baby girl, Corrinne – and then she'd get a lift north with a guest who was going that way later. Tony and Sandra looked fantastic in their wedding clobber, and the weather was glorious. There were tears – from me, of course (again), whilst doing a reading at the ceremony – and my speech went down a treat after everyone had been wined and dined.

Chris made it most the way north and jumped in a taxi for the last part of the journey, arriving at the hospital about 11:30pm. The little fella didn't bother poking his head out for another 26 hours, by which time I'd been back in St Helens myself for about nine hours, after having danced the night away at the wedding, polished off a full English breakfast the next morning, and stopped for a leisurely lunch outside Stoke with Mum and Dad … and I found time to drop all the wedding suits back off at Moss Bros on the way!

'8lb 3oz. Mum and baby doing fine. No official name yet,' came the message from Chris at 4am the next morning.

They named him Theo. I nipped to the hospital to see how everyone was. He was a lovely looking baby. He'd been a bit of a bugger coming out, and Graham hadn't fainted at the birth, which was always a possibility, but Corrinne was knackered and glad it was all over.

Then I flew back to Spain on my own and stuck a wash on when I got home at midnight – I was a dab hand at the washing now!

The next day I went to art class and did a drawing of Chris, so I'd have something to remind me of her these next four weeks – I'd transitioned now to coloured pencils, and after doing an online course on shadows and highlights, I had a stab at a drawing of Chris. Years ago when we visited Australia, she had a right old cough and sore throat and sounded like Deirdre Barlow off *Coronation Street* for a while – a real raspy voice. Well now

I'd made her *look* a bit like Deirdre Barlow too with my pencil drawing – to be honest, it wasn't the best.

The landlady, Olivia, came round that afternoon and showed me how to harvest and crack open the almonds off the tree we planted two years earlier. I had quite a big pile by the time I'd finished, and they were delicious and so fresh. I promised to keep some bagged up for when Chris returned.

After 48 hours in Spain I had to be back at the airport again first thing in the morning – this was starting to get a bit ridiculous! I had to get myself over to Sweden where an old friend and work colleague, Jan, was having his 50th birthday party. His family had a beach house on a small island called Oaxen in the Himmerfjärden bay in Sweden's southern archipelago, otherwise known as the middle of bloody nowhere! This time round I had to make use of the full complement of Planes, Buses, Trains, Cars, Boats and Shanks's Pony ("on foot") to get there. Honestly, I could have flown to the Antarctic by the time I got there.

After a great night of revelry with old friends, a welcoming host, free drinks, great food (and lots of Dad dancing!), we dashed across the island at midnight to catch the last ferry. On the other side, we now had to find a taxi to take us the 14 miles back to the sleepy fishing village of Trosa, the closest accommodation we could all find, but that proved a challenge at that time of night. Incidentally, I had to pay extra for bedding on check-in … how typically Scandinavian.

After an anxious 40-minute wait for the taxi (and with Swedish horror movies playing in my head where travellers meet an unfortunate death in the woods), a taxi finally turned up and we had to bribe the driver to let all six of us squeeze into his saloon car.

When I'd been researching how to get to and from the tiny island, I'd even considered hiring a push bike for two days, and when I saw the unlit roads on the drive back to Trosa, I was damn glad I hadn't made such a foolish decision, which could very well have been the end of me.

It was very late when we arrived in Trosa, but my other old mate and colleague, Rainer, a very laid-back Finn, convinced me to have a nightcap with him – oh boy, the Finns can drink! The local brewery in Trosa had a cheekily named beer on sale called Brexit, and I couldn't resist one. It came with free crisps but no trade deal or freedom of movement, and it left a bitter aftertaste!

Despite being an expensive trip – £7 a pint and £18 for a burger – I was glad I'd made the effort for a very dear friend, but I was also now very happy to be back in Spain.

37

We Have a Leak

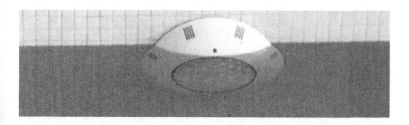

Water, water, everywhere, but not a drop to … swim in – at least not in our pool!

I woke up to find the pool level 18 inches lower than the night before. We must have a leak. Bugger! That's all I need – I'm supposed to be house hunting today; we should have been moving out in three weeks, but Olivia gave us a one-month extension due to Chris being away on baby duties. She and her boyfriend have decided they want to move into the villa after we'd lived here three years. We were gutted as we love the house and location (but maybe not so much the work involved with the garden).

To be fair, Olivia has been great, and she gave us notice a few months ago, as she knew we'd be upset about it. But right now, I had a new problem to deal with, so I sent her a photo of the pool. I don't know where it's leaking from but it's already down to the pool lights. I reckon if the level stops dropping when it gets to the bottom of the lights, then it must be leaking behind the lights somewhere. Olivia can't get here until tomorrow with the plumber, so I guess I'll find out later.

The level was below the lights the following morning, so it's a mystery. Olivia arrived with the plumber, and after much scratching of heads, he decided he was going to need a digger. He reckoned one of the pipes must been leaking into the earth somewhere.

His mate came round the next day and dug a dirty, great, six-foot-deep hole behind the pool. He couldn't find a leak from the pipework there, but the huge hole was filling up with water now, so he had to start digging some of my carefully laid lawn up along the side of the pool. Eventually, he did find the source of the leak in the pipework and went off to buy some new pipe and sealant.

After making his repairs, he asked me to use my water pump to empty his big hole of water so he could assess it again tomorrow. I spent a couple of hours clearing the hole for him, pumping the water further down the garden. At one point, I disturbed a snake! I must have been filling his den with water. It was about three feet long, and I took a video so I could send it to Chris. I googled it later and discovered it was a Western False Smooth Snake that lives underground, eats small reptiles and isn't poisonous or a danger to humans.

That was a relief. Although I'm known in our family as a bit of a snake wrangler. On safari with Chris in Tanzania, I'd spotted a snake in our safari lodge on the rim of the Ngorongoro Crater. It was about a foot long and heading into the bathroom. I followed it in and realised there was a hole behind the base of the sink unit where the pipework came up. The last thing I wanted to do was to head for a sleepy pee in the middle of the night, only for this thing to come sneaking out of the floor to get me, or even worse, be lurking in the loo when I sat down – ooh! I can feel my balls shrivelling up just thinking about it!

I quickly grabbed a towel and tossed it over it, like a northern Steve Irwin – that should stop it moving and keep it calm, I decided. I then grabbed a plastic bag, turned it inside out, carefully lifted the back of the towel and grabbed the snake's tail through the plastic bag. I pulled the snake out from under the towel slowly, rolling it into the bag at the same time. Closing the top of the bag, I returned to the living room dangling it proudly in front of me … although Chris recalls me sweating profusely and taking big gulps of air.

While I was playing the hero, she was just sat on the bed flicking through her wildlife book to try and identify it. I took the snake out to where the safari drivers were all congregated.

'What's in the bag?' one of them said.

'A snake.'

You should have seen them all scuttle out of the way quickly. One of the braver souls stepped forward and wanted to look at it, so I opened the top of the bag briefly for him to take a peek.

'It's a baby cobra!' he announced.

Shit, I thought – where the hell's mummy cobra then?!

'What shall I do with it?'

'Release it over there.'

I wandered over to the treeline and tipped the snake out onto the ground and made a hasty retreat.

'Baby cobra, my arse!' Chris said when I returned to the room. 'This is it here.'

She held open a page of her wildlife book, and there it was … the mildly venomous Centipede-eater.

We found ourselves back at the same lodge several years later on another safari. On entering the room, I bent down and started opening all the cupboard doors.

'What are you doing?' Chris asked.

'Checking for snakes.'

A moment later, I snapped one of the doors closed with a bang.

'Oh shit!' I said.

Chris jumped on the bed all of a panic.

'What is it? A snake?' she cried.

'No. Worse than that. I've just farted and followed through in my shorts!'

Apologies, dear reader … African food hygiene had finally caught up with me on that trip, I'm afraid.

Back in Spain, when I was done clearing the hole in our garden, I started refilling the pool (thankfully using the garden hose from the community irrigation supply rather than the mains supply, so it wouldn't cost me anything). By evening, and with the pool in operation again, there was still water leaking from the exposed pipe, but it only seemed to happen under pressure when the pool pump was running.

The plumber covered it in more sealant the following day and it seemed to do the trick. I was left with a huge unfilled hole in the ground that remained there until the day we moved out six weeks later, but at least the pool was fixed now, and I could have a swim again.

With no need to stay in anymore for workmen, I decided to go and watch the sunrise over neighbouring Cártama. Friends Laura and Shell that we'd met in the walking group were doing some more strenuous walks these days with one or two hardier hikers like me. I met up with them before dawn and we scaled the *Sierra de Los Espartales*, an eight-kilometre circular route with 440 metres of ascent in total. It was a great walk, apart from the unfriendly shrubs we waded through halfway up that left my shins bleeding – I always hike in shorts, regardless of the weather or time of year, but maybe I need to start packing shinpads on Laura's walks!

Later that week, the *Feria de Málaga* was on again, and I'd promised myself last year that I would return some day on public transport to get in the party mood more. There was a bus service to Málaga from Alhaurín El Grande that took about an hour, and by lunchtime I was swaying along to a live soul band in the city centre with a beer in my hand. I had lunch at my favourite tapas bar, followed by more beers and live music. I didn't bother going to the fairground to continue the party as my last bus home was in the early evening.

All in all, I had a great day out, probably drank a little too much, and fell asleep on the bus home. I didn't miss my stop, though, as Alhaurín El Grande is the end of the line, and I was woken by the driver.

38

House Hunting

Here we go then, back on the hunt for somewhere to live. My first thought is we won't find anywhere better than where we are now, and rental prices have been going up, so it's going to cost us more. Also, moving house when you've got your own furniture is a right pain, and the fewer times you have to do it in your lifetime the better.

Now then, ordinarily, Chris wouldn't let me pick out a pair of curtains, never mind a whole bloody house, so I had no idea how this was going to work out. I was home alone and had to conjure up the perfect villa from somewhere. Wish me luck!

Chris spotted one on Facebook and sent me the details. It didn't look too bad on the photos – it had an extra bathroom and was €150 cheaper than we were paying now ... where do I sign?! The pool was above ground, but it looked like it had a sundeck surrounding it. I contacted the owner and arranged to view it.

The house turned out to be smaller than the photos portrayed. It was down a quiet lane with lovely views, but the road was very narrow, there was no driveway, and there was just enough room to park Chris's Mini outside (as long as a fire engine didn't want to get past). Ah well, worth a try.

I had more problems when I contacted local estate agents. We weren't planning to move out for several weeks, what with Chris being away until the beginning of September. When they get a house on the market, they won't bother taking you unless you're ready to move, and preferably within 14 days. In that case, how was I supposed to find our next place in the sun? Also, many of the properties came fully furnished, and the owners were often reluctant to remove the furniture.

While I was browsing estate agent's windows in town, I bumped into one of the guys from the walking group. He did a bit of gardening for people and told me there was a house we could probably rent that he worked on. He called the chap up and I waited half and hour to meet up with him, then followed him out to his house.

The house was a good size, with a lovely pool at the back and he had fruit trees and olives in a separate enclosed part of the garden. The place was furnished, but he had a big double garage standing empty and he sounded willing to put it in storage for us. The only downside was that he thought he might wish to sell up in a year or so as his wife's health was suffering, and she was back in the UK receiving treatment. I didn't want to be doing all this again in 12 months, so I declined his offer.

Nothing online was inspiring me, and I was starting to wonder if we'd have to put the furniture in storage and book a hotel until we could find somewhere we liked.

Eventually, I found another place worth looking at. It was a decent size over two floors. There was no agricultural land to worry about, and the terrace was a nice size with a pool and a bit of astroturf. The only downside was the road noise – it was up a steep driveway off the main road that runs down to Fuengirola, and even inside the house I could hear the odd lorry labouring up the hill.

Meanwhile, Chris had been busy in the UK too. Corrinne's husband, Graham, is a good builder in his spare time and can't sit still, having learnt most of his skills from his dad, but he hated decorating, and especially hanging wallpaper. Thankfully, Chris is a dab hand at it and quite enjoys it (weird, I know), so she papered baby Theo's room for them.

She'd also been commissioned to do another dog portrait, this time for her Fire Watch boss and friend, Jill, whose Cocker Spaniel, Max, had passed away not long ago, so she was cracking on with that when she wasn't helping with the baby or decorating.

I went to view another house, this one just a couple of minutes away. It was just round the back of the recycling centre, which ordinarily might have put you off, but I'd used the place a few times myself and, unlike the ones in the UK, this one didn't get a lot of traffic and always seemed quiet enough, with no lingering odours. I'd measured our furniture and worked out what size the rooms would need to be to accommodate everything, and so armed with my new toy, a laser tape measure, I followed the agent inside. The house was a bit on the small side, and the way it was configured, we just wouldn't have been able to fit our lounge and dining room furniture in. Next door had a big dog too that looked like it had a fine pair of lungs on it, so that was another one ruled out.

I decided to have a break from the house hunting and went to the footie again with Allan from the walking group. It was the first home game of the new season for Málaga CF. They'd missed out on promotion last season so were still playing in the third tier of Spanish football. Today, they were up against Canarian side, Las Palmas, but didn't play much better than last time I saw them. I was hoping the away team might be a bit jetlagged, but it's only a two-and-a-half-hour flight away. A late penalty secured a draw for Málaga CF, but it looked like they might have a long hard season ahead of them again.

I got back on the job hunt that weekend and fired off a few more job applications. I also received my 9th agent rejection notice, sadly. Undeterred, I put the aircon on in the back room and sat in there all day working on another edit of the book, only coming out for food, toilet breaks and to try and balance the chemicals in the pool since I'd filled it up recently.

With the house hunt on hold now until Chris returned, I went over to the UK to join her for a week and see how Corrinne and baby Theo were getting on. They were both doing fine. We did the usual rounds visiting our other three girls and their families and my parents, and then it was back to Spain to continue the house hunting.

Within a few days of returning, we'd almost exhausted our online search and were drawing blanks at every turn ... too small, fully furnished, too expensive, wrong location. There was one I liked the look of in the other Alhaurín, Alhaurín de la Torre. It had an elevated position on the side of the Sierra de Mijas, with great views over the valley from a huge picture window in the lounge. It was just that the small side garden (and more importantly the pool) lost the sun mid afternoon thanks to the mountain, so we ruled that one out.

Finally, we found one to go and view together. It was within budget, and from the photos available, it looked to have a good pool and garden with large, covered terrace. We were a bit confused about the room configuration from the photos but were keen to see it in the flesh. We met the estate agent at their office in Coín and followed her car for a few miles before turning up a dirt track. I took the turn gingerly in my Lexus, and Chris immediately had concerns about getting her Mini up the road on a regular basis. We'd call this type of road "unadopted" in the UK – you need to choose low gear and navigate round the holes and bigger stones. We stopped a couple of hundred yards up this path and waited for the agent to open the gate to the driveway, then followed her in.

The plot was a good size, with landscaped garden and pool area at the front of the house, although it was in desperate need of some attention. There were lots of leaves and other debris in the pool, and the trees and shrubs needed trimming.

'The owner hasn't been down for a while,' the agent said apologetically.

No shit, Sherlock!

Inside, the house had a really strange layout. The front door opened onto the living area which was long and narrow, with access to the kitchen and bedrooms cutting across in front of the fireplace, where in winter I'd ideally be sitting in my armchair. It was only two bedrooms really, but there was a dressing room of sorts that led through to the main bedroom that we could have made into a study, but putting a bed in there wasn't going to work. The kitchen was very tired and didn't appeal to us.

Worse, though, was the state of the bathroom. Oddly, it was immediately on the left of the living room as you came into the house, with only a curtain covering the doorway, with the bedrooms on the opposite side of the living room. The bathroom was small and hadn't been cleaned for a very long time, and there was a grubby pair of grey underpants hanging from the shower head! The least the owner could have done was send in a gardener and some cleaners to make the house presentable. There was no way he was going to get anyone to rent this from him in this condition unless he knocked another €400 off the rent.

We stepped out onto the terrace in despair, wondering if we were ever going to find somewhere to live.

'What about the other house I enquired about in Coín last week?' I asked the agent. 'Is the owner still adamant that he can only rent it out furnished?'

That one had looked a really nice house. It was €300 more than we were already paying, but there didn't seem to be much around at the moment that fitted our criteria.

'He did actually agree to rent that to someone else, but after they paid their deposit, we never heard from them again. They also wanted it unfurnished, and he agreed in the end. Let me call him and see if he's home now.' She put the call in.

'He says you can come to see it if we go now. He has another viewing at 2 o'clock but if you like it and agree a price with him, then he'll tell the other couple not to bother coming.'

'Right, let's go,' said Chris.

Having seen the photos of this property a week earlier, she was more than keen to go and see if the photos did it justice. We arrived at the house 15 minutes later.

'Right,' I said to Chris as we parked up at the end of a short lane, 'we both liked the photos, and it looks like it's got everything we need.'

It had three bedrooms, a second bathroom in the garden by the pool, and even an outside kitchen and bar area.

'If it's as nice as the photos when we go in,' I continued, 'please don't appear too enthusiastic, as we can't really afford it, and I need to get the price down.'

The owner, Roberto, came out to meet us in the lane. Roberto spoke great English, and we chipped in with some Spanish to make a good first impression. As we approached the house, he clicked his remote control, and the solid gate slid open, revealing the side of the house, the pool and landscaped garden. No strimming needed here, I thought, as it had printed concrete all around the property.

Chris took in her first sight of the pool area, fringed by a couple of palm trees and private walled garden with shrubs around the border, and she let out a little squeal of delight. I had to nudge her to remind her we hadn't negotiated the price yet.

We trailed Roberto around the property taking it all in. The floor tiles weren't very appealing, and the living room walls were mustard-coloured. The kitchen also had dark wooden cabinets, but the room itself was more than twice the size of our existing kitchen. All three bedrooms were a good size, with cream walls and a feature wall in a bright colour.

'Don't worry about the wall colours,' Roberto assured us. 'Feel free to paint them all if you wish.'

The bathroom was larger than our current one, too, with a walk-in shower, large sink unit, toilet and bidet. The bathroom suite was a 70s avocado shade, but liveable. We'd probably been spoilt at our current villa which was newly constructed with bright white walls inside and out, and complementary light cream-coloured floor tiles, giving it all a neutral, contemporary feel. This house had been constructed in the 70s, and although Roberto had painted the outer walls white, the floor tiles inside were very dark. But we were sure we could make it look more appealing simply by painting all the internal walls white.

What made this house great, though, was the outside living space. The covered terrace was very large, with traditional coloured tiling all around it, and built-in tiled seating round the outer edges for a large family gathering. Our terrace furniture (consisting of sofas, armchairs and coffee table) would easily fit in the space. There was a large marble table in one half of the terrace, and Roberto said that would have to stay because it weighed a ton and would be too heavy to move. The house was furnished, but the furniture could be moved to a property Roberto was going to rent out on the coast.

The outdoor kitchen had everything you'd need for outdoor living, including a large built-in barbecue, oven and hob, sink unit, dishwasher and a tall fridge. It was separated from the pool area by a long bar. Adjacent to that was another small building with a laundry room and a second bathroom. There was also a shed for all my crap that was at least five times larger than Olivia's.

I told Roberto we liked the place and that we were looking to move at the end of the month. We could also supply an excellent reference from Olivia, if needed. However, the property was slightly out of our budget, and would he accept €100 a month less if we signed a three-year lease.

Roberto said he liked us, and he could see that we would look after the house well, and thankfully, my offer was acceptable to him. If we could sort out the paperwork with the agent and get the deposit to them from the bank by 1 o'clock, he'd tell the other people not to bother coming to view the house.

Chris and I were absolutely thrilled. We drove straight over to our bank in Alhaurín. We had to go inside to withdraw the money over the counter. There was a long queue with only one person on the counter as usual. It was clear we'd be here for at least 20 minutes before getting up to the counter, so I messaged the agent and explained we might not get back to her office before 1 o'clock, but that we were definitely coming over to sign the contract.

As usual in Spain, it was all cash transactions, and we had to pay a deposit equal to two months' rent and pay half a month's rent as commission to the agent. We signed a three-year lease on the house and returned home content that we'd found somewhere at least as good as Olivia's property, which somewhat softened the blow of having to move out.

I was delighted, as I could kiss goodbye to the bloody strimmer that was like a conjoined twin every one week in six! And there was only a bit of watering to do once or twice a week at the new place, whereas it would take me the best part of an hour several nights per week currently.

Fate had dealt us a kind hand … now if it could just find an extra €200 a month for the rent increase, I'll be forever in its debt!

39

Another Fine Mess

A message pings in from Tony …

'Drew. We're in hotel Gran Elba from Friday to Monday. If you can make it, would be good to see you.'

'Tony and Sandra are over in Málaga this weekend,' I said to Chris. 'Fancy a night out on Friday and we'll stay over?'

'Yeah, I'm always up for a night out in Málaga.'

I messaged Tony straight back …

'Great. We'll book a hotel and get back to you,' I said.

A few days later, I'd booked a room and decided where best to meet them.

'We aim to get into Málaga about 6pm tomorrow,' I texted. 'Let's meet in Taberna La Malagueta in Plaza del Obispo next to the Cathedral for drinks at 7:30.'

'Sounds great. Can't wait.'

We were just about to set off for Málaga on Friday afternoon when Chris noticed something strange on Facebook.

'Where are we meeting Tony later?' she asked.

'In a bar next to the cathedral.'

'In Málaga?'

'Yes.'

'Then why has Sandra just posted a photo on Facebook from a bar in Estepona?'

'Eh? Let's have a look … oh, yeah! Let me check my messages again.'

I found Tony's original message and read it again carefully.

'Bugger!' I said. 'I thought the Elba in Estepona was just called Hotel Elba or something; when I saw the word Gran in front of it, I thought he'd booked into the Gran Miramar again in Málaga, like they have done the last two times!'

'You idiot! So, we've booked a hotel in Málaga and they're staying in Estepona?'

'Erm. Looks like it. And I've prepaid the hotel. I'm going to have to book one in Estepona now.'

I was feeling a bit of a fool at this point, and quickly went online to find a hotel, and the cheaper the better, seeing as I'd already paid for one in the wrong city. I then messaged Tony.

'Cockup on my part. Thought the hotel you mentioned was the one in Málaga. Booked one in Estepona now. Meet us in Restaurante Central Beach for a drink at 7:30. By the way, you even agreed to meet us in a bar next to Málaga cathedral!'

'You never said the cathedral was in Málaga. I thought you lived over here!' he replied.

'Well, there is no cathedral in Estepona!'

'Doh! I've just read back the messages and noticed you mentioned Málaga. However, I did give you the name of our hotel. In future we should let the girls make the arrangements!'

He was probably right.

To be honest, the weather forecast for Málaga this evening was for heavy rain, whereas Estepona looked clear, so it was just as well we were heading away from the weather front.

The Estepona hotel I booked was very central, but it was very basic, and the bed was awful, but I guess you get what you pay for. Understandably, Chris wasn't happy and blamed me – I tried to keep a low profile.

Tony and Sandra were finally on the hunt for a nice villa in Estepona, which is why they were back here now. We had a great night out, as always, and there wasn't a drop of rain in sight. The same couldn't be said for Alhaurín and the surrounding areas, though, as they'd experienced a *gota fría*.

A *gota fría* (cold drop) is a violent storm in which rain appears to drop from the sky ceaselessly at speed. It's caused by heavy rain clouds building up on top of each other before they all release their rain at the same time. Naturally, it causes severe flooding of the affected areas.

According to online news reports, the storm began over Alhaurín El Grande at three in the morning with enormous hailstones the size of ice cubes falling over the town. The combined force of the hailstones and rainfall brought a river of rocks crashing down from the mountain, littering the roads and damaging anything in its path, including walls, houses, vehicles and power cables. Cars were swept away in greater numbers than last time the town was hit with torrential rain, and the municipal swimming pool will now need a new roof.

The nearby town of Alhaurín de la Torre was hit with 87 litres of rainfall per square metre in just half an hour, triple the intensity of a typical torrential downpour. As described, water literally pours out of the sky as if you're stood under a waterfall.

When we arrived home, we found a scene of chaos in our garden. The sofa and chairs from the terrace had been blown into the garden, the cushions were soaked through, and the garden itself was completely waterlogged. The pool was of course full, which is better than it being empty!

One of the Eucalyptus trees had gone crashing through into the neighbour's garden over the other side of the stream at the bottom of the garden. On our right, José's garden wall had been knocked down into our garden by the force of water rushing over the land. All of our irrigation pipes for the olive grove had been washed to the other side of the garden and lay in a heap up against Luis's fence. Chris's Mini had several golf ball-sized dents in its roof, and the house had had paint chipped off the walls.

It looked like the Somme on a good day.

'Maybe instead of renting another house, we should have just built an ark,' I said to Chris as we surveyed the damage.

Before we'd left for Estepona, we'd had the foresight to switch off the power to the pool pump and the gate, so we at least hadn't fried the electrics.

As you can imagine, the cleanup took us the rest of the weekend, and Olivia coopted Luis's son to help clear the fallen Eucalyptus with his chainsaw. If we'd have still been in the house next year, I could have burnt that wood after it had dried out. Ah well, never mind.

In contrast to people who lived halfway up the mountain, we'd gotten off lightly. Some of them had seen their cars float away or their homes flooded. And our local bar at the end of the lane had been flooded out again.

A couple of weeks later, I found out my footie mate from the walking group, Allan, had died while out cycling. Poor chap. Heart attack. He can't have been that much older than me. He was loving living over here too. It just shows you, death can creep up on us at any time, so don't put off until tomorrow what you can do today – i.e. if you've always wanted to live abroad when you retire, then retire early and do it now, before it's too late.

Spare a thought too for another friend from the walking group who, arriving back at Málaga airport, was expecting Allan to meet him and take him back to his place to collect the car he'd left there, as Allan lived quite close to the airport. He was without his car for another couple of weeks because the police wouldn't give him access to the apartment to collect his car keys. So I reckon Allan had the last laugh there. RIP Allan, mate.

40

Moving House

Moving house took us a week, and we were only going five miles away. It wasn't that we had so much stuff to move, it was just that we had some overlap on the rental contracts. This allowed us to move all the smaller items and boxes ourselves over several trips, and just leave the furniture removal for one day.

We hired a local 'woman with a van' who was absolutely brilliant. She was a big strong northern lass – built like a 'brick outhouse', as we say up north – and she brought along a young lad to boss about. I'd already been out and bought a load of bubble wrap and had wrapped all the sturdy, oak, wooden furniture, as it was the only thing we owned of any real value … it should still be in perfect condition when we've shuffled off our mortal coils.

We did the main move a couple of days before we had to hand the keys back to Olivia, which then allowed us some time to properly clean the house and touch up any marks or scuffs on the walls with some fresh white paint. As the advert would say, a clean, tidy, professional couple!

I'd spent the previous week strimming the garden, so that was all neat and tidy, and in the same condition as it was when we'd taken the place on three years earlier. There was still a dirty great hole behind the pool, but only because Olivia hadn't arranged to have that filled in yet.

I was going through the shed, sorting out what was coming with us and what I could leave behind.

'You're not bringing those to the new house, are you?' Chris asked me.

I was pulling out some fence posts and netting that I'd used only once to create a child-proof fence around the pool on the one occasion that needed it.

'Course I'm bringing it. You never throw wood away. That'll come in handy one day. And the netting.'

'You're just a bloody Womble, you!' she countered.

'Wombles are much-loved creatures, you know.'

'I'll have to start calling you Uncle Bulgaria.'

I had a load of gardening equipment I hoped I'd no longer need in Spain (unless we had to move on again in three years and ended up with another piece of land to manage), so I bit the bullet and just left it all for Olivia ... a lawnmower, the petrol strimmer she went halves with me on, various garden implements, the extra hose pipes we'd bought, a sprinkler for the lawn, and the rather splendid woodstore I'd made during our first winter.

She'd taken a shine to my water pump that I'd used from time to time to clear most of the floodwater out of the pool pump housing, but that was coming with me in case I had a similar problem at the new house.

Olivia was also inheriting her house back complete with air conditioning that it didn't have when we moved in. When we'd paid to have that installed (at not inconsiderable expense), we'd created a separate agreement so that it would, in effect, depreciate over three years, and she'd only have to pay us a proportion of the original cost if she asked us to move out before then. It felt wise to do so at the time, given that we were renting the house under a (technically illegal) rolling 11-month contract. And here we now were, three years on, and now bereft of said aircon system. The new house had aircon in all the bedrooms, so we wouldn't miss it.

After clearing the house out, we gave it a deep clean and touched up the paintwork, and then we sat on the terrace on a couple of camping chairs and watched our friend Rick play a starring role on daytime telly. He was appearing on ITV's *Tipping Point*, or what I call 'shove halfpenny' when I can't remember the title. We didn't have internet installed at the new house yet, so we had to watch it at Olivia's instead on the iPad. Rick hadn't told us beforehand that he'd only gone and won the game show and walked away a couple of grand richer ... the milky bars are on Rick next time we see him!

When we were done cleaning, we met Olivia and her boyfriend at the house to hand over the keys. She was absolutely thrilled we'd left the house spotless and ready to move in, and said we were the best tenants she could have wished for. Despite this, for some strange reason, she had the decorators arriving in the morning to paint all the walls white again, even though they were already white, and we'd just touched them up.

With our furniture now arranged in the new house, and all our clothes and other stuff already unpacked, we had visitors on our first night in the new house ... Jill and Ian called round with some gifts. It's traditional in Spain to give a bottle of olive oil as a housewarming gift, apparently, so she'd bought us a fancy little bottle of extra virgin olive oil.

Chris told me that giving olive oil as a gift is a symbol of abundance, prosperity, peace and wellbeing – but as long as it tasted good when I dunked a chunk of crusty bread in it, that's all that mattered to me.

Jill also brought us a candle. As a resident of Coín herself, did she know something about the electrics that we didn't?! And to save us having to prepare dinner, she also brought round a tray of homemade lasagne. That's what friends are for ... making your dinner!

I started to wonder if the candle was to heat up the lasagne if the power did go off. The power did in fact trip out a few times in those first couple of weeks, and we had to get the *potencia* increased to 5kW. The house had previously been let out as a short-term holiday let, and I bet the guests had never bothered putting the oven on at the same time as the kettle.

'Your lane's a bit bumpy,' Ian said at one point.

He wasn't wrong. After leaving the main road, there was about 200 yards of tarmac and then it was lumpy bumpy all the way down into town from there.

'Yeah,' I said, 'they could do with tarmacking it to be honest. I know they recently tarmacked one of the other local roads because we walked along it with the walking group not so long ago, so maybe we're next on the list.'

'Did we ever tell you about the time they tarmacked our road not long after we'd moved in?' Jill asked.

'No, why? Did they make a mess of it?'

'Not quite. They just didn't tell us they were going to do it. The urbanisation was new and there weren't many plots built on yet – ours was one of the first. We'd gone out for the day in the car, and when we got home, they'd installed pavements and tarmacked the whole street, raising the level of it all by about a metre. We couldn't get the car on the driveway.'

Jill and Ian's urbanisation is built on a steep hill, and they live off the uppermost road. Their house was below the level of the road, and now everyone who walked past the house could also see over their 6-foot garden wall.

'The builders just left us a wooden board to climb down into the property!'

'You're kidding!'

'No. We had to pay someone to come and raise the driveway and add another 3-foot to the garden wall.'

'That's bonkers!'

After Jill and Ian had left, Chris and I sat relaxing on the terrace with a glass of red. Chris was admiring our new surroundings, with the outdoor kitchen and bar, and extra bathroom … I was just looking forward to not having to strim anything ever again and to a relatively maintenance-free garden. The only downside of the garden was we didn't have the same views of the Sierra de Mijas, but we had a totally private garden, and I could go for an all-over tan now if I so desired!

'We did well to find this place in the end,' Chris said.

'I know. And we walked past this house on our very first walk with the rambling group.'

'Oh, yes. You're right. We did, didn't we? It must be fate that we live here now then.'

It is indeed fate. And it was my least stressful house move to date.

The new house wasn't without its foibles. We'd christened the outdoor kitchen on that first night in order to heat up the lasagne in the oven, as we couldn't get the oven inside the house to switch on. Nor in fact would the extractor hood switch on.

We asked Roberto to call in next time he was passing to take a look. It turned out they were in fact working. The extractor fan not switching on was symptomatic of crazy Spanish wiring. On entering the kitchen there were two identical switches on the wall, one of which turned on the overhead light, while the other one didn't seem to do anything. However, that had to be in the correct position for the electricity supply to reach the extractor hood, apparently. Why would anyone need two switches for an extractor fan, one on the fan itself and the other a light switch? Very odd.

Even dafter – and I don't think you'd come across one like it in the UK – was the operation of the oven. There were three dials on the front of the oven, one for choosing between oven, grill and/or fan assisted mode, another for choosing the desired temperature, and the third one was a timer switch. What we didn't know was that this oven (that I think was previously installed in Noah's ark) wouldn't work at all without the timer being on. So every time you wanted a bit of cheese on toast under the grill, you had to turn on the timer. Very odd indeed. The timer also only went up to two hours, so if you wanted low and slow while you buggered off to the pub for a few hours, you'd find the oven switched off when you got home and a half-cooked dinner!

The utility room also had one of those 'slow' light switches that our second bedroom at Olivia's had. I think the wire must have run from the switch in the utility room, three times round the garden, then down to the town and back before delivering the electricity to the lightbulb as it could take fully two minutes for the light to come on.

Such is life in the *campo*.

We also didn't have a fire in the fireplace, as Roberto had removed the pellet burner before we moved in. He said we'd be better with a log burner and told us to find one we liked, and he'd go and buy it. As it turned out, the dimensions of the fireplace were such that we could only find one log burner that would fit inside it. It was about half the size of the one in Olivia's house, but having said that, the living and dining room here were smaller, so we were hoping this small log burner would be able to heat the place adequately in the winter.

That wasn't a foregone conclusion, however, as this house had single glazing, whereas Olivia's had double glazing throughout. And as we know from bitter experience, Spanish houses are not designed to retain heat but release it. For now though, it was October, and we were still mostly living outdoors on the terrace and cooking in the outdoor kitchen, making use of the patio heater outside to maintain a comfortable temperature when sitting out in the evening.

We didn't have long to wait for our first foreign visitors. Sandra's best friend for more than 30 years, Gail, and her husband, Tony (not to be confused with my best mate Tony), were renting a swanky villa in Benalmádena for a couple of weeks, so we invited them up here for a paella.

It was a little cool on the terrace, so we put our other patio table and chairs by the pool in full sunshine and enjoyed a pleasant afternoon of good food, fine wine and great company. Later in the week, we went down for a night out round the old town of Benalmádena Pueblo with them. This was our first visit to the old town, and it was so pretty – a complete contrast to the tourist area on the coast a few miles down the mountain.

We walked into town from their villa and dined at a lovely little restaurant in *Plaza de España*. Benalmádena Pueblo is another whitewashed Andalucian town, and it's always a delight to stroll the narrow streets of these places, browsing the restaurant menus as you pass by, and stopping for a drink when the mood takes you. It's a very simple, unhurried way of life, and the main reason we live here.

Like Tony and Sandra before them, I don't suppose it'll be too long before Gail and Tony are on the hunt for their own

Spanish dream property too. If so, let's hope they don't take as long as it seems to be taking Tony and Sandra.

41

Getting My Lip In

'It's time I got my lip in,' I said to Chris.

'Why now? I've not heard you play your trumpet for ages.'

'Because I've just joined a salsa band.'

'What?! When did you do that?'

'Just now. I saw an ad on Facebook from a Dutch pianist in Fuengirola. He's putting a band together.'

'But you've never played salsa before. The closest you've got to salsa was those half a dozen dancing lessons we had in Bury.'

'And I was a natural at that, the teacher said.'

'Yeah, right! I don't think that's quite what she said. She just asked you if you'd had lessons before.'

'Yes, after she'd seen these snake hips move.'

'Snake hips? Your physique is more steak and chips than snake hips.'

'Charming. Anyway, I've played a bit of Latin jazz with the big band over the years.'

'Salsa, though? Aren't you being a bit ambitious? I thought you were going to join one of the town's marching bands – you liked that one in Alhaurín that wore the army uniforms.'

'Well, I'll never know if I don't try. I won't be screeching in the higher register like Maynard Ferguson, but with a bit of practice, I should be able to nail some salsa tunes.'

Our new house was a little further from its closest neighbour than the old house, and with the walled garden and the blinds down, I felt a bit less inhibited blowing my trumpet. I stuck a mute in to tone it down a little, but at least I could give it some welly, even if Chris wasn't very appreciative.

I went to meet Herman at his house. He had an amazing open plan first floor, with a black grand piano in the room and fabulous views down the mountain overlooking the Fuengirola coastline. Downstairs was a room with his electric piano in, and in the adjacent room I could see he had all sorts of percussive instruments. He was a really likeable guy. I'd been writing out the trumpet parts for half a dozen songs he was interested in doing first, and I was quietly confident.

Herman had invited a Brazilian singer and Argentine percussionist to the first session. I enjoyed playing the music with them, and although we were light on band members yet, it didn't sound too bad. One evening, we all went to see the singer perform with a guitarist in a bar in Torremolinos, and she was a terrific live performer.

We had another couple of rehearsals, and then the singer's other commitments got in the way a little. Sadly, it all fizzled out soon afterwards when she decided she had too many other things on, and we struggled to find another singer to sing this style of music. But I maintained my solo practice sessions playing the same songs at home to keep strengthening my lip after so long out of the game. I even bought a different mouthpiece that I hoped would improve my lip stamina in the upper part of my range.

I'm still in touch with Herman, who has branched out as a solo concert pianist now, writing and performing his own compositions and doing some work with choirs. I wish him well but I hoped it wouldn't be too long before I found another outlet for my playing.

42

The Patter of Tiny Feet

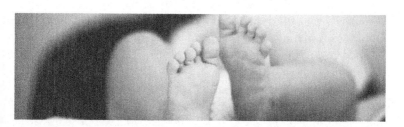

We had a trip to the UK again to see baby Theo and to bring him and his mum back to Spain with us for a couple of weeks. This was our eighth UK trip in 10 months during 2019, which was a few too many for my liking. Little did we know what would hit the world in 2020, so in hindsight, I shouldn't complain.

While in the UK, we met our daughter Rachel's new boyfriend for the first time. Karl seemed a smashing lad. Down to earth and polite. The poor lad got a baptism of fire, though, as our other three daughters and their families were all present too, and when all four girls get together it can get a bit raucous. He survived the ordeal, and it didn't put him off, which is always a good sign.

Theo was as good as gold on the flight back over with us. Corrinne and Theo were the first guests to stay at the new house. Corrinne thought the fantastic outdoor space more than made up for the dark mismatching floor tiles and the avocado bathroom suite. We'd painted all the interior walls white already, so at least it was brighter inside now than before.

After visiting the Dominican Republic for Chris's 40th birthday celebration many years ago and seeing all the hotel's palm trees covered in pretty little lights, I'd always wanted to have my own palm trees decorated the same way. I'd therefore bought two sets of lights and strung them as high up our two palm trees as my little step ladders would allow. The swimming pool also had lights, and there were spotlights dotted around the garden. With the added fairy lights on the palm trees, the garden look quite magical when the sun went down.

The weather was still great in October, and we took them down to La Cala for Theo's first day at the beach. Corrinne slathered him in factor 50, and we sat him inside a little beach tent we'd bought him while we did a bit of sunbathing.

Chris was still doing her Fire Watch shifts, so one afternoon I took Corrinne and Theo down into the old town of Coín for a wander round and some coffee and cake. There seemed to be a bit more to the old town of Coín than there was with Alhaurín's old town, which had most of its popular restaurants concentrated in the newer part of town, whereas you could quite happily wander round Coín's old town and get yourself lost down the narrow streets.

The other difference between the two locations we'd now lived in was that we had a steep climb up into Alhaurín, whereas Coín was a steep downhill walk. I could see us quite happily strolling down into Coín on a hot summer evening and taking a taxi home afterwards to avoid walking up the hill. In Alhaurín, because the initial walk was sharply uphill for 20 minutes, we were always a little discouraged from making that walk on a hot summer night, and would instead drive into town and leave the car overnight and get a taxi home in the dark because there was no street lighting outside the centre of the towns.

Graham flew over to join us for the second week of the holiday, although I suspect he'd also relished having a quiet time at home and a good night's sleep the previous week while Theo was over here with us. Graham is like a Duracell bunny – he won't lie down and sunbathe; he always wants to be busy doing something. He'd asked me to have some jobs ready for him to work on when he got over here.

The first job on my list was to get the TV put up on the wall in the lounge somehow. I'd bought a bracket for it, but the configuration of the lounge wall either side of the fireplace was challenging, with built in cupboards with glass tops, over which were an array of shelves for books, etc., made out of some kind of hard white plaster/concrete – we had no idea what it was, really. I wasn't quite sure how best to affix the TV to it so it would pull out from the wall on the bracket and give us a good viewing angle across the room.

Graham reckoned we could bolt a piece of wood to the side of one of the vertical plaster/concrete bits and attach the TV to that. My main concern was to not damage the property and make it look seamless when complete, and easy to repair when taken down if and when we have to leave.

The local wood merchant was very helpful. I'd drawn a diagram with dimensions to show the woman on the counter. She disappeared into the warehouse and returned with an offcut length of wood she gave us for nothing, and when we got it home, it fit absolutely perfectly in the gap we had assigned to it. Graham made the rest of the job look easy, hiding the bolts and routing the wires into the cupboard underneath and moving the Wi-Fi router for us. We were very pleased with the result.

'What's next?' Graham asked.

'I've seen this lovely thick piece of oak down on the coast that will make for a fine seat top for some bar stools,' I said.

'What about the legs?'

'I HAVE SOME FENCE POSTS FROM THE OTHER HOUSE,' I replied loudly, so Chris could hear me … and hopefully appreciate the value of my wombling persona at last.

Next day, we bought the oak slab and had it cut to size before bringing it home. I gave Graham my design idea, some power tools and left him to it while I lit the barbecue, and before lunch was ready, we had three nice new stools to sit on by the outside bar. I just needed to stain them when I had a minute, as Graham doesn't do the menial jobs.

I wish all our guests could be put to work on the house like this!

43

Mojácar Out of Season

While Theo jetted off for his second foreign holiday, this time to Cancun's Moon Palace Hotel, where his parents were married five years earlier, Chris and I decided to belatedly celebrate our own wedding anniversary with a night away in Mojácar in the neighbouring Almería province.

We took the coast road, as it's the shortest route, although it's still 200 miles and a four-hour drive away. Normally, we'd prefer the inland road past Granada when we're heading in this direction because the Almería coastline is littered with polytunnels, making it a not very attractive route. However, on Mum and Dad's recommendation after staying in the area some years ago, we decided to stop halfway at Cabo de Gata, a national park on the Almería coastline.

Almería is known for its desert climate and the location for some famous spaghetti westerns, like *The Good, The Bad and The Ugly*, and that climate extends down to the coastline and the national park. We headed for the small town of Cabo de Gata, a 20-minute drive from the motorway. We drove past the town at first as the road skirts around the eastern edge of the town and then takes you down alongside the coast towards the salt flats. We weren't sure where Mum and Dad had stayed that had made them recommend it to us, but we assumed it would be around the town of Cabo de Gata itself, perhaps.

We turned around and drove back up the road and into the town, which is quite small, and at this time of year, quite deserted. We had a walk along a short prom that overlooked a flat, narrow strip of sandy beach and there didn't seem to be much open along the front. It was a very sleepy town with just a couple of bars on this section of the promenade. We stopped for a drink and a few plates of tapas before walking up to the other end of the promenade.

We concluded that the old folks must have stayed somewhere further along the coast than this, as there wasn't much to recommend the place, really, and there was a lack of facilities for your average British tourist in the town. There were more touristy spots in front of the salt flats several miles away, but we didn't feel it was worth spending any more time here, so we turned around and headed back to the motorway and onward to Mojácar instead.

A couple of hours later we arrived in the resort of Mojácar Playa and our hotel for the evening, the Parador de Mojácar, a modern hotel in the Parador chain that's right on the main road that runs alongside the long, sandy beach. The room was very spacious, and the hotel was very quiet due to the time of year. We dumped the bags and went for a stroll. Crossing the road, you are immediately on a sandy parking area adjacent to a thin strip of beach. There is no promenade here, as such, just the beach on one side of the road, and the pavement on the other.

We followed the road north for a while to get a feel for the area. It was a very clean resort, as most of Spain is, and it looked like it would be a popular summer destination for the Spanish and foreign tourists alike. I knew a lot of Madrileños had holiday homes along the Spanish coastline, and I would have expected this place to be no exception.

A few miles inland, we could see the town of Mojácar Pueblo clinging to the hillside of the Sierra Cebrera, but we decided we'd just relax down on the coast. We found a bar and stopped for a drink and to take in the sea air.

The average temperature here in the winter months is reportedly between 10°C and 18°C, and it never drops below 4°C. And thanks to the sea, the summer temperatures in the area hover around the high 20s and low 30s, so it's a lot cooler than the desert-like 40s further inland, and for that matter where we live in the Guadalhorce Valley. So if we ever decided to escape the heat in the summer, this wouldn't be a bad place to come and stay.

After changing for dinner, we strolled out in the same direction and headed for a small commercial centre that had some nice-looking restaurants attached. We chose to eat at an Argentine grill called La Estancia (which I confess I googled at the hotel to check out their menu). We had empanadas to start and steaks for main course, with a side order of a nice spicy Chimichurri sauce, washed down with a bottle of Argentine Malbec, of course.

Conversation turned to memories of my Uncle Harold who used to live with my Auntie Enid up in the hills around here in a town called Arboleas. It was 10 years earlier that he'd passed away, and I still miss him a huge amount. I remember coming over here to visit them the year before he died. I had business in Madrid but had decided to fly down here first just to go and visit them both. They had a lovely villa up in the hills behind the town.

Sadly, what should have been a happy visit to see them turned into a family tragedy. On the way back from dining at a local restaurant, I received a call from the UK to inform me that our niece, Vicki, had died following severe complications after the birth of her daughter. Chris and I had only visited her a couple of nights earlier in the hospital and she'd been in good spirits, but she'd developed a blood clot in her leg that cruelly stole her from us. I was beside myself with grief, and Harold and Enid were an incredible source of comfort for me at that moment, and for that will be eternally grateful.

We have wonderful families on both sides, and many of them have shaped me to be the man I am today, not least my Uncle Harold. I get my musical talents from his and Mum's side of the family; Harold loved to sing in the pubs and clubs that he managed or acted as compere for, and his father, my Grandad, taught me the mandolin at a young age. God bless both of you, Harold and Vicki.

After breakfast, we headed out of the town to the north and passed through more beachside neighbourhoods with hotels, bars and restaurants, so we must have been staying at the very southern end of the resort. Just beyond Mojácar Playa is the port town of Garrucha, and a little inland from there, the popular town of Vera, separated as it is like Mojácar from its coastal beach areas. I imagine this coastline has a very different feel to it in the height of summer, but at the end of autumn it's a very peaceful place to spend some time.

44

Peak Perfection

In the weeks that followed, we had the usual Christmas lunch engagements with the art group and the two walking groups we patronised (plus the now obligatory Christmas lights night out in Málaga with Kim and Martin).

With regards the hiking, I was heading out more and more now with Laura's more adventurous group, as the walks were much more challenging and interesting – Chris usually declined the invitation to join me because of her fear of heights.

A particularly strenuous walk of late was the hike up the *Pico de la Capilla* in the *Valle de Abdalajís*, the summit of which stands at 1,186 metres. This trip was a full day out, starting with an hour or so in the car to reach the starting point.

There was much to love about this walk, including a large herd of ibex we spotted early on, the vultures catching the late morning thermals, and the fabulous views from the summit. There was a lot of scrambling up and down the challenging terrain too, which was littered with large, limestone rock formations reminiscent of the El Torcal region of Antequera.

We had a couple of falls in the group, though nothing too serious, and one member of the party lost the sole of one of his hiking boots early on in the walk, but he soldiered bravely on with one boot. Our intrepid guide, Laura 'Sherpa Tenzing', led four of us up to summit with her, leaving the others having a tea break at base camp 3. What goes up must come down, however, and my knees took a bit of a hammering on the way down – I always find coming down long steep slopes much harder on the body than getting up them in the first place.

I was glad when we reached the town and our planned watering hole after almost eight hours on the mountain. We were running about an hour over time thanks to the nature of the terrain, the minor injuries to attend to, and a boot missing a sole. We were supremely catered for at Restaurante Los Atanores, and it proved a very welcoming place to recharge our batteries before heading home. This walk will live long in the memory for me.

And with regards my output from the art group, I'd recently been sticking with coloured pencils so I could draw some of our younger family members' portraits.

My great-niece Ella had taken a shine to my galleon painting (that Mum had actually hung in her living room, as promised, and not the loo!), and she'd said in passing that she wished I would paint her. The comment got back to me, so when I presented her with a pencil portrait, she was so thrilled. I've now just finished one of my grandson, Caleb, that I'll take over as a surprise for him when we go back to the UK for our usual Christmas family gatherings.

And before we headed for the colder Christmas climes of Northern England for the last time this year, I also found time to apply for two more jobs (fat chance) and send out five more agent submissions for my novel (even fatter chance), receiving an 11th rejection in return. Happy Christmas!

45

Something Weird is Going On

At the start of 2020, we raided the savings to treat ourselves to a fortnight in the Dominican Republic with Kim and Martin. We should have been going to Costa Rica, but thanks to TUI buggering up our flight arrangements and changing the capacity of the plane eight weeks before our departure, we ended up having to cancel the trip of a lifetime to the tropical jungles of Central America and instead ended up on a beach in the Caribbean.

I know, it's a tough job, but someone's got to do it … but joking aside, we were gutted we wouldn't be seeing a part of the world we'd never explored before.

The real worry at the time though was we were hearing more and more disturbing things about a new virus that had taken hold in China and may have already spread outside the country. This made us very wary travellers.

Kim had been suffering from a persistent cough when we'd met up in December for the Christmas lights, and soon afterwards I had the same cough myself which I took with me to the Dominican and came back with. We refused to believe that we'd already contracted the virus at that early stage, and certainly wasn't displaying any other symptoms than an annoying dry cough that a few short months later would make everyone stare at you with fear and mistrust. After all, we hadn't been to China or in contact with anyone we knew that had been to China.

Before long, however, there were reports that the Chinese were barricading residents inside their apartment blocks. Fear was growing worldwide about this new deadly virus, and the first case in Italy was confirmed in February. We'd have to be a bit more vigilant from now on, I thought.

Meanwhile, Tony and Sandra were over again looking for a holiday home, this time in earnest. They were staying at the swanky Anantara Villa Padierna Palace Golf Resort outside Marbella. We went down to meet them for lunch and were ushered up to their room, which was rather splendid.

'We've been upgraded to a Junior Suite,' beamed Tony, as he poured us both a glass of wine.

'They probably did some background checks on you before you arrived,' I said. 'These posh hotels employ people to investigate their clients to see if they're worth pampering, so they've probably been all over your LinkedIn account.'

Shortly after their stay, the hotel was added to the elite group of hotels voted "The Leading Hotels in the World", so maybe they got upgraded because they thought Tony and Sandra were mystery shoppers for the brand. Either way, it was a beautiful hotel.

The hotel must have also brought them a bit of luck, as that weekend they found the holiday home they'd been looking for: a nice, detached villa high up on a hill with spectacular views overlooking the southern coastline of Estepona. They were thrilled with it and put an offer in, so fingers crossed for them both – they'll save a fortune on hotel bills if it goes through!

While they were over, they had a run inland to visit us in our new home these last four months. For February, the weather was great, with temperatures in the high teens, so Tony and I left the girls sunning themselves around the pool while we went off for a round of golf.

'I see the pound dropped 1.4% on Monday after your put in your offer on the villa,' I said to him. Even a relatively small variation like that can add several thousand pounds to the price.

'Yeah. That wasn't great. The seller lives in the UK, so we're going to see if we can agree a price in sterling.'

Their offer on the villa was accepted, and they'd booked to return in May to complete on the sale. Sure enough however, within 6 six weeks the pound had slumped by another 10%, thanks to what we now call COVID-19 taking hold across Europe. The villa sale fell through as a result. But every cloud has a silver lining – Tony had paid the deposit on the villa through his lawyer, which when refunded back to him was a few grand more than he'd paid, thanks to the currency fluctuation – he's a jammy swine!

Tony is the kind of guy who can spend all night at a roulette wheel and walk away a winner. Given that, I'm surprised he's not an avid gambler. We once went together as teenagers to watch Manchester United play in an FA Cup tie. We didn't have tickets and were wandering around outside the ground asking various touts how much they wanted. We weren't flush so needed a good deal. Then some random guy approached Tony and asked if he needed a couple of tickets. He gave us his two tickets he couldn't use, and he wouldn't take any money from us. We couldn't believe our luck.

When he pops his clogs, Tony will probably already have his name down on the guest list at the Pearly Gates, and St Peter will welcome him in with open arms, saying he's reserved him the best room in Heaven, complete with a full sports TV package and a free bar!

Meanwhile, the same weekend that Tony and Sandra had discovered their dream place in the sun and were looking forward to starting a new adventure in their lives, I was off on a new journey of discovery myself. When we'd been in the Dominican Republic in January, I'd answered an ad on Facebook for musicians to form a new band to write their own mix of jazz funk and R&B music, and tonight I was heading off to meet up with the other band members who had responded to the ad.

Probably not the best time to be starting up a new band admittedly, as two days earlier, Spain had confirmed its first COVID case when a German tourist on the Canary Islands had tested positive.

I met the other musicians and singers at a bar in the centre of Málaga, although we had to change venue once everyone had arrived as there wasn't space enough for us to congregate together safely on the terrace. We just had a general chat to establish what the style of music would be and to ensure everyone was happy with the plans. There were some that were perhaps not ideally suited to what we were proposing to do, and it remained to be seen who would ultimately be chosen to take part in the project, but I was hoping I'd make the cut.

Joining such a band was a bit of a ballsy move by me, given that, apart from one of the singers, the other prospective members of the band were all Spanish, so I was throwing myself in at the deep end with the language.

When one person is talking to me in Spanish, then I try to hang onto their every word, and so long as they're not talking extremely fast, then I have a chance of understanding about 50% of the words, and I can usually get the gist of what they're saying. However, when the conversation is coming at you from all angles in local dialects and at speed, I haven't a scooby doo what's going on for the most part. At times, I was asked if I was understanding the conversation, and I had to admit I was getting about 30% of it (if that), so I asked the band leader to summarize the key points for me in a text message later.

We left the meeting feeling positive, but unable to confirm when we'd be able to meet again with our instruments to start writing songs together. It was at least nice to put some faces to names.

46

Spider Bites

Apologies to other arachnophobes like me ... cover the photo with your hand and carry on reading quickly to the next page ... or just toss the book in the air and scream!

This story starts so innocuously and ends like a disaster movie! We'd been out for the day in Málaga, meeting up with my trumpet-playing mate, Andy, and his wife, Ali, who were on holiday in Nerja. On returning home, Chris went to the loo and felt a little nip on her bum. Now here's the thing ... she didn't think much of it, didn't know what it was (or even if she'd dreamt it), and therefore did nothing about it ... including not mentioning it to me at the time, which I'm not sure I'll ever forgive her for.

The next day we went out with the rambling group and came across a chain of pine processionaries, a very destructive species of caterpillar that destroy pine forests. They're a common pest in this area, and the local authorities often spray the forests from aeroplanes when there's evidence of their nests. They walk down from their tree nests with synchronicity towards the end of the winter months and march off in single file in a chain formation, nose to tail – figuratively speaking, as they don't have tails (or probably noses for that matter!) – in search of a suitable place to burrow underground and pupate before turning into moths.

When threatened, the caterpillars fire harpoon-like hairs off their backs with pinpoint accuracy. Contact with human skin causes a severe rash, but for small mammals, like dogs, they are often fatal when inhaled. When the processionary caterpillars are known to be on the march, the walking group don't bring any dogs out with them. As a result, apart from taking a photo at a safe distance, we carefully avoid them.

The following day, I woke with a small lump on the outside of my left knee. It had a black head, and the flesh around it was red. With my own in-house nurse on hand, I naturally decided to get Chris's professional opinion.

'I think one of those caterpillars might have fired a hair at me yesterday,' I said.

'Don't be daft. We didn't go anywhere near them. And you'd have felt it at the time.'

'Well, I think something's bitten me, then,' I said.

'Where?'

'On my knee.'

'That's strange, I thought something bit me on the bum while I was on the loo yesterday when we got back from Málaga.'

'What? And you didn't think to tell me at the time?'

'I thought nothing of it, but this morning it's a bit sore.'

'Let's have a look.'

Bum cheeks were bared, and we compared our lumps. At this point, they both looked quite similar, although mine was more raised, perhaps because there wasn't much flesh around my knee joint, whereas the swelling on Chris's bum cheek looked more internal.

The first thing I did was pull the bed covers off to check for creepy crawlies under the covers. Nothing. I got down on all fours and scanned under the bed.

'You don't think it's a scolopendra, do you?' I asked.

Although I've never seen one in the flesh, scolopendras are not uncommon in southern Spain, and they're known to have a bite that leaves a swelling and long-lasting pain. They're a poisonous species of centipede. Thinking about it, if we'd have rehoused that Centipede-eater snake from Tanzania, we wouldn't have to worry about scolopendras.

'A scolopendra? Probably not. They're too long. I'd have noticed something like that around the toilet.'

'Well, what was it then? A spider?'

193

I could already feel my skin scrawling at the very mention of the thing.

'Maybe. Perhaps it was a brown recluse.'

'Well, if it was, they're not that bloody reclusive if they've managed to bite both of us. What do they look like?'

'They're no more than an inch long and brown. They usually hide on the underside of leaves and sneak out to catch any prey landing on the leaf.'

As you've gathered, Chris is our resident Spanish wildlife expert when she's not fighting fires.

'So you're saying it could have been hiding under the toilet seat when you sat down?'

'Maybe.'

'Then how's it bitten my knee?'

'Maybe you sat down, and it dropped into your trousers?'

'Wouldn't I have felt it though?'

'Maybe not. Especially after a few wines!'

'So what do we do?'

'It'll probably burst and form a scab, that's all.'

I wasn't convinced by that rather blasé prognosis and wondered if I shouldn't seek a second opinion from a Spanish professional, but I let it drop for now.

'You can't tell the girls about this,' Chris said.

'Why not?'

'Because they'd freak out and never visit us again, especially Corrinne and Steph.'

Every time I went to the loo afterwards, I checked under the seat for any lurking brown recluses … and I killed every damn spider I saw for weeks to make sure I got the bugger that bit me!

To take my mind off it, I fired up the laptop and applied for two more jobs I wasn't qualified for nor had prior experience of but what the hell, I wasn't any more successful with the jobs I *was* qualified to do, so I had nothing to lose.

Mum called to check up on us and I told her we'd been bitten by ants while out walking when we sat down for a rest stop. There it was … the lie was now in circulation!

At art class a few days later, I showed the old girls my knee and one of them suggested calling at the pharmacy for some silver ointment. After completing another pencil portrait, this one of my granddaughter Amelia, we headed over to see the pharmacist. He had a look and couldn't say for sure what the bite was from, but probably a spider, and he gave us some cream to try.

Two days later, Chris's bum cheek had an even larger red patch and an angry looking black head on top of her spot. Mine by this time had burst open with an area of sloughing about an inch wide.

By the weekend, something very weird was happening to my knee. The affected area was now a couple of inches wide, and the wound had a white centre, while the surrounding bit looked like an Italian salami with more white bits dotted throughout the red area, and the outer rim was turning black. Beyond the immediate wound, the flesh was red, and the redness appeared to be spreading ever outwards. The spot on Chris's bum was larger and had also popped, and it was starting to show signs similar to mine. This wasn't good. I reckoned we were being eaten from the inside out!

I googled brown recluse spiders and discovered it was one of the most dangerous spiders in Spain. They're also called violin spiders because of the markings on their back in the shape of a violin. I felt like someone should be playing a sad tune on a violin for me right about now, actually. And funnily enough, it said that you may not notice being bitten at the time, but it will soon become very painful, and it often leads to an open sore developing that takes months to heal … well Halle-bloody-lujah!

This nasty, little, eight-legged arachnid has a necrotic venom, making the skin around the bite DIE! Jeepers – it even said that over time the wound may grow to 10 inches in diameter. Meanwhile, gangrene sets in and the tissue eventually sloughs away! I'd read enough.

'I think it's time we went to the hospital with these,' I said.

So the next day, off we went to the Hospital Valle del Guadalhorce, a fairly new hospital with an A&E department. We showed the lady on the desk all our ID, including our private health cards, and we waited to be called through. We weren't sure they'd see us with our private health insurance, but she never said anything to the contrary. She asked for our home address and told us to wait to be called through.

I was the first to be seen by a doctor, who had a quick look, pulled a face, said she thought it was a spider bite, and then I was ushered through to another room where a nurse was waiting.

'¡*Madre Mía!*' she exclaimed upon seeing my severely infected knee, before calling out for a second opinion (or reinforcements – who knew?).

'¡*Mira este! ¡Mira este!*' Come and look at this, she was shouting to anyone and everyone.

'¡*Madre Mía!*' a second, much older nurse exclaimed. '*Araña,*' she declared, confirming what everyone else had said; this was the handiwork of a spider.

Nurse 2 buggered off to leave nurse 1 to deal with the wound. She donned a pair of gloves and started squeezing the life out of my knee, trying to get as much puss and other crap out of the wound as possible. What happened to a local anaesthetic, for crying out loud? And crying out loud I was! This is Spain, you wuss – get on with it.

I gripped the table with all my might as her squeezing became more and more vicious and determined, but I could really have done with a stick to bite down on. I couldn't suppress the painful yelps I emitted every time she went in for the kill. Finally, when she could extract no more pleasure from her work, she dressed the wound and sent me back out to be seen by the doctor again, who presumably was going to give her marks out of 10 based on how high up the 'yellometer' she'd got me to scream.

Chris received the same diagnosis from the doctor and looked almost frightened when she was ushered in to see the same nurse. She was greeted by the same chorus of *Madre Mías* from the nurses, but instead of squeezing the life out of her bum cheek, they chose a different implement of torture, a bloody great syringe filled with iodine, that they thrust deep into her flesh at least a dozen times.

I can't imagine what the treatment is if you get bitten on the end of your willy!

The doctor gave us prescriptions for antibiotics to fight the infections and told us to get the wounds re-dressed at the health centre on a regular basis.

Feeling I could now impart even more local knowledge to would-be holidaymakers, I went home and applied for a job as a rep with Jet2. 'Right campers, we're now approaching your accommodation. Remember: check the toilet seat for bloody spiders,' I'd tell everyone before they disembarked the coach for two weeks of sun, sea and spider bites – now that would make a great title for a book!

Chris and I took ourselves off to the medical centre the next day to have the dressings changed.

'¡*Madre Mía!*' the nurse exclaimed when she peeled away my dressing. I've decided this must be a familiar cry of horror in Spanish health facilities. Unsurprisingly by now, she followed this up with, '*Araña.*'

Yep, it was a dirty, rotten spider that did this to me. She did a bit of squeezing of her own, and I did my damnedest not to yelp, but I was holding my breath and screaming internally. Chris received the same treatment … *Madre Mía* followed by some squeezing and a new dressing. The nurse wanted to see us daily after that first visit to check on our progress, and as she split her time between two health centres in Coín and Alhaurín El Grande, we had to make sure we turned up at the right one on the right day.

I passed my automated, online interview questions with Jet2 and was called in for an interview at their Torremolinos office. After 24 job applications (not counting the failed attempt at getting a cushy job as a golf course marshal), I was ready for my third job interview on foreign soil. On the day, I put on my jolliest Hi-de-Hi-like holiday smile and went into the interview.

One of the guys at the art class was a holiday rep for them, and I dropped his name in the conversation. There was one tricky question that didn't seem that related to the job, but other than that, I didn't think I handled the interview badly, so it was a question of waiting to see if I got selected to go on their week-long training course in Alicante.

Just in case I'd overegged it again though, I applied for job number 25 when I got home, this time with the British Consulate in Málaga, helping fellow Brits navigate Spanish officialdom if they got into difficulties, and with COVID on the horizon, I expect their switchboard was going to get busier.

47

Countdown to Lockdown

While the world was going crazy, we decided to have a weekend visiting Karen and Rick at their holiday apartment up in Murcia. This was our second visit to see them in the small seaside town of Santiago de la Ribera on the banks of the Mar Menor.

The resort seemed very quiet, even though we were still in February, but the climate on the Mar Menor is very pleasant at this time of year, with temperatures usually up in the high 50s and low 60s. This year, the weather was more like April, with the mercury hovering around 70°.

Chris was happy to see Karen, her old nursing workmate, as she could now show off her bum wound and get the sympathy she probably wasn't getting from me, as I was too busy feeling sorry for myself. My knee was starting to give me some pain while walking, so I added pain killers to my daily dose of antibiotics. With Chris dressing my wound for the next few days, Karen took over bum dressing duties.

To take our minds off our woes, our visit happily coincided with the town's *Ruta Carnavalera de la Tapa y el cóctel*, where the local tapas restaurants vie for the prestige of being chosen as the restaurant offering the best tapa dish or cocktail. This made for a very pleasant first evening on the town, strolling from bar to bar sampling their star dishes and drinks.

Diners taking part in the festival (that runs for about three weeks) are called *taperos*. You're given a map of the route and the dishes on offer, and each time you try one, your map is stamped. When you've finished participating, you can choose your favourite three tapas and the best cocktail, and if you manage to get 12 stamps on your map then you're entered into a prize draw. Doing this kind of thing takes you to tapas bars you may not have visited before, so it's a good way of discovering new restaurants.

On the Sunday, the festival culminated in a procession of floats and dancers. With this strange virus circulating around Europe now, it all seemed a bit surreal to be watching such a procession taking place. Nowhere in Europe was in lockdown as yet, and it still wasn't clear how far and wide the virus would spread, and how deadly it would prove to be.

We returned home the following day and headed back to the health centre for a dressing change and more torture. Chris's wound was healing nicely and the nurse said she didn't need to come again, but she was loving squeezing my knee so much, I was still required to turn up daily, although later that week when I arrived, the receptionist told me the nurse hadn't turned in, and I should try again tomorrow.

She still didn't turn in the next day, so either she'd had enough of looking at my puss-filled knee and decided to apply for a job as a holiday rep with Jet2, or she'd succumbed to COVID, given we'd had our first confirmed COVID case on mainland Spain the day before, and maybe she was victim number two. Or maybe she was just pulling sickies to avoid catching it in the first place.

When I arrived home untreated for a second day, Chris sent me back out to the pharmacy to buy what she needed to dress my wound herself. I wouldn't swear to it, but I'm sure there was a glint in her eye at the thought of inflicting more pain on me!

The rest of our time that week was spent mostly watching TV reports of COVID getting worse in Italy, and more cases being found across Spain, including the first confirmed case in our own small town (my nurse perhaps?!). It was all getting a little close to home now.

The old girls at art class were all getting quite nervous about the situation, and we spaced ourselves a little further apart this week. I was still trying to perfect my coloured pencil portrait techniques, with limited success. I did a portrait of my newest grandson, Theo, which turned out ok, but I was no Tomasz Schafernaker, the UK weatherman who is a master at this sort of stuff. Go and check him out – some of his portraiture is stunningly realistic.

By the weekend, it was time to get out there and have some fun again in the fresh air, so we went down to the Coín beer festival on Sunday afternoon. There was live music and a good selection of Spanish and international beers on offer. I got a bit tiddly and bought a couple of one-litre beer glasses to add to my beer glass collection. Chris stayed sober as she'd decided to drive, which saved us a walk back up the very steep hill full of ale.

By the following Friday, cases of COVID had been confirmed in all 50 of Spain's provinces, and things were starting to look serious. Two days earlier on 11th March 2020, Italy was the first European country to go into lockdown, and there were rumours that Spain would soon follow suit.

In the meantime, the new band I'd joined had scheduled to meet that night for a first proper discussion with all the confirmed band members, but we postponed it because of the rapidly deteriorating situation.

In fact, Chris told me that same day that Murcia had just confined half a million residents to their homes, thanks to the fleeing hordes from Madrid descending on their coastal holiday homes before they got locked down in the capital, in the process extending the spread of COVID. I couldn't help thinking we maybe shouldn't have gone up there ourselves last week.

Where would it all end?

48

Lockdown!

When it happened, it happened very quickly – the next day, in fact, Saturday 14th March 2020.

We had flights booked to the UK for a week in four days time, but it was looking like we wouldn't be able to get there anytime soon if we went into lockdown like Italy, and so we headed down to Fuengirola to get some e-cig supplies for Chris just in case. As a former health professional, Chris used to be a smoker, like many in that profession who regularly told their patients to stop smoking! To be fair to her, when she was home she never smoked inside the house and always went out by the back door. That considerate nature, coupled with the fact she was smoking menthol cigarettes, meant that the smell didn't linger on her clothes.

In the final few years before she kicked the habit, I was her drug dealer of choice for tobacco, as I was flying in and out of the EU every week on business, so a sleeve of 200 cigs was a regular gift when I returned home. At least the habit was costing the household budget a lot less that way, and it was the only reason I was supplying her.

Personally, I'd never been a smoker, save for the odd cigar after a black-tie dinner when the master of ceremonies would announce 'Gentlemen, you may now remove your jackets and smoke'. But even then, it was more peer pressure and doing something out of the ordinary. I had the odd cig in my youth when offered one, but it didn't really appeal to me, and nor did smoking pot, which I was also introduced to in my teens.

Chris had tried all sorts to give up in the past, from patches to hypnosis, but nothing had worked until e-cigs came along, and she quite quickly adapted to using those instead of the real thing. She also used the discrete version that didn't engulf everyone within a three-metre radius in a billowing cloud of smoke or vapour (or whatever it is that comes out the end of them). Nor was she into the crazy flavours – it was tobacco or nothing for Chris … and living with me probably made her dependent on at least one kind of drug!

We were just heading to a pharmacy for more wound dressings for my knee when the Spanish radio station we were listening to cut to an important message: the country was going into immediate lockdown!

'Oh shit!' I said, as we passed a pharmacy and looked for a place to pull in and park, just as a police car pulled out of a side street behind us. 'Are we still alright going in the pharmacy?'

'Yeah,' Chris replied. 'I don't think we're going to get locked up for that.'

'But that's the point – we ARE getting locked up, for God knows how long!'

'Well let's hurry up, get what we need and get home then.'

After a flying visit into the pharmacy, Chris drove us back up the mountain in the Mini while I scoured news websites for more information. Spain's Prime Minister, Pedro Sánchez, had just upgraded Spain's State of Emergency, the details of which were as follows:

The Spanish government has decreed a 'state of alarm' across the entire country in response to the coronavirus pandemic.

As of today, Saturday, freedom of movement will be severely restricted, with citizens required to stay at home for the next 15 days.

All of Spain's regions and autonomous communities will be put under upgraded status of alarm.

Officers will be given special powers to make 'checks' on people, goods, vehicles, buildings and establishments while the state of alarm is in effect.

The Royal Decree issued today says citizens will only be able to use public roads for the following reasons:

1 Acquisition of food, pharmaceuticals and basic necessities.

2 Visits to health centres.

3 Travel to the workplace to perform work or business-related activities.

4 Return to the place of habitual residence.

5 Assistance and care for the elderly, minors, dependents, people with disabilities or especially vulnerable people.

6 Visits to financial entities.

Due to force or need.

7 Any other activity of an analogous nature duly justified.

8 The circulation of private vehicles on public roads will only be allowed to carry out the aforementioned activities, or to refuel at petrol stations.

So that was it, we were stuffed! Locked up for 15 days. And all because some Chinaman had eaten a bat (or so we were led to believe).

And I could kiss goodbye to my new life as a holiday rep now too with the airlines grounded, as I would surely have been Jet2's first choice candidate. As it happened, I never heard back from them, but as a glass half full kind of guy, I put that down to other more important global events taking precedence over airline recruitment just at this moment, and they'd surely be itching to sign me up and give me a red blazer once this thing blows over in a couple of weeks ...

On the way home, we had a quick pitstop at an English deli to pick up a freshly made pork pie, a Cornish pasty and a custard tart for lunch as a final cheeky treat before we were confined to the house.

Arriving home, we checked the cupboards and realised we didn't have much food in, and the supermarket shelves were probably being emptied as we spoke.

'Right, I'm off out to the supermarket,' I declared. 'Any requests?'

'Staples like rice and pasta, tins of tomatoes, some meat and veg, and some cartons of long-life milk,' Chris reeled off the top of her head. 'Oh, and more facemasks and hand gel.'

I raced down to our local Mercadona supermarket, where it looked like they were running heats of *Supermarket Sweep* – but with no sign of Dale Winton – and just like old Noah had done before me, I thought two of everything would be a good idea but threw in six bottles of red wine.

I must have hand-gelled myself four times on the way from the checkout to the car ... and said a few Hail Marys for good measure! Even though I wasn't a practicing Catholic anymore, it wouldn't hurt to hedge my bets.

On the drive home I started to wonder how easily the virus was really transmitted if people were catching it left, right and centre. I knew it was respiratory, which meant droplets of air containing the virus were passing around, but did that mean that the air outside the car had COVID droplets in it? I turned off the car's aircon just in case.

Yes, I know I'm a pathetic idiot, but I wanted to remain a LIVE pathetic idiot, not a DEAD one!

As I pulled onto the driveway, Chris was standing behind the bar in the outside kitchen with her marigolds on as if she was about to operate on me.

'What are you doing?' I asked.

'I'm going to wash all the shopping in hot soapy water.'

'What, even the veg?'

'Especially the veg?'

'And the bags of crisps?'

'Yes, everything.'

'You can't wash a box of cornflakes,' I protested.

'EVERYTHING!'

Jeepers, this was serious stuff. I'd left home an hour ago and come back to find my wife had turned the simple act of putting away the shopping into a military operation.

'Where's the wine?' she asked as I was putting the last of the bags onto the bar top.

'Here,' I said, lifting a wine carrier up.

'NOT THAT SIDE!' she shouted. 'That side of the bar is for clean stuff.'

'Sorry!'

'How many bottles did you buy.'

'Six.'

'Is that all? That's not going to last till the middle of the week, never mind 15 days. And why've you bought more toilet rolls?'

'I didn't know how many we had already.'

'We've only just opened a pack of twenty-four.'

'Well there weren't many left. It was carnage in the shop. I had to wrestle an old dear for that packet. If I'm going out of here in a box, I'm not going out with a dirty bum!'

Toilet tissue was in such demand right now, I bet Lou Rawls was getting a lot of hits on Google!

'Where's the meat?'

'Ah! There was no chicken or mince meat anywhere. I even drove up to Carrefour where I spotted some chicken breasts behind the meat counter so took a ticket, and there were 90 numbers before mine! So I knocked it on the head and bought a pre-packed chorizo instead.'

With a full lockdown now in place and international travel banned, we wouldn't be flying to the UK next week anymore. Nor would my parents be flying back with us for a holiday. Rachel also had flights booked to come and visit us soon, and no doubt that was likely to get cancelled.

Later that evening, I messaged Tony the bad news about us being locked down in case he hadn't heard yet.

'Sounds grim,' he replied. 'Keep safe. It's all fine and dandy in the UK. Just been to the pub and it was rammed. Don't know what all the fuss is about.'

With comments that like, he could have been Boris Johnson's Press Secretary!

'Don't be surprised if this time next week you're in lockdown over there, too,' I felt confident prophesizing – although, as happened, Boris was able to delay the inevitable for another nine days while he released all the old people from hospital so the could pass it round the nursing homes and cull a few thousand state pension payments.

'Right, you've convinced me. We're going panic buying tomorrow,' Tony said.

'Don't tell Chris I said so, but don't forget loo roll – that'll be the first thing to fly off the shelves when the shit hits the fan!' which seemed a rather fitting way to describe the situation.

'Have you got plenty of wine and gin?' Tony asked.

'A case of beer, nineteen bottles of wine (sorry … make that seventeen now) and one and a half bottles of gin.'

'Buy a fishing rod,' he joked.

'They had none in Aldi. They were even limiting trombones to one per household – that's how bad it is here!'

'Can you get me a trombone before they run out?'

You can't beat a bit of British, stiff-upper-lip humour in the middle of a global crisis.

The weekend passed with us glued to the TV (and counting down our wine stocks). There didn't seem to be any good news anywhere … other than the UK's annual Cheltenham Festival – a four-day horse racing bonanza – was in full swing and very well attended, no doubt with people coughing and spluttering all over each other!

In fact, the only silver lining to this very grey cloud was that I'd had the presence of mind to have a haircut when I got back from Murcia, believing it wouldn't be long before we got locked down. Readers may recall I like to wear my hair short and spiky, so the last thing I wanted was to come out the other side looking like Chris Waddle in the 80s!

A few days into our Spanish lockdown, it was becoming clearer what the lockdown rules meant in practice. You were confined to your own town, and a trip to the shop for groceries was limited to one person per household. As Chris didn't trust me to wash the shopping properly, I was the nominated shopper.

We were also allowed to collect our mail, as houses in the *campo* don't get mail deliveries to the house. However, since moving to Coín five months earlier, we hadn't moved our PO Box from Alhaurín, and I wasn't sure if that allowed to me to go there if I now lived in Coín. We hadn't been to check the post for at least six weeks, so I thought I'd chance it, just in case there was a literary contract waiting for me!

Things didn't bode well when I got to the end of the lane to join the main road that cuts between the two towns. There was a *Guardia Civil* officer writing out a fine to some old bloke who had ventured out for a walk. If he'd had a dog with him, and his house was nearby, and the dog hadn't done its business yet, he would have been allowed to walk until the dog had done a whoopsie in its favourite spot, but then he would have had to turn round and go home again. No dog? No whoopsie? No can do!

I furtively headed towards Alhaurín when I came off the main road, keeping my eyes peeled for roadblocks. Happily, I made it into town without coming across one. I picked up some mail nipped in the pharmacy and was heading back when I policeman flagged me down in the centre of Alhaurín.

'*¿Dónde va?*' he demanded to know.

I told him I was on my way to do my shopping at Mercadona. He countered by asking me why I'd literally just driven past the road that leads to Mercadona's underground car park. Quick as a flash, I told him I didn't want to use the lift from the car park due to COVID and was planning to park on the road at the front of the shop instead. He paused to mull over my response and then waved me on. Phew! Thank God he didn't ask for my name, as I might have panicked and forgotten to give it him the wrong way round.

He watched me as I took the exit from the roundabout that took me past the front of the shop. I sailed straight by it and chose a different route out of the town centre. Thinking I may have to do this trip again in the future, I spent 20 minutes trying to find a route home through the *campo* that would allow me to avoid the key roundabouts where a roadblock was likely to be positioned, but to no avail – they were all dead ends, thanks to the Rio Fahala crossing my path at every turn.

'Any post?' Chris asked as soon as I returned.

'Just your credit card statement.'

'Is there any *good* news?'

'Yeah, the Eurovision Song Contest has just been cancelled.'

I was glad to be home and not dodging the police anymore. At least there'd been no roadblocks, or I may have been led away in handcuffs. I went indoors to do my Spanish homework for later. Our Spanish lessons had moved online due to the lockdown, of course. Interesting fact: did you know the Spanish for handcuffs is *esposas*, the same word they use for wives?! Pure coincidence? You decide.

When the weekend arrived, I settled down to watch some live music on Facebook. A musical couple on the coast had organized a two-day online music festival called Rock The Lock Down to keep everyone entertained. Musicians and singers of all abilities had nominated themselves for a slot, and it all went remarkably smoothly, with some great performances. Afterwards, people continued to post videos of themselves performing, and it helped to cheer everyone up and let them focus on something positive.

Meanwhile, in the UK, Boris was under increasing pressure to implement his own nationwide lockdown. My brother, Mike, had driven up from the Isle of Wight to Manchester to visit Mum on her birthday. Then Boris went on telly, wished her a happy birthday and declared a national lockdown. Mike rang Mum and Dad and told them they had an hour to pack their bags, as he was taking them back to the Isle of Wight for the duration of lockdown. A week later, the ferry service linking the UK mainland to the Isle of Wight was suspended.

They had a lovely holiday down there. The weather was great, and Mike and Ann had a big house and garden with a swimming pool. They were almost certainly much safer in that isolated island environment than being up in Manchester, so we were relieved they were being taken good care of.

The weather in Málaga meanwhile was bloody awful. At least it kept the Spaniards indoors, and overall, compliance with the rules in Spain was adhered to and policed 100 times better than it appeared to be in the UK.

Tony pinged me a message to see how we were doing.

'It's Day 14 in the Big Brother House,' I replied. 'Drew is growing restless as the weather is shit. Meanwhile, Chris is in the Diary Room worrying about her roots showing. Other than that we're fine - well stocked with essentials like wine and crisps. How about you?'

I left him to read it out to himself in a Geordie accent.

'We're all good,' he replied. 'Awaiting a delivery of wine from Laithwaites.'

It was nice to see that we'd both got the essentials covered!

Online shopping was much more advanced in the UK than in Spain, although the pandemic sparked a bit of entrepreneurial spirit here, and a few people started to offer a delivery service on their mopeds.

Ten days after Spain locked down, the official death toll here from COVID surpassed that of China – although there was little confidence in what China had been reporting as, according to the newspapers, they'd been trying to hush it up for months.

I was starting to get a little paranoid about catching it now, so I went out and bought a temperature scanner. Then the press were telling us that low blood oxygen levels were a key symptom of having contracted the disease, and so I was off to the pharmacy again to pay over the odds for a bloody pulse oximeter – at this rate, we'd be able to open our own sodding medical clinic!

There was nothing we could do but hunker down for a bit while the boffins came up with a reliable vaccine, I suppose.

Back in the UK, schools were closed, and most people were either off work or "working from home" (yeah, right). With nothing much better to do, and with the sun shining, they were probably sat in the garden all day getting steadily pissed whilst trying to teach maths and geography to their kids before realising what a shit job teachers must have trying to teach their unruly offspring. So I reckon in about 20-30 years, the country's going to be being run by kids who were homeschooled by alcoholics – which would probably be an improvement on our current politicians.

My car was due its ITV test (Spanish MOT) this month too, but that got cancelled when they closed all the test centres. The insurance company wrote saying not to worry, it wouldn't invalidate my insurance, and the government confirmed that they wouldn't issue fines for noncompliance while there was a state of alarm in place, which was a relief.

During the early part of the lockdown, Alhaurín El Grande had yet another bout of severe flooding, and the videos of cars smashing into each other like bowling skittles as they were washed down the steep narrow streets looked even worse than last time. Jeepers, we were living through Armageddon! I wondered if I shouldn't order a bible from Amazon for my Kindle and start reading the Book of Revelation.

Whilst we'd been in the Dominican Republic at the start of the year they'd had a similar bout, so this was three severe flooding events in the space of the last seven months! At least this time we were spared the cleanup operation at our villa in Coín. The pool was full, of course, but apart from that, there was no other damage or cleanup needed.

What on earth is going on with the world? And what else could possibly go wrong?

49

Medical Mysteries

Well, this …

'Do the COVID symptoms include lumps under your armpit?' I asked Chris.

'It's respiratory, so unless you've grown a pair of lungs under there, then no. Why? What's up?'

'Erm … the clue was in the question ... I've got lumps under my armpit.'

Chris inspected two lumps under my left armpit and couldn't explain their sudden appearance.

'I don't know what's caused those. Best go and see the GP.'

'Do you reckon it's a side effect of the spider bite?'

'No, nothing to do with your spider bite.'

I wasn't convinced, so spent the rest of the day googling spider bite side effects. Remarkably, nobody else had previously recorded such a link between the two conditions, but I wasn't being put off – maybe I was the first such patient and would forever more be known as "Patient Zero" and be classified as medical mystery.

The GP pooh-poohed my spider bite theory too and gave me some antibiotics and ointment. I'm surrounded by sceptics. Maybe I've just got COVID, and I'm the first ever concurrent COVID and spider bite victim, and this is how it manifests itself. The possibilities are endless.

With the treatment, the smaller lump shrank quite quickly and didn't hurt, while the larger lump became quite painful.

developing a head that burst, releasing some pus, but then healing up after a short time. As you might have expected, nurse Chris delighted in squeezing this new lump on my body – it was her favourite sport since she wasn't allowed out of the house to find her own entertainment.

Three weeks later, another lump appeared under the same armpit, which had me running off to the GP again for more antibiotics. He gave me a different type this time, and they didn't work at all. Within a week, the lump had grown at least twice as large as the previous one. It was extremely red and angry, and the pain when Chris got her hands on it was excruciating – I was having to do some heavy breathing between squeezes! In addition to lots of pus, there were white, hard lumpy bits coming out too. I went back to the doctor and begged him for some more of the original antibiotics and he relented. They alleviated the problem gradually over the coming week, and the relief was palpable.

While I was still treating this second outbreak, another lump cropped up above my groin. Shit! These things are working their way south on my body … probably in an effort to join up with the spider bite host on my knee! Thankfully, this new lump didn't have time to develop into anything serious and the antibiotics killed it early on.

However, just as the antibiotic course finished, a lump appeared under my other armpit. Although I'd finished the course of antibiotics, the box had some extra tablets – as did the first box of the same stuff – so I cut out the middlemen (GP and pharmacist) and started another course of antibiotics, and that seemed to sort it out again.

Two more lumps appeared three weeks later again, one on my bicep and another on the side of my chest. This time, I had no spare antibiotics and couldn't get an appointment with the GP for nine days, so I just had to rely on the ointment I had. Maybe I should start block-booking GP appointments every few days and cancel them the day before if I'm lump free! This wasn't good, though, clearly.

When I got to see the doc, he arranged a blood test and stool sample. My bloods were fine – in the peak of physical fitness apart from a gammy, spider-bitten knee (that was still being dressed regularly by nurse Chris) and a pock-marked body! The brown stuff was also an excellent sample, apparently. This time the lumps didn't get any bigger, and they disappeared after a while.

Then, guess what happened ... Chris got a lump like mine under her armpit – I KNEW it was that bloody spider. Now the medical fraternity couldn't ignore us any longer, surely!

Just as she got hers, I got two more bloody sore ones on my left moob and left shoulder. With all the holes in my body, I was starting to look like a bloody colander! The doc scratched his head in disbelief, then gave me a longer course of antibiotics and a different ointment. He also prescribed me some probiotics because my immune system will have been collapsing in on itself quicker than a pile of Jenga bricks.

He was kind enough to let Chris have a few happy pills too. Chris, however, wouldn't let me squeeze her spot, which I thought was a bit mean, as she'd been having hours of fun playing Whac-A-Mole with mine for weeks!

You're probably getting as fed up with these lumps now as I was at the time, so we'll skip over lumps 9 to 13 and cut to the chase ... when lumps 14 and 15 appeared to put me in serious pain again, I got an appointment with a dermatologist instead of the GP, and they were finally able to come up with a rational diagnosis to dispel my spider bite theory once and for all ... I had Hidradenitis Suppurativa ... I know, what the hell's that?

According to our very own NHS in the UK, the condition is characterised by boil-like lumps, blackheads, cysts, scarring and channels in the skin that leak pus. It tends to start with blackheads, spots filled with pus and firm pea-sized lumps that develop in one place.

EUREKA! That's exactly what I've got. But I was none the wiser why I'd suddenly developed this awful condition, other than because of that BLOODY SPIDER!!

It had only taken five months to get there, but now I had a name for my affliction – there was even an online support group and everything! I imagine they all meet up annually to compare war stories round a campfire. It was a relief to find out I wasn't alone (and Chris didn't have any reoccurrence of hers, thankfully), but the long-term prognosis didn't make for happy reading.

'According to this website, I could be in for a lifetime of pain and misery,' I sobbed to Chris.

'A bit like our marriage, then!' she joked, although I knew she loved me really (I think).

My condition continued to flare up for a couple of months, but with much smaller lumps and less frequently – maybe it knew we'd pinned it down, and it was finally giving up the ghost. I got another appointment with a different dermatologist, and she suggested going for laser treatment under the armpits, as she believed the infections were appearing in my hair follicles.

So, although many of the more recent lumps had not been under the armpits (or anywhere near a group of hair follicles), what did I have to lose? And it was only €9 per session (and a fiver in petrol as the clinic was miles away). I'm happy to report that, whilst undergoing laser treatment (which continued for about two years), the lumps didn't return. That could have been pure coincidence, but regardless, I'M CURED, and I could kiss a stranger in the street (once this COVID thing has blown over, of course!).

50

Going Stir Crazy

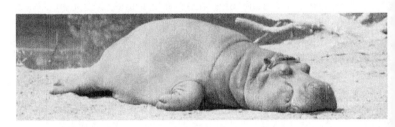

Lockdown was getting boring now. Apart from my regular dance with the devil trying to get the shopping in without bringing back a deadly virus – and now my periodic GP visits – there wasn't much to do.

We soon got fed up watching news reports of the death toll climbing the world over, and we weren't allowed out for exercise, unlike everyone in the UK, who were all out walking, running, cycling and buying pets ... or driving up to Barnard Castle to test their eyesight. We couldn't go anywhere that wasn't essential to our survival.

On 2nd April 2020, Spain recorded 950 deaths in a single day, the most of any country to date. On 3rd April, the FCO cancelled all recruitment, so that was my chance of a job at the British Consulate up the swanny too.

Oh dear. What to do? I know, let's organise a family quiz night.

'What app are we using?' I asked the girls on our family WhatsApp group.

'Zoom,' our tech savvy daughter, Andrea, replied.

'Haven't got that, and I don't fancy downloading it. It's Chinese. Probably comes with a free virus! I've got Skype, and your mum's got something called House Party.'

'Don't need to download anything. Just use your web browser.'

'OK. Let's hope we don't get zoombombed by a sex pest.'

Zoombombing was a new phenomenon on the Zoom video sharing app. Zoom had taken off big time since lockdown started, and it turned out it wasn't as robust as it wanted us to believe. It was being criticised for a range of privacy issues, like saying it used end-to-end-encryption when it didn't, and it shared user data with Facebook. But anyone and everyone was getting on it to keep in touch with friends and family. However, like anything on the web, you get undesirable characters who just want to exploit the technology, and Zoom video calls were being gatecrashed by pillocks who wanted to flash their willy or shout abuse at you.

It didn't help when idiots like Boris Johnson were tweeting pictures of a Zoom call that included the nine-digit call reference number for any Tom, Dick or Hooray Henry to pile on with their willies hanging out! Although, being a politician, he's probably used to seeing people with their willies hanging out at the kind of parties they reportedly like attending. And these are the people running the country and keeping us safe – God help us!

As you'd expect, everyone had problems connecting to Andrea's Zoom meeting, with them all using different email providers, web browsers and hardware. After an infinite amount of toing and froing and waiting for everyone to get their dinners on the table, we got underway and had lots of fun, considering the world was gripped by a pandemic. It was a little light relief from watching the death toll shoot up.

There was lots of banter going on as the whole family is so competitive, and our eldest, Steph, and her teenage daughters won the quiz. Odd that, I thought.

'I want a recount,' I moaned. 'Funny how Steph kept disappearing off the call! I even learnt the names of the bloody seven dwarves, and it never came up. I did more revision for this than I did for my 'O' Levels in 1980!'

I was branded a sore loser and had to take it on the chin. And poor Corrinne and her family went to bed hungry as Pizza Hut failed to deliver their dinner. They got a knock on the door from the pizza delivery man at 11:35pm when they were all in bed, and he was told in no uncertain terms to go and stuff his stuffed crust where the sun doesn't shine.

This was also the time of peak meme – an image, video, piece of text, etc., typically humorous in nature, that is copied and spread rapidly by internet users. Facebook was also full of crap and conspiracy theories, not helped by Donald Trump suggesting his medical experts look into whether injecting people with disinfectant could cure them of COVID! And if you think I've just made that last bit up, go and check for yourself if you don't believe me.

One meme I saw illustrated all the tosh perfectly, and went something like this:

This is what Facebook sounds like: The Germans invented 5G so they could use bats to spread chemtrails to distract you from the lizard paedophile ring in the monarchy. However, the Chinese caught the bats and used them to send telepathic viruses to humans to control the population. Prince Charles wrote to the House of Lords to say he had Coronavirus because Charles himself flew both planes into the world trade centre because his dog got autism from William's MMR vaccination and Jimmy Saville cured cancer but kept the cure secret. He kept it secret because Paul McCartney died in 1969, and John Lennon faked his own death to become TuPac.

Enough said! The world's gone mad and millions of people are talking bollocks.

Our son-in-law, Graham, started up a gardening business while all this was going on. The UK were having great spring weather, and of course everyone wanted to be outdoors, but they soon realised how shoddy their gardens were. We were alright, as we had a pool and outside bar and dining area, but we couldn't use it as the weather here was still awful, the pool was cold, and we needed a patio heater to sit outside in the evening. Somehow this Coronavirus appeared to have messed with the global weather patterns too (only joking – don't go starting another conspiracy theory along those lines).

When we did get a dry day, I walked five kilometres round the garden one afternoon whilst reading my Kindle. Now, I'm not bragging, we don't live on an estate with a five-kilometre perimeter, I just walked a 25-metre stretch of the garden 200 times, liked a caged tiger.

Despite me wishing we could go out of the house together and get some exercise, I had to feel sorry for my sister, Janet, who would normally be helping her two daughters with childcare duties. As it stood, she was resigned to only seeing the grandkids through the window of a car.

While we westerners were feeling sorry for ourselves, ordering takeaway meals and having Zoom calls, spare a thought for the remote African villages during all this. The Ugandan community I sponsored were short of food, so we organised several rounds of fundraising to buy them staples such as poshu and more livestock to support themselves. They'd gone into lockdown one week after the UK, and it must have been an awful time for them. All the kids were sent home from school, and so where they would normally have been being fed at school, there wasn't enough food at home for them. We did our best to make sure essential food supplies got through to them, and we continued supporting them with weekly food drops until the lockdown had ended.

Back in Spain, after seven weeks of being confined to our properties, the Spanish government announced a small concession – we could all go out and exercise – whoopidoo! This would be a blessed relief for a population complying with Europe's strictest lockdown restrictions. However, different age groups had to leave and return to their home within specified time parameters, according to the following strict instructions:

Adults may take a stroll either alone or with one other member of their household, as long as they remain within a one-kilometre radius of their home.

Adults may also go out for individual exercise – such as running or cycling – once a day, without making contact with third parties, and with no limit on how far citizens can go, as long as they remain within the same municipality. All kinds of sports are allowed as long as they are practiced individually.

Both walks and exercise must take place between 6am and 10am, or between 8pm and 11pm.

In a bid to minimize crowds and protect at-risk groups, such as seniors, the government has set time slots for outdoor activity.

Adults are allowed to go outside between 6am and 10am, o
between 8pm and 11pm; children between 12pm and 7pm; an
people who need to go out with a caregiver and seniors over 7
years of age have their own time slots of 10am to 12pm and 7p
to 8pm.

Following the news we could go for a walk, I went online t
find a free map drawing tool that would draw me a map with ou
house in the centre of a circle with a one-kilometre radius.

'Right,' I said to Chris, who hadn't stepped foot outside th
property for seven weeks now, leaving me to do all the hazardou
shopping trips after which she strip-searched me for viruses, 'w
can walk up to the woods, turn left and walk along that first lan
in the woods.'

'Can we go to the *Nacimiento* and do a loop?' she asked. Th
Nacimiento was a local landmark with a duck pond that feature
on a popular circular route from our house.

'No, that's 300 metres outside the circle, I'm afraid. We'
have to just go to the end of the circle and then come back th
same way.'

It turned out a one-kilometre radius was quite restrictive whe
you lived in the *campo*.

'What if we run?'

'You can go to the *Nacimiento* if you run, but if you'r
walking, then you can't. And I haven't run that far since we di
the Edinburgh 10k four years ago.'

'What if we walk to the edge of the radius and then run th
last 300 metres to the *Nacimiento*.'

'Sorry. No running in pairs. We'd have to split up if we run.'

'Bugger, we'll just have to walk to the one-kilometre lim
and back then.'

We waited until 8pm on the dot that night and then set off.
was really weird seeing other people out walking in pairs. Wit
Chris not having seen a soul for seven weeks, I was worried sh
might rush over to touch someone to check they were real, bu
she didn't, thankfully. It was very liberating though, and imagir
how good this must have felt to all those poor people who'd bee
cooped up in an apartment block.

When we'd gone about as far as we were allowed, you could almost see the *Nacimiento* further down the hill.

'Shall we risk it and carry on?' Chris asked. 'I can't see the *Guardia Civil* patrolling the *Nacimiento*.'

I tried to put on a Clint Eastwood accent for my reply.

'You've got to ask yourself one question. Do I feel lucky? Well, do you, punk?'

Even though I wasn't pointing a .44 Magnum at her, the most powerful handgun in the world, that would blow her head clean off, Chris made the right decision, and we started to go back the way we'd come.

We soon spotted the lower path down on our right that we would normally follow back from the *Nacimiento*. There was a rough-hewn path down the steep hill, probably made by cyclists and walkers making a shortcut in the past.

'Let's go down here and take the other path back,' I suggested.

This was a much nicer route back, and didn't break the rules. There was more to look at and appreciate in the countryside (including the barking dogs every 50 yards guarding their properties). We took the drainage subway under the main road and continued along the path, past some remote houses and small farms, skirting the fields at the bottom, and we eventually emerged on another lane close to home.

'Ooh, look … there's a honkey!' I exclaimed with glee.

'A what?'

'A honkey. You know, a cross between a horse and a donkey.'

'No, you pillock, they're called mules! They come from breeding a male donkey with a female horse.'

'Oh! Well, maybe this one's a honkey, from a horsey dad and a donkey mum.'

'I think you'll find they're called hinnies, hun.'

'Well, I've definitely heard of a honkey.'

'I think that's what Huggy Bear from Starsky and Hutch used to call white people.'

'Oh, yeah. Maybe you're right.'

'There's no *maybe* about it – I know I'm right.'

And here endeth the first lesson!

We went home and jumped in the pool, which was finally warm enough. With the air temperature hitting 31° today, the pool was finally up to my new lower limit of 24°, which was about 10° warmer than that time I sat in the pool at the other house for an hour showing off and ended up with a mild case of hypothermia.

And now that we were exercising again (if you can call a two-kilometre walk exercise), I decided to bake my favourite cake the next day, a coffee and walnut cake covered in butter cream, which I ended up eating entirely on my own as Chris isn't a fan. Oops, sorry!

51

A Novel Idea

'I've got a great idea for a novel,' I said to Chris.

'You haven't finished the first one yet.'

'I have. It's all good to go when it lands on the right desk.'

'How many agents have you sent it to so far?'

'Twenty-five.'

'And how many rejections have you had?'

'Eleven. The other fourteen are probably giving it some serious consideration as we speak.'

'If you say so. Anyway, what's your idea for the new one?'

'Well, I'll probably write a sequel to the first novel, but after that I'm gonna write one called *Terminal Vigilantes*.'

'What's that about then? Someone going round smashing up computer terminals.'

'Noooo, don't be daft. It's about people diagnosed with a terminal illness. Some shady government department is tipped off about their diagnosis. They research the candidate and see if they've been the victim of a grave injustice in the past.'

'Like what?'

'Well, let's say some guy's daughter was murdered years ago, and the murderer got off with it or received a light sentence. With a few months left to live, what he wouldn't give to see that scumbag killed before he pops his clogs, eh? But the thought hasn't really occurred to him, and even if it has, he wouldn't know where to start. I know *I'd* want to do it if I could. So the agent gets him chatting in the pub and convinces him he can help him deliver some rough justice at last.'

'And what does this shady government department get out of it?'

'Well, in return for kidnapping the murderer, taking him to a remote location, and letting the dad deliver some brutal punishment before killing him, the dad has to promise to do something for the agent afterwards in return.'

'And what's that then?'

'Assassinate a prominent politician, a kill that has positive geopolitical ramifications for the UK.'

'What, like the president of the US?'

'Exactly – especially the current one! They train and arm the guy, get him in the place to do it, and he's happy to do it, of course, even though he's likely to get killed in the process. After all, he's going out of here in a box soon anyway. Hence the title *Terminal Vigilantes* – vigilantes with a terminal illness.'

'Not a bad idea, but let's see how you get on with the first novel, eh? I thought you wanted to be a holiday rep anyway?'

'Nah. The travel industry will be on its knees for years now. Writing's much more fun.'

'Holiday reps get paid, though.'

'Don't worry about that. There's money in writing. I just need a break.'

'And how many jobs have you applied for so far?'

'The same as agent submissions, twenty-five.'

'And you haven't got one yet.'

'No, so statistically, I've got a one-hundred percent rejection rate from the job market, and so far, only a forty-four-percent rejection rate from literary agents.'

'So you think you're doing better with literary agents, do you?'

'The statistics don't lie.'

'I wish I had your optimism.'

'Hey kid, what've I always said? Stick with me, I'll make you famous!'

'Well, you'd better get back in the office and carry on writing then.'

I went back to the office and fired up my laptop. Despite the agent rejections, I had been feeling more positive of late. Over the last 18 months, I'd kept in contact with Major Michael Jenkins MBE, the army veteran and author. I'd read the first two books in his trilogy, and after sending him some valuable feedback on those ones, he'd asked me to be one of his beta readers on the third instalment. I was absolutely thrilled to be in a position to offer him some independent feedback.

Now, you've probably realised by now that I don't do things half-heartedly – when I do a job, I do a proper job – and so, after completing the beta reader questionnaire that was distributed, I went on to pretty much do a copyedit of the book, also referring back to character threads from the first two books where I felt there was perhaps some inconsistency in the backstories.

When he'd had chance to go through all my comments, he sent a very appreciative reply in return.

'Wow! This is superb feedback, Drew. I'm gobsmacked! You have no idea how much this helps (well you probably do!), but this is so, so helpful, very accurate, and incredibly detailed, which an author needs. It's a lonely journey, so beta reader feedback like this is awesome. I'm looking forward to adjusting a few things now in the coming weeks. Thanks so much, you deserve lots of beer from me!'

Sadly, with him in Wales and me in Spain, and a travel ban in place, I wouldn't be able to share a beer with him anytime soon, something I would have loved to have done. Sitting down and chewing the espionage fat with a man of his background and stature would have been an absolute thrill for someone like me, although he probably wouldn't have been able to tell me much, as I don't think the official secrets act has an expiry date.

In fact, he was so thrilled with my input, in the same email he told me he'd just recovered the rights back from his publisher to the first book in the trilogy, and he wanted to put out an updated second edition. But first, he wanted me to copyedit it. He must really think I have a talent for this kind of work, and I couldn't have been happier – it was a real boost to my confidence.

He offered to send me a crate of good wine for my efforts, but living in Spain as I do, surrounded by great wine, that would have been like taking coal to Newcastle, as they say in the northeast. Seeing him succeed was reward enough for me, and if he was able to give me some more military advice over time then all well and good.

For me, reading another author's work and being able to provide useful feedback to them is such a rewarding thing to do and especially so in the middle of a pandemic, as it takes your mind off all the things you'd normally be sat around worrying about that you can't control.

Before I did anything else though, after being locked down for seven weeks, I was badly in need of a haircut, but we weren't allowed to go to the barbers. I could have a go at the front myself, but with the best will in the world, I'd have no chance of taking a pair of scissors to the back of my head without ending up in A&E. Sadly, I got rid of the clippers I used to own when we left the UK – Steph used to come round and do my hair as she was an ex-hairdresser turned nurse, so could cut my hair *and* treat me for cuts if the razor slipped!

'Chris?' I shouted across the garden.

'What?' came a cry from the far end of the pool.

'Can you cut my hair for me, please?'

'Are you serious? Aren't you worried I'll make a mess of it?'

'Well, it's either that, or you're going to be married to a man with a mullet.'

'Oh God, no, go get me your clippers?'

'I gave them away, back in the UK.'

'Then how am I supposed to give you a short back and sides?'

'There's a little pop-up trimmer on my electric razor.'

'Are you having a laugh?! You want me to cut your hair with a little moustache trimmer? You must really trust me.'

'You'll be fine.'

Chris got out of the pool, dried herself off and wandered over.

'What about the top bit?' she asked, poking and prodding at my bonce.

'You can do that bit with scissors.'

'But I've never cut hair before, apart from my own fringe from time to time.'

'Don't worry. I'll give you some instructions.'

'But *you've* never cut anyone's hair before, either? What makes you qualified to give me instructions?'

'I've been in the chair a thousand times – I know what they do. They wet it, comb it up in all directions, run it through two fingers and then cut round the fingers. It's dead easy.'

It wasn't dead easy!

Nor was trying to cut thick clumps of hair off with a pop-up moustache trimmer – it kept jamming in my hair. When she'd finished hacking at my head, I put a few photos on the family WhatsApp group.

'Aw, well done, Mum. You've done a good job there,' one of the kids commented.

'You don't know what I asked for,' I replied.

'What did you ask for?'

'Well, I didn't ask to look like John Lydon!'

'Who's he?'

'Lead singer with the Sex Pistols,' I said.

'Never heard of them.'

Bloody Millennials, I thought – they're all culturally dead after about 1980.

I gave up and went back to the office to lose myself in a good book. Soon afterwards, I was able to send my author friend my analysis and recommendations for a second edition of book one, and he was again thrilled with my input.

'Blimey, Drew. Just going through your notes and amending. Superb stuff, you really know your onions – you ought to be a copyeditor.'

Having now dipped my toe in that water, it was something I'd be keen to do professionally, so at some point, I need to do some research on that, perhaps, and maybe get a qualification. In the meantime, I needed to get back to editing my own novel one more time.

In the words of the author Virgina Woolf, 'writing is like sex. First you do it for love, then you do it for you friends, and then you do it for money.'

How true!

Now, in the words of Jerry Maguire, 'SHOW ME THE MONEEEEEYYYY!'

52

Going Out

'Shall we go down to the coast?' Chris asked.

Málaga province had just eased the restrictions slightly, and so long as the residents of Coín didn't raise the COVID incidence rate above the threshold, we'd be allowed out of our municipality at last.

'Yeah. Let's go to Fuengirola for a walk along the prom and fish and chips at The Crispy Cod.'

We probably had fish and chips on the coast as a treat only a couple of times a year, and this time it felt like it would be an extra special treat. Plus, the weather had finally bucked up and stopped raining. We rang ahead, as you had to book one of the limited tables outside.

When we got down there, I thought we'd misinterpreted the easing of the measures – it felt like we'd just stepped into a film set for the remake of *28 Days Later*.

We hadn't passed any roadblocks, but the place was like a ghost town. The beach was cordoned off with tape, and there was hardly a soul walking along the prom. Those that were out and about had to follow the blue, painted signs on the floor that reminded you to remain two metres apart.

If you wanted to walk east, then you had to walk along the promenade adjacent to the beach. And if you wanted to walk west, you had to walk on the other side of the road alongside the shops and cafes.

The fish and chips were well worth the wait. It was our first meal out in three months, and if I was to get hit by a bus on my way home, then I would have died a happy man. As far as last meals go, fish and chips has to be up there with a Sunday roast dinner.

Today was also made noteworthy by Andalucía not registering any more new COVID cases.

Lockdown measures were also easing in the UK, with the government saying it was time to unlock and trust the common sense of the British people, just at a time when a man had entered the *Guinness Book of Records* by sticking nine creme eggs up his bum! Yeah, the British are known for their common sense, clearly. Even the government couldn't be trusted as they kept holding drinks parties in the garden of Number 10.

At least my brother, Mike, could finally take Mum and Dad back up to Manchester, two months after he'd driven them down to the Isle of Wight, which was probably a bit longer than he expected to be entertaining them. The main thing is he'd kept them safe and sound and virus free (and cemented his place as #1 son too, probably … grrr!).

The following week, on 1st June, Spain was able to report no new COVID deaths, which seemed like a significant milestone, and maybe a turning point in the pandemic. I had some more good news that day too: I received feedback on my writing from someone who knew what they were talking about. It turned out that my friend from Árchez, Martin, had a sister who was formerly a professional proofreader, and she'd agreed to review my novel for me.

It was very kind of her, considering the material wasn't in her preferred reading genre, but she did a great job of highlighting things that I could improve. This information will be invaluable in avoiding the same errors as I continue to write, which will of course benefit you, the reader, too. So on your behalf, dear readers, I sent Judith a few nice gifts by way of a thank you.

Judith even thought the book was "screen worthy", and Martin agreed, saying that when he'd read the novel himself, he'd been picturing Jason Statham as the main protagonist. Wow! Hollywood here I come! Jason? If you're reading this, contact my agent – if I ever get one! (did I mention you're my favourite actor?)

To celebrate my impending stardom, we went for another walk, and this time, with no distance restrictions, we continued as far as the duck pond at the *Nacimiento* before returning home through the fields, although there was no sign of the honkey/mule/hinny (delete as appropriate).

The mood had lightened significantly that week, and the members of our new band decided it was time to meet up for the first time. Still concerned about COVID transmission, we met outside in a public space and sat on the grass with a beer getting to know each other a little better.

There were some new faces from that first meeting we'd had in Málaga back in February, but everyone was friendly and eager to get started. However, given the practicalities still of rehearsing in a confined space, we decided we'd start life as a "virtual" band, collaborating online only as we wrote our first songs – it was safer that way and would give us something to actually play the first time we met up for a rehearsal at some date in the future.

As Spain was opening up more and more, they allowed barbers to start up again. I was looking even more like John Lydon these days, with my hair growing to different lengths in all directions, so I booked myself in for a much-needed haircut. It was maybe the best €9 I've ever spent! I was so happy, I stopped at a café on my way back and treated myself to a plate of churros and chocolate.

My friends in the Nkuringo community in Uganda were unable to enjoy such luxuries, regardless of the fact they were still locked down. I'm sure they don't know what churros are, but I know the kids would love them warm and smothered in chocolate sauce. Gotta be tastier than poshu, right?!

53

Going Out Out

The phrase "Going Out Out" was coined by Micky Flanagan years ago, way before anyone knew what a lockdown was, or had ever heard of a furlough scheme, much less understood what it was – although getting paid 80% of your wages for sitting at home on your backside watching Netflix was something everyone soon got used to, and they were understandably horrified when they had to go back into work to earn their salary again.

"Going Out Out" was how the cockney comedian described nipping out for a drink in the afternoon, but eventually staying out all night getting pissed.

On 21st June 2020, 14 weeks after we were locked down, the Spanish state of alarm was lifted, and we were finally going out out!

The original state of alarm had only covered the first two weeks of lockdown, and it was renewed consecutively six times hereafter. But now everyone was free at last to go anywhere in the country. You could just see the divorce lawyers rubbing their hands as they were about to be inundated with new business after thousands of wives had discovered they'd actually married a layabout. [Don't even *think* about it Chris!]

We had to continue wearing a face mask on public transport and in enclosed public spaces where we couldn't remain 1.5 metres apart, but other than that, we were let loose.

And Spain was even allowing British tourists back into the country without needing to self-isolate. I'm not sure whether that's a good idea or not, knowing how reckless British holidaymakers can be, especially after at least three months without a holiday, and with oodles of cash sitting around after being furloughed and not being able to go out and spend it. We might be getting the tourist pound back into the economy, but I suspect they'll be bringing a lot more than cash with them and we'd be locked down again before you knew it.

'It says here that we are now living in a phase called the "new normality",' I said to Chris over my brew that morning.

'Well you've got no chance then, as you've never been normal.'

'And I'm not about to start now, either.'

But if I'm not normal, then I must be abnormal, I thought. I checked the dictionary definition to see what that really meant and discovered that someone abnormal is considered "unusual" especially in a way that is "worrying". I didn't like the sound of that at all – it made me sound like the village idiot, and although I walked a bit fast sometimes, my feet weren't pointing at ten-to two like our own resident village idiot in Coín … and I wasn't in the habit of shouting at passing cars like him either. So I continued reading and found a definition further down that I was much happier with … from now on, I was to be known as someone who was "extraordinary" – yep, I'll have a bit of that!

By way of celebrating the end of a national lockdown, we set off for a lunchtime walk, through the fields where the honkers lived, bypassed the *Nacimiento* and wandered down to the first bar we came across. We had a nice cold beer at the first place, then carried on walking to the next bar, where we had a glass of wine from a bottle that tasted like it had probably been opened on the day lockdown started, so of course, we had no option but to move onto somewhere better.

We then headed into town to one of our usual haunts and had some tapas and another drink (or two) … just what you might call a selfless act in support of our local economy! At this point we were going to walk home again, but it would have been a shame to waste a beautiful afternoon by having a siesta, so we set off again down the next little backstreet and found a bar we hadn't visited before. This one served olives on a stick with garlic and chilli peppers with each drink, and they really brought out the flavour of the wine. After that, I'm not really sure what happened, but we must have carried on, to the extent that the following day I could tell we'd been out out!

After six months without a visit to the UK now, Chris was desperate to get her hair done. She'd usually have it cut and dyed back in the UK, as she thought Spanish hairdressers were not as familiar with blonde hair as UK hairdressers were, and she didn't want to come out of a salon with orange hair. Oddly, she wasn't up for letting me have a go at it during lockdown, especially after she'd butchered me, so Kim offered to do it for her up in Árchez. Kim was a nutritionist now but had previously been a hairdresser, and she was someone Chris could trust. Hair dyed and cut, we all went down to the coast at Algarrobo for lunch.

Seeing as the country was getting back to normal, the job market seemed to be opening up again, so I applied for my 26th job, this time as a Marketing Copywriter (which was something I could almost convince myself I was suitably qualified for). People may have also exhausted their lockdown stockpile of books, so I sent out agent submissions 26, 27, 28 and 29 for my novel that had been re-edited following Judith's recent comments.

It didn't take long to realise I wasn't going to get a reply about the job, but at least one of the agents wrote to me briefly – another 'thanks, but no thanks' rejection letter.

Now that the state of alarm was lifted, the walking groups started up again with masks and a plentiful supply of hand gel. There was much fist bumping and elbow knocking going on amongst our fellow walkers in the car park. Our first walk took us to the forest surrounding the *Refugio De Juanar*, a short drive away. It was a popular walk with the group for its forest paths and spectacular views down to Marbella. If you were very lucky, it was also a place to spot the odd ibex. After three months of having the run of the mountain to themselves, we were delighted to come across a huge herd of the lovely little creatures crossing our path.

In fact, nature had taken over the world during lockdown. Dolphins were spotted playing with each other in Estepona marina while there was no human activity. In Wales, some sheep were caught pushing each other on a kiddies' roundabout in a deserted playground. In the US, a coyote was spotted on the Golden Gate Bridge. And in Hong Kong zoo, two giant pandas mated for the first time in 10 years because hundreds of people were no longer gawping at them as if they were at a popular dogging site!

The walks continued to stay mostly around the local area for the first few weeks, as nobody wanted to get too adventurous, and car sharing outside your family bubble was frowned upon. There is so much beautiful countryside where we live, that it's never a chore to choose a local walk anyway.

Everyone was full of chat on the walks, as although they hadn't really been anywhere for months, everyone had lockdown tales and opinions to share. We started getting quite friendly with a lovely lady called Tina. Her husband, Bob, was a sax player, so we agreed to meet up for coffee and a chat to see how we all got along as a foursome. Tina will talk to anyone, so it's not a problem making conversation with her, and Bob was a chatty and very pleasant soul too. Here were two people we both thought we had lots in common with and would be happy to get stuck in a lift with … so long as they had facemasks on, of course!

Bob, in particular, seemed as daft as me, so I didn't even need to play down my "extraordinariness"! I have to admit, everything was starting to feel a lot more like a new normal after all, even though I might have been far from it in the eyes of many.

Even the old girls at art class thought it might be time to get the band back together again, starting with a lunch date at a different bar to our usual one, as this one had an outside covered terrace, and we could spread out a bit. After a successful lunch, we agreed it would be safe to restart the class there the following week. However, for a change, instead of everyone painting what they wanted, Julia was requested to lead the group from the front in a more formal class where we all painted the same painting in the style of the inimitable Bob Ross.

For those unfamiliar with the renowned American artist Bob Ross, he paints amazing landscapes in oils, using a technique called "wet-on-wet" that allows you to complete your painting in 30 minutes! Wow! He's faster at knocking this stuff out than I am! He was a loveable character – a bit like Rolf Harris without the didgeridoo (or the unsavoury past!). He hosted a tv painting show called *The Joy of Painting* (not to be confused with *The Joy of Sex*) that's still very popular today … as I'm quite sure *The Joy of Sex* is too!

Julia's Bob Ross class was great fun – we painted a mountain overlooking a lake with a woodland path in the foreground … your archetypical Bob Ross subject, in fact. Now we just needed to find 10 buyers in Coín for the same painting!

Meanwhile, it was also time for my new band to get together to play something for the first time – how exciting. We chose a couple of jazz funk cover versions to start with, just to see how we all sounded together as a unit. There was a full rhythm section, three brass players and a singer. The rehearsal room we'd booked had air conditioning and was a good size, so we spread ourselves out around the perimeter walls and had the air conditioning on full blast to keep changing the air regularly.

I really enjoyed myself, and I hoped we would continue to gel and write some great songs together. Let's hope this new normal continues and we can soon get back to the *old* normal.

54

Back to Borisland

With Spain now open to Brits, Boris eventually relented and le Spain send people back the other way without having t quarantine. We just needed to have a PCR test done at the airpo the day before and fill out a Passenger Health Check form online

I was just googling Málaga airport PCR tests when an ema pinged in. It was my 13th – and ultimately final – agent rejectio notice. Sod 'em – literary agents clearly need a slap in the fac with a wet fish for them to see what's in front of them. I sha have to go the self-published route at some point in the futur Ah well, no cut for the middlemen.

A few days later we headed to the airport to have a long fluff stick poked up our noses. It was carnage when we got there. Th entrance was manned by a security guard who was checking yo had the right to be there, and then we were directed to a separa area that had been set up especially to deal with the testing.

After about 30 minutes of queuing, we reached the front des and had our passports and flight bookings checked. Then w were ushered round the back. Some bloke in a lab coat – whic must make him medically qualified to do what he was doing – s me down and proceeded to shove his tickling stick up my hoot and into my brain for a shufty around. I didn't apologise when coughed all over him as a result.

Results were due within the hour by email. Chris got he while we were driving home. I didn't get mine back all mornin but eventually it arrived, and we were declared fit to fly. We then had to upload that to our flight booking, and we were good to go.

The following day, we were all packed and ready to head off to the airport. We hadn't seen any family members in 3D smellyvision since Christmas, seven months ago, our longest stint without hugging a snotty grandkid! I must admit, the thought of mixing again with them while COVID was still rife filled me with dread.

'What are you doing?' Chris asked me, as I was photographing the inside of my wardrobe.

'Taking photos.'

'Why? Are you finally selling some of those shirts you've had for 20 years?'

'No. It's for the insurance claim in case we get burgled.'

'I thought you already had photos of everything. You catalogued it all after the last burglary.'

She was right, of course. After the trauma of the burglary last year, I'd made a full asset register of everything of value. It was all in a spreadsheet with photos, make, model and serial number. Last time, I wasn't sure what had been taken for sure, and I was traumatised for days.

'That was just all the valuable stuff. TVs, computers, trumpets, all the tech. I didn't take photos of all the clothes, and I didn't realise till too late that they'd nicked my Barcelona football shirt.'

'Bloody Virgo!' she muttered as she left the room.

I heard her, but I let it slide. She'll be thanking me when we come home to a ransacked house in two weeks and some lowlife has rifled through her knicker drawer again.

I then went in the garden and photographed the inside of the shed from every angle, getting all my power tools in shot. Virgo and proud! I wonder if they make t-shirts with that slogan on. My English teacher will be going nuts I just ended that last sentence with a preposition – what is that all about, anyway?)

The airport was just as chaotic as the day before. Chris had us masked up with the proper gear – N95 masks and visors – we looked like we were going to give someone's teeth a clean and polish. And although everyone had some form of mask on – and some of those homemade cloth ones that had been worn fo weeks and never seen the inside of a washing machine – we wer the only ones showcasing the full-face visor look. Everyone wa staring at us … I looked that daft, I felt like one of those model at London Fashion Week wrapped in tin foil with a tea cosy o my head!

I spotted a Gypsy King in the departure lounge … no, not on of the Spanish guitarists … Tyson Fury, the boxer, aka "Th Gypsy King". He must have been holidaying in Marbs with hi wife. He was a big bugger in real life. I'm a fan. I should hav got a photo with him, but I was a bit starstruck, and he probabl wouldn't have come anywhere near me looking like this.

Just before we boarded, Chris made me change my mask for new one as I'd been wearing that one for two hours now. On th flight, the insanity of the situation was not lost on me whe people started removing their masks to tuck into a sandwich an a glass of wine. It seemed to me that half of humanity deserve to be wiped out by the pandemic just to improve the gene pool!

We landed in Manchester, and it was pissing down. Th weather hadn't changed since we were there last December that's Manchester for you. It's as bleak as this most of the yea and still looks like a Lowry painting half the time. It was an od family visit all round, with restrictions on activities and mixing.

It's a good job we arrived when we did, as four days late Boris announced that anyone arriving from Spain was no long exempt from self-isolation, so anyone already on their holiday in Benidorm would now need another two weeks off work whe they got back while they sat at home for 14 days. Well, I d predict that Spain opening up in June would spike the COVI infection rate again, and as a result, Boris is closing the stab door again to the people that brought it over here in the fir place, probably.

It was Mum and Dad's diamond wedding anniversary whi we were there. That's 60 years married, which is quite a achievement. My brother, Mike, drove up from the Isle of Wigh and my sister, Janet, joined us too for a small celebratory lunc If they can steer clear of COVID, then let's hope we're back he in five years to celebrate their 65th.

A week into our two-week stay, I get a message from our PO Box in Spain saying I'd received a letter from the Spanish tax office, *Agencia Tributaria*. Shit! That's never good news. I also knew that when you got a letter from them, it was a registered letter, and for whatever action they wanted you to take, the clock started ticking the moment it was signed for by the person at the PO Box who collected it from Correos on my behalf. It seems the Spanish authorities were keen for me to prove something to them about my resident status or more likely, pay a fine for some half-baked reason. Marvellous!

I was stuck in the UK for another week before I could find out what they were claiming I'd done wrong. It completely ruined my second week. I'm a worrier at the best of times and go around telling people my glass is half full, when I don't even usually have a glass, never mind anything in it!

All sorts of scenarios were flooding through my mind. Had I inadvertently reported my financial situation wrong. Was my Modelo 720 worldwide asset declaration missing a vital piece of information, and they were now going to throw the legal book at me and extort a fine from me 100 times the value of that undeclared asset?! Did they not realise I was a struggling out of work writer? I thought about absconding and not going back, but then I looked out the window at the August drizzle and soon dropped that thought.

I couldn't tell you what we did that last week as my head was firmly wedged up my jacksie. I do remember baby Theo having his first birthday while we were there. At the time in St Helens, it was permissible to have people in your garden, so he had a garden party for a few family members.

We did the same nose poke travel rigmarole for the return journey, probably administered by some kid on a young offenders' day release scheme, and the following day we boarded our flight home with my fate in the balance.

55

I'm Having an Identity Crisis

We touched down in Málaga, and I half expected the *Guardia Civil* to come down the aisle to escort me off the plane, but they didn't, so my indiscretion can't have been that serious.

The following day I was at the door to our PO Box as they opened up, and I was barely out the door again before I'd opened my letter. It looked very official, and I instantly knew I'd been placed on the naughty step. My Spanish was improving slightly, so I could get the gist of the allegations delivered in an accusatory, official tone across three pages, but I'd need to translate the rest of it when I got home.

My crime? To have the temerity to submit a Modelo 030 (whatever that is) with my names the wrong way round. But the wrong way round how? Wrong way round compared to reality, as was the case with every official document since the pillock at Fuengirola police station buggered up my initial registration three and a half years ago? Or wrong way round compared to the official names that the Spanish state thought I had, i.e. back to front? At the top of the letter they listed my name and surname the wrong way round, but I was still none the wiser.

Near the bottom of page one they'd highlighted the phrase *10 días hábiles* in bold. I knew what the first two words meant, and I assumed the last word meant "working". So whatever they wanted me to do, I had just 10 working days to do it, or they'd send the boys round. Correction: today was Tuesday, the clock had started ticking a week last Monday, so I now had fou working days left after today, where a working day for a Spanish civil servant ends at 2pm so they can knock off for a long boozy lunch and a kip before dinner time, and getting appointments with officialdom during a global pandemic was harder than finding loo rolls in the supermarket.

The last page of the letter listed nine "Articles" covered by two "Laws" and one "Royal Decree" that I was reportedly currently in contravention of – so even the Royal Family was having a go at me. As a result of the severity of my crime – and no doubt the severity of any punishment – I felt a bowel movement coming on so had to dash home sharpish!

'What've you done?' Chris asked.

'I'm an imposter. My names are the wrong way round, which is what I've been trying to tell everyone for three and a half years, and if I don't put it right by Monday, I'll probably be battered senseless in a *Guardia Civil* training camp and sent home on the next boat.'

'Don't panic, we can sort this out.'

'Don't panic? Even the King's been informed, apparently. They're never going to name a street after me now, unless they build a prison on it!'

'Give Michelle a call. She'll know what to do.'

Our Spanish teacher was usually a very calming influence and knew her way around the Spanish system better than most. But first, I translated the document myself, and especially the bit that mentioned the punishment for non-compliance.

Apparently, failure to comply in the manner and timeframe requested could be considered a "serious" (I didn't highlight that word, they did!) tax violation and punishable by a pecuniary fine. I didn't like the sound of "serious", but I liked the sound of "pecuniary" even less – it sounded to me like they had a wheel of fortune in the office with a range of huge fines on it ... someone would give it a big spin on a Friday lunchtime before they all buggered off to the pub, with everyone in the office standing round it singing "round and round the wheel spins, where it stops, nobody knows"!

I checked what "pecuniary" meant as it sounded to me very much like "punitive" in that they would derive real pleasure from making the fine as painful as possible. As it happens, it just means "involving money". Phew! But surely, any fine would involve money. So why say "pecuniary fine"? I think I'll write to them and tell them to stop using pleonasms in their correspondence (look it up!).

I sent Michelle a copy of the original letter in Spanish – after all, she's a Spanish teacher, she can translate it herself. I added a comment to relay my feelings: "They're a bunch of bloody fascists – 10 days?! Don't they know people take holidays? And in the middle of a bloody pandemic!". I also sent a copy to my tax accountant to see if they knew what was going on and what I should do. Then I went for a lie down in a darkened room while I awaited a reply.

The tax accountant confirmed that, at my request, they'd completed Modelo 030 to advise the tax office that my tax return forms had my names the wrong way round. And this was the outcome of that submission – I had to change my names at the police station and provide evidence. So this was all my fault after all, was it? It seems if I'd just kept my mouth shut, I wouldn't be in a blind panic right now.

Michelle confirmed the same as my accountant and asked me to send her copies of my passport and NIE so she could get the ball rolling. Later that day, she'd made some progress.

'Right, I've got you an appointment with the tax office on Monday at 1:30pm.'

Well at least she'd bought me as much time as possible there, as they'd be setting the dogs on me half an hour after that if we couldn't get this unfortunate matter smoothed over to their satisfaction.

'But what am I going to tell them that I haven't been trying to tell them for years?'

'You're going to present them with a document with your names the right way round.'

'What, like my passport?'

'No, confirmation of your TIE application from the police.'

A TIE (*Tarjeta de Identidad de Extranjero*) was the biometric identity document issued to non-EU nationals, which post-Brexit meant us. I didn't have one yet. Like most Brits already here, the time, you didn't actually need one just yet, so long as you still had a valid green Residency Certificate with no expiry date, but mine had my names the wrong way round, so clearly wasn't acceptable.

'Oh! Is that the plan?'

'Yes. You need to get proof that you're correcting the mix up with your names, and the only way to do that is at the police station, so you may as well apply for your TIE card at the same time.'

That kind of made sense, to kill two birds with one stone, but I still wasn't convinced I was going to be able to beat the deadline.

'I've completed form EX23 for you,' she then said. 'That's your TIE application form. And I've done Modelo 790 for you too.'

'What's that for?'

'That's the form you use to pay for your TIE application. You can do that at the bank. I did mine at the Unicaja ATM in Coín. And you've got an appointment at Málaga police station at 11am on Friday morning, so you need to pay it before then.'

'Is that everything then?' My head was spinning – I could feel Linda Blair coming on again!

'Just one more thing.'

There's ALWAYS one more thing!

'What?'

'You'll need an up-to-date *Padrón* certificate from the town hall before Friday too.'

Great. The *Padrón* certificate is the first step in everything you do legally over here – it proves you live where you say you do and can't be more than three months old when you present it. And dealing with the town hall is like trying to get membership at the local golf club – you're more likely to get blackballed by the Captain of the Ladies' Team.

'But they've been working by appointment only during the pandemic,' I said, 'and I don't fancy my chances with that lot.'

Even before the pandemic you had to go and fill the request form in at the main desk, go upstairs to the finance department to pay the fee, then go back down to the main desk to submit your

application, at which point you had to wait days before you coul
go back and collect your certificate. You had more chance c
crossing a picket line during the miners' strike in the 80s c
getting a full day's work out of a British Leyland employee!

'I think you can apply online at the moment,' Michelle said
offering a glimmer of hope.

'Is that going to be any quicker?'

'I don't know. You can give it a try.'

'And if I can't get a *Padrón* certificate by Friday.'

'You're going to jail, you won't pass GO, and you won
collect £200!'

She didn't say that, but she was probably thinking i
Regardless, we tried to fill the request in together online, eve
though we had two chances, slim and none!

'Am I putting my name the wrong way round on the form?'

'I would if I were you. They won't give you a certificate wi
your names the right way round until you've got your TIE.'

I pressed the SUBMIT button and half expected a laughin
emoji to appear on the confirmation page.

'Do I just wait in hope now, then?'

'I'd call them first thing in the morning if I were you and t
and get an appointment too.'

Chris made me my favourite dinner that night to try and tak
my mind off it – or kill me … the dish is a stuffed chicken brea
on a potato rösti with tarragon sauce. It's from the popul
cooking program *Ready, Steady, Cook!*, and we've affectionate
christened this recipe *Ready, Steady, DIE!*, thanks to the arter
clogging properties of the sauce that uses (for two people) half
pat of butter and half a tub of double cream!

Next morning, I'd received no email back from the town ha
but I had received another email from my accountant. The new
was even worse than first thought, as she reckoned day 10 w
actually this Friday not the following Monday. I refused
accept that they would treat day one as the day the letter w
signed for, as that would be less than a full working day – ev
the Spanish tax officials aren't that mean, are they?!

This whole thing was getting out of hand now, so I rang t
town hall to make an appointment. I tried for ages to get throug

but it was constantly engaged. Eventually, I got through to someone and started the conversation as I always do when dealing with a Spanish official … in my best clear King's Spanish diction (not Coíno drawl, where they drop half the letters and sound like a Cornish cattle auctioneer), I tell them I'm English and my Spanish isn't perfect, and then I try and tell them what I need.

The usual response is not a reply but a question that I don't understand, and I then have to impersonate Manuel from *Fawlty Towers* … '*¿Qué?*' I usually have to say, bent slightly at the waist (even on the telephone) with my ear tilted upwards and a blank look on my face. This time it wasn't a question I received back, more of a flat refusal … there were no appointments before Monday.

'But that's the day of my execution,' I wanted to say.

I tried to explain why I needed one before Friday, but they cut me off in mid sentence.

'*No es posible,*' they said.

I half agreed with them – it *wasn't* possible to do all this shit by Monday lunchtime, with or without a bloody pandemic, but it wasn't me calling the shots, unfortunately. As I began to plead my case a second time, a different voice came on the line. I pressed REWIND and started from the top again. I was given the same response from this second person. They were probably even high fiving each other as they declined my request. And then they hung up on me.

'Any luck?' Chris asked.

'No. I'm going to jail, I won't pass GO, and I won't collect £200!'

Then, just as I was wondering what to choose for my last meal, an email pinged in from the town hall. Are they sending me a laughing emoji after all? Apparently not, but I was none the wiser at first – it just said there was a new notification online about my application for a *Padrón* certificate and that I should login to my citizen profile on the government website to read it. When I did so, I could barely believe my eyes. There was my new *Padrón* certificate to download. EUREKA! One down, three to go. What's next? Pay for my TIE application at the bank. I had a brew first to calm myself down a bit, then I drove into town.

I was almost smiling when I reached the Unicaja bank. I joined the queue for the ATM outside. I had no idea what I was doing really … and neither did the ATM, as every option I tried to choose it said I had to scan something, but the barcode on the form didn't elicit a response. There were murmurings behind me as the queue was getting longer, so I came away, had a little rethink, and rejoined the back of the queue to have another go.

The second time was no more successful, so I went in the bank instead and joined another queue. Some old dear at the front was emptying a big jar of copper onto the counter to pay her leccy bill, and it took ages. The next few in line weren't much quicker. After a 20-minute wait, it was my turn.

'*Quiero pagar este, por favor,*' I said, presenting my Modelo 790 form.

'*¿Tiene una cuenta con Unicaja?*'

I told her, no, I didn't have an account with Unicaja, but here were 12 shiny euro coins as payment in cash.

'*No es posible,*' she said.

Did she have a brother working the phones at the town hall, I thought? Defeated, I moped out of the bank. My Spanish bank didn't have a branch in Coín. I know, I'll try the Santander bank I have a UK account with them, so that should suffice, right?

There was a big queue of pensioners in the Santander bank but nobody at the ATM inside, so I thought I'd chance my arm again. I had no luck with this one either, so reluctantly joined the queue to speak with the bank clerk. I waited another 20 minutes for my turn in this queue – don't old people have a lot of time on their hands? You'd think they'd be in a hurry to do everything before they die!

I asked the lady behind the counter if it was possible to pay the fee on my Modelo 790 form, even though I only had a UK Santander account.

'*Sí, es posible.*'

Bloody fantastic. I laid my cash on the counter.

'*No es posible hoy,*' she said.

What? It's not possible to do it today? Whyever not? The bank is open, I'm here in front of you, I have the form completed and signed, and I have the right money. Why couldn't I do it today? Did they want pesetas?!

Apparently, you could only pay this form on a Tuesday or Thursday, and only between the hours of 09:00 and 10:30. Today was Wednesday, and it was now 11:30, so I'd lucked out on both counts. Deflated, I went home.

'Everything ok?' Chris asked.

'No. I have to go back tomorrow.'

'Why? Were they shut?'

'No. You can only pay bills in a leap year on a day with a "T" in it, and only between the hours of midnight and half past when the bank's shut. Oh, and you have to roll up one trouser leg and drink a pint of water from the other side of the glass!'

'You what?'

I clarified: 'Bill payments Tuesdays and Thursdays only, nine till half ten.'

'Have we teleported back to the nineteenth century or something?'

It certainly felt like it. Chris made me another brew and mopped my brow.

I went back to Santander at 09:00 the next day and successfully paid the bill and got it stamped. Two down, two to go.

Friday came, the day of my police appointment.

'Can you come with me?' I pleaded.

'Sorry,' Michelle replied. 'Normally I would have done, but since COVID, interpreters aren't allowed to accompany you. You have to do this all on your own.'

I arrived at the offices of the *Comisaría Provincial Policía Nacional* in Málaga in plenty of time. There was an unruly mob of people outside, all jostling for position. I thought I'd come to the wrong place at first and that I'd joined the hordes waiting to snap up the latest iPhone from the Apple store, but no, this was in fact the police station.

I had Michelle's advice ringing in my ears: *As you approach the entrance to the right of the column on the far right (the area for foreigners), DON'T enter the big queue against the wall [i]f there is one, but stay at the side of the column. An officer wi[ll] come out at exactly the appointment time and will call out th[e] time and check your name off a list.*

I couldn't actually see *any* queuing going on. It looked lik[e] they were all trying to get to the front of the bar in a night club. [I] held back a little and watched the process unfold. A femal[e] police officer came out of the main door and shouted a[n] appointment time, at which point, everyone surged forward, and [I] mean *everyone*! While the officer ticked some names off a lis[t] another burly officer would let them through the crowd contr[ol] barrier. When the door closed behind the last lucky applicant, th[e] wall of people muttered expletives under their breath and steppe[d] back a little.

The same thing happened again 10 minutes later. Did all thes[e] people have their names the wrong way round or something? [It] was ridiculous. Whatever happened to social distancing? I wa[s] getting very anxious … I could understand now why the Fla[t] Earth Society were worried this two-metre social distancing ru[le] could push some people over the edge!

It was going to be my turn next, so I staked a claim on [a] position as close to the barrier as I could get. As long as I wa[s] within earshot, I'd been in with a chance. I wouldn't have long [to] make my presence felt when the door next opened, so I used m[y] time usefully and rehearsed my lines in my head: TWO PINT[S] OF LAGER AND A PACKET OF CRISPS, PLEASE!

The door opened, and I was lifted forward a yard witho[ut] even moving my legs.

'*ONCE!*' the officer shouted.

That's me – 11 o'clock. I wanted to raise a hand, but my arm[s] were pinned to my side, so I just shouted my name out. S[he] spotted me in the crowd and told the bouncer to let me in. As [I] stepped through the barrier I turned to the crowd with a sm[ug] look on my face as though my name was on the guest list [at] Stringfellows.

I followed the guy in front and took a seat in a waiting roo[m.] Within minutes, I heard my name shouted out from down t[he] corridor, so I scuttled off in search of the voice's owner. I to[ld] the only spare seat available on one side of a Perspex partition – don't you wish you'd bought shares in Perspex in 2019? – and a bored official stared back from the other side. I passed all my application paperwork under the partition and launched into my well-rehearsed spiel: when I'd registered in Fuengirola originally, the police officer had made a mistake and put my names the wrong way round on my NIE certificate.

He didn't look impressed. I wondered if it had been wise to lay the blame firmly on the police, although they had taken my passport at the time so it should have been obvious. This guy pondered my request for a moment and then declared that I couldn't do that without changing my name first. But that's exactly why I'm here, to change my names the right way round and get a new ID document that would satisfy the tax office.

I passed him the letter from *Agencia Tributaria* which he looked at for all of two seconds, before saying I needed more documents.

'*¿Qué documentos?*' I asked.

'*Pasaporte histórico,*' he replied.

What?! A historical passport. What the hell is one of those? He's having a laugh, surely. I showed him my passport and pointed out it was the same passport that had been used to register for an NIE in Fuengirola.

He took my passport from me and wandered off into a back room to consult someone. It was then I noticed that he was wearing shorts and flip flops, as well as a polo shirt. This guy was just some penpusher they'd drafted in to clear the backlog of applications, obviously. Another head appeared around the corner of the door, this one sporting a police uniform. He scrutinised me. I smiled back.

The penpusher returned, collected up all my documents and told me to go and wait in the waiting room again. After an anxious wait, I was called through again and took my seat. Good news, it was indeed possible to complete my application after all. Phew! I made extra sure to point out again that the new ID *must* have my surname and first names the right way round, as per my passport.

When he'd finished shuffling my papers, he stamped my application and gave me a printout with an official stamp and summary of my application to present when I collected my new ID card in 35 days' time. RESULT! Three down, one to go.

However, when I got outside and checked it over, I wondered if I'd wasted my time again ... in true Spanish bureaucratic fashion, my names were printed in separate boxes at the top of the page, but there was absolutely no indication as to which was my surname and which was my first name.

"Trust the process", basketball player Tony Wroten of the NBA's Philadelphia 76ers said in a radio interview a few years ago. Well, if this works out, and my new TIE card comes back with my names the right way round, then you could say that my basketball came off the backboard and wobbled round the rim three times before finally dropping through the hoop as the game clock clicked over to zero.

The appointment with *Agencia Tributaria* was a bit of an anticlimax in the end. I turned up, presented a copy of the letter they'd sent me and a copy of the stamped document from the police station, and that was it. However, despite jumping through hoops to get all this done in the time allowed, as I sit and write this book four years later, my names are still the wrong way round on my tax returns!

So I did all that running around for them, and in the end, they couldn't even be bothered to update their system.

I give up!

56

Double Trouble

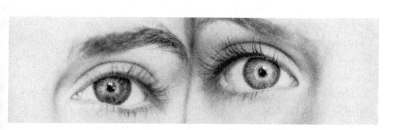

Now that airlines were operating again, Tony and Sandra flew in to get their holiday villa purchase back on track. I was looking forward to seeing a lot more of them over here once the purchase went through, so it's just as well the *Agencia Tributaria* didn't try and bankrupt me or deport me. We met up a couple of times as it had been several months since we'd seen them.

Chris and I booked into a nice little hotel in Málaga to have dinner and drinks with them. They were naturally staying in the five-star Gran Hotel Miramar again. Ours had everything we needed, including a TV remote wrapped in cellophane, a nod to the "new normality". We dined outdoors and sauntered along the marina afterwards. We felt much safer in Spain than we had done back in the UK and whilst travelling.

The ITV stations were also open once more, so I popped down to Fuengirola to get my car belatedly examined. I thought they might give me 12 months after it passed the test, but they used the original due date of April instead, so I'd be back here again in eight months.

I bet the insurance companies made a tidy profit during lockdown too, as nobody could go very far, and at least half the nation's cars probably never left the driveway in all that time. Hence, no traffic, no accidents, no payouts. Quids in! Just don't expect the premiums to come down next year.

Back in the UK, our eldest, Steph, was tearing her hair out with the kids. The two 17-year-old twins were sending her up the wall – just as she'd done to us at that age … karma, as Chris likes to remind her! – so we agreed to take the pair of them off her hands for a couple of weeks. They'd have to quarantine for another two weeks when they got back now, of course, but that didn't bother them.

Apart from staying in bed all morning, leaving their rooms in a right mess, running the aircon all day with the windows and doors open, and using a new towel every time they needed one, Grace and Lucy were absolutely no trouble at all and a pleasure to have. Just two typical teenage girls, really … makeup handprints on the white walls, hair bands all over the place. It came as no surprise to us as we had four girls of our own.

They spent their mornings in bed, and their afternoons eating or doing some kind of activity. We went to the cinema one afternoon and were the only ones in there. The evenings were spent eating, drinking and night swimming in the pool. I wish all our guests were this easy to handle, although a bit of tidying up wouldn't go amiss next time girls.

On their last full day with us, Chris was very busy with the Fire Watch group as a huge fire in Estepona had engulfed the Laguna Village shopping complex and burned it to the ground, ruining the livelihoods of around 20 shop owners. The nearby five-star Kempinski hotel had to evacuate all its guests, and 30 homes were evacuated. The fire had started on the other side of the A7 coastal road, and the high winds had made it easy for it to jump the carriageway and ignite the thatched roof of Laguna Village.

At first, we speculated that it was probably started by someone throwing a lit cigarette out of a car window, which is a common cause of wildfires in Spain, but it transpired that someone was stealing electricity for their home, and the cable they'd laid had sparked a fire on the property that quickly spread to neighbouring fields and then jumped across the carriageway. The homeowner will no doubt be prosecuted as a result.

With COVID back on the rise, we were once again keeping a keen eye on the number of cases. By the end of August 2020, Spain had reported almost 29,000 deaths, representing 7% of all confirmed cases. When compared to the UK (41k dead 13%)

252

France (31k dead 13%) and Italy (35k dead 14%), we were doing much better in Spain. From my point of view, the lockdown had been severe and very well policed, with no exercise and limited movements of people. Germany had fared much better still with just 9,000 deaths (4%).

As for the figures coming out of Russia (1.7% death rate), they were hard to believe. As well as the underreporting of COVID deaths, doctors believed to be whistleblowers were mysteriously falling out of hospital windows.

Our own little town of 22,000 people had so far respected the rules remarkably well and reaped the benefits. From 84 cases so far confirmed, only two people have sadly died.

This thing isn't over by a long stretch, clearly, and we still need to maintain our vigilance in larger groups. The outdoor living in Spain is definitely a plus point. Let's just hope they develop a vaccine soon.

57

And Relax

With the twins safely home and self-isolating in their bedroom for 14 days (which will have just felt like a normal day to them) we were alone once more, so took ourselves off to the beach a La Cala. With the sun beating down and the sea gently lapping against the shore, one could almost feel like the last six month hadn't happened and it was all some weird dream.

It's from this very beach, actually, where my novel opens wit the kidnapping of the protagonist's family. I had a quick loc round for dodgy-looking characters, just in case. None to t seen, thank goodness. And ... relax!

Whilst lying there, it was a good time for me to reflect on o last few years in Spain. It had been a rollercoaster of a ride, fa sure, with so much happening.

We'd had two more great years in Alhaurín El Grande ar really come to love the place, but we'd ultimately had to mov on. In the end, after struggling to find somewhere suitable, v were very fortunate to find another super villa and another sup landlord in Roberto in the neighbouring town of Coín. We been at the new place almost a year now, and we were ve happy with the location. I was especially happy I didn't have spend about 40 days every year strimming an acre of weeds!

Tony and Sandra had found their dream holiday home Estepona and were due back next month to collect the keys. V look forward to seeing a lot more of them, and who know perhaps one day they'll make the move permanent.

Chris had gotten herself a job on the Fire Watch group, albeit unpaid, and I was working as a writer, also unpaid (for now, but watch this space!). Having failed miserably to secure gainful employment in Spain, I was actually enjoying being a writer – Jet2's loss is your gain, dear reader! My thriller was complete (link at the end of this book), and I'd received encouragement from the few that had so far read it, including a decorated serviceman and a former proofreader – certainly enough to keep me writing and in a positive frame of mind.

At this point in our Spanish adventure, in September 2020, I set aside the novel and began writing the first book in this travelogue series, *Tapas, Tears & Tribulations: A Year in Andalucía* (that I hope you've already read). I was determined to see my books published, even if I had to go self-employed and release them via the self-publishing route. And the fact you're reading this now is proof that I kept that promise to myself.

In the last three years, save for a six-month COVID blip, we've managed to see a lot more of Andalucía than we did in our first year, visiting some beautiful towns for the first time, from coastal holiday hotspots like Estepona, Sanlúcar de Barrameda, Nerja and neighbouring Frigiliana (which we finally found at the third attempt), Mojácar and Tarifa beach (plus a bit of Cádiz by accident), to magnificent inland towns and cities steeped in history like Granada, Córdoba, Antequera and Ronda. We are indeed blessed to live in this part of the world.

We also discovered a lot more about our local area thanks to the hiking groups and have explored some more of the towns on our doorstep, like Mijas Pueblo, Benalmádena and Fuengirola, not forgetting Málaga city of course, which has become a firm favourite, vying with Barcelona and Valencia for our affections.

Our family has expanded further with the addition of our second grandson, Theo, and we're delighted to see Mike and Ann finally marry, along with our best friends Tony and Sandra tying the knot (and Chris managing to stick around at least for my Best Man's speech).

I'm playing my trumpet again (much to Chris's delight!), and I'm hoping by mixing with Spanish musicians on a regular basis, my oral Spanish will also improve.

My artistic bent has also taken me in an unexpected directio[n] with the art group. I've absolutely loved painting [*Chris: yo[u] mean copying!*] the pop art stuff and drawing my grandkids i[n] coloured pencil, but I'm not kidding myself that I'd ever make [a] decent artist. I just don't have the natural ability to do it by ey[e] without referring to a photo, and even then, I'm measurin[g] everything to try and get the scale correct. I'm no Bob Ross, fo[r] sure, but I'm also no Rolf Harris either, thankfully! It's also bee[n] great to see Chris blossom as an artist and produce some reall[y] fine pet portraits for family and friends, probably thanks to h[er] having at least one good eye now!

And what lessons have I learnt these last three years?

Well, I've learnt to let Chris choose the restaurants by ju[st] wandering up and seeing what the menu looks like.

I've also learnt to read Tony's text messages more carefull[y] so even though we may not be booking the same hotel, we [at] least book ones in the same bloody town!

I've learnt that my golf game hasn't really improved muc[h] despite the golf lesson I had, but I play so infrequently that it'[ll] be a while before I can even compare myself favourably [to] someone like Maurice bloody Flitcroft!

I've learnt how ridiculous the Spanish driving licen[ce] application test is in determining who is considered fit to dri[ve] over here and why it's a good idea to try and second guess wh[at] the Spanish drivers are planning to do, especially the old ones.

I've learnt not to trust tax accountants (although I didn't tru[st] them before moving to Spain), especially ones that can affo[rd] office space in Marbella.

I've learnt that when it finally rains in Spain, it bloody we[ll] rains and you'd better be prepared for it, and that it's not a go[od] idea to park your car on the side of a mountain with a stor[m] brewing.

And what else have I learnt these last three years? ... Oh! I'[ve] learnt how to use a washing machine. [*Chris: at last!*]

And I've learnt not to drink the seawater while I'[m] swimming, especially just after *San Juan*!

But above all else, the biggest lesson I've learnt in the last three years is to KILL SPIDERS ... and check under the toilet seat before sitting down!

[*Chris: I'd like to add that I don't condone the indiscriminate killing of wildlife!*]

[*Drew: erm, what about mozzies?*]

[*Chris: alright, with the exception of mosquitos, I rescue wildlife from the house and terrace (including spiders) and release them in the garden*]

[*Drew: ok, are you all done now? Can I type "THE END"*]

[*Chris: yes*]

THE END

* * *

[*Chris: oh, one more thing...*]

[*Drew: too late – save it for book 3*]

[*Chris: we're doing this all over again?*]

[*Drew: we are indeed!*]

About the Author

Before emigrating, I'd lived what most might describe as a pretty unremarkable life: I'm a musician whose popstar dreams were dashed (more than once) at a young age and who found success ultimately in IT. Resident in Spain since 2016, I've loved writing funny poems all my life, thanks to the inimitable Pam Ayres, and when I found I had a bit more time on my hands, I thought I'd turn my hand to a more expansive writing career, writing amusing travelogues and action thrillers.

I enjoy the writing process, and like most writers, I don't write to be famous or earn a million – although that would be very nice, of course, even if the Spanish state would end up keeping more than half the proceeds – and so I'm really writing to entertain the reader.

I do hope you enjoyed this second instalment of our Spanish adventure. If so, please remember to leave a review as they're the lifeblood of a self-published author.

If you'd like to contact me, then you can do so via email at DrewJohnsonAuthor@gmail.com or via the Twitter/X app at @DrewJohnsonAuth.

Thanks for accompanying me on this journey. *¡Hasta luego!*

Other Books by the Author

You can find the first book in this travelogue series *Tapas, Tears & Tribulations: A Year in Andalucía* on your local Amazon store here:
mybook.to/TapasTearsTribulations

You can find my first novel *Eye For An Eye* (written under the name Andy Hughson) on your local Amazon store here:
mybook.to/EyeForAnEyeAndyHughson

And if you like well-crafted spy thrillers, please take time to check out the books of my dear late friend, Major Michael Jenkins MBE, on your local Amazon store here:
mybook.to/MichaelJenkins

Acknowledgements

Thanks are due first of all to Chris for letting me continue t
write about our adventures (and helping me remember some c
the stuff I'd forgotten!). And for that same reason I would hav
forgotten even more if it wasn't for WhatsApp conversation
(thank God my lot don't using "disappearing message" settings
and Facebook posts. Thank God too that I'm a Womble and hav
kept years of email trails and bank statements to jog my memor
of where we were when and what we did!

Some photos are from www.unsplash.com and are used on th
understanding they are "Free to use under the Unsplash License'
In particular, the author would like to thank the followin
photographers for their work, the use of which the auth
believes has helped to enrich the book for the reader:

Karol Chomka, Jakub Uzieblo, Chris Unger, Egor Vikhre
Ricky Kharawala, M.S. Meeuwesen, National Cancer Institut
Steve Johnson, Sheelah Brennan, Ahmed Zayan, Dimitry B, Er
Park, Simon Hermans, Markus Winkler, Crawford Jolly, Carme
Carmen, Ricardo Gomez Angel, Frank McKenna, Malopez 2
Max LaRochelle, Nik, Shivam Baraik, Lucas Albuquerqu
Elliott Van Buggenhout, Jimmy Conover, Scott Graham, Franc
Antonio Giovanella, Andreas Rønningen, Annie Spratt, Kimsc
Doan, Laura Roberts, Valeria Zoncoll, Glenn Carstens-Pete
Ryan Snaadt, Michal Balog, Aarón Blanco Tejedor, Janko Ferl
Livia Chirila, Veri Ivanova, Jas Min, Freestocks, Tim De Pau
Thom Milkovic, Tim Mossholder, Yutacar, Maskmedicare Sho
Ethan Wilkinson, Alexander Grey, Roman Raizen.

In addition, images in the following chapters have been us
on the same understanding courtesy of Wikimedia Commons:
Ch22: Malopez 21 tinyurl.com/mr2wz7yd
Ch46: CDC tinyurl.com/24ysc9ad

All remaining photos were shot through the author's lens.

Printed in Great Britain
by Amazon